Sustainable Land Management

SOURCEBOOK

D1614064

AGRICULTURE AND RURAL DEVELOPMENT

Seventy-five percent of the world's poor live in rural areas and most are involved in farming. In the 21st century, agriculture remains fundamental to economic growth, poverty alleviation, and environmental sustainability. The World Bank's Agriculture and Rural Development publication series presents recent analyses of issues that affect agriculture's role as a source of economic development, rural livelihoods, and environmental services. The series is intended for practical application, and we hope that it will serve to inform public discussion, policy formulation, and development planning.

Other titles in this series:

Forests Sourcebook: Practical Guidance for Sustaining Forests in Development Cooperation

Changing the Face of the Waters: The Promise and Challenge of Sustainable Aquaculture

Enhancing Agricultural Innovation: How to Go Beyond the Strengthening of Research Systems

Reforming Agricultural Trade for Developing Countries, Volume 1: Key Issues for a Pro-Development Outcome of the Doha Round

Reforming Agricultural Trade for Developing Countries, Volume 2: Quantifying the Impact of Multilateral Trade Reform

Sustainable Land Management: Challenges, Opportunities, and Trade-Offs

Shaping the Future of Water for Agriculture: A Sourcebook for Investment in Agricultural Water Management

Agriculture Investment Sourcebook

Sustaining Forests: A Development Strategy

Sustainable Land Management Sourcebook

THE WORLD BANK
Washington, DC

Cover photo: Erick Fernandes/World Bank.
Cover design: Patricia Hord.

ISBN: 978-0-8213-7432-0
e-ISBN: 978-0-8213-7433-7
DOI: 10.1596/978-0-8213-7432-0

Library of Congress Cataloging-in-Publication Data

Sustainable land management sourcebook.
     p. cm.
  Includes bibliographical references and index.
    ISBN 978-0-8213-7432-0 — ISBN 978-0-8213-7433-7 (electronic)
      1. Land use—Environmental aspects. 2. Sustainable agriculture. 3. Rural development—Environmental aspects.
I. World Bank.

HD108.3.S874 2008
333.73—dc222   2008022135

CONTENTS

Preface   ix

Acknowledgments   xi

Abbreviations   xiii

PART I
SUSTAINABLE LAND MANAGEMENT: CHALLENGES AND OPPORTUNITIES   I

Chapter 1 **Overview**   3
              Structure of the Sourcebook and Guide for Users   4
              The Need for Sustainable Land Management   5
              Definition of Sustainable Land Management   5
              Drivers and Impacts of Global Change   6
              Production Landscapes: The Context for Land Management   9
              Land Management Trade-Offs   12
              Confronting the Effects of Land Use   13
              Selecting and Using Appropriate Indicators for SLM and Landscape Resilience   13
              Diversity of Land Management Systems and Poverty Alleviation   13
              Future Directions for Investments   16

PART II
MAJOR FARMING SYSTEMS: INVESTMENT OPTIONS AND INNOVATIONS   21

Chapter 2 **Introduction**   23

Chapter 3 **Rainfed Farming and Land Management Systems in Humid Areas**   25
              Overview   25
              Potentials for Poverty Reduction and Agricultural Growth   25

              Investment Note 3.1   **Science and Local Innovation Make Livestock More Profitable
                                            and Friendlier to the Environment in Central America**   27

              Investment Note 3.2   **An Approach to Sustainable Land Management by Enhancing
                                            the Productive Capacity of African Farms: The Case of the
                                            Underused and Versatile Soybean**   34

              Investment Note 3.3   **Balancing Rainforest Conservation and Poverty Reduction** 39

              Investment Note 3.4   **Groundwater Declines and Land Use: Looking for the
                                            Right Solutions**   45

Investment Note 3.5   **Environmental Services Payments and Markets: A Basis for Sustainable Land Resource Management?**   **51**

Innovative Activity Profile 3.1   **Species Diversity in Fallow Lands of Southern Cameroon: Implications for Management of Constructed Landscapes**   **56**

Innovative Activity Profile 3.2   **Domestication and Commercialization of Forest Tree Crops in the Tropics**   **60**

Innovative Activity Profile 3.3   **Avoided Deforestation with Sustainable Benefits: Reducing Carbon Emissions from Deforestation and Land Degradation**   **65**

Innovative Activity Profile 3.4   **On-Farm Integration of Freshwater Agriculture and Aquaculture in the Mekong Delta of Vietnam: The Role of the Pond and Its Effect on Livelihoods of Resource-Poor Farmers**   **71**

Chapter 4   **Rainfed Farming Systems in Highlands and Sloping Areas**   **77**
Overview   77
Potentials for Poverty Reduction and Agricultural Growth   77

Investment Note 4.1   **No-Burn Agricultural Zones on Honduran Hillsides: Better Harvests, Air Quality, and Water Availability by Way of Improved Land Management**   **78**

Investment Note 4.2   **Beans: Good Nutrition, Money, and Better Land Management— Appropriate for Scaling Up in Africa?**   **83**

Innovative Activity Profile 4.1   **Fodder Shrubs for Improving Livestock Productivity and Sustainable Land Management in East Africa**   **88**

Chapter 5   **Rainfed Dry and Cold Farming Systems**   **95**
Overview   95
Potentials for Poverty Reduction and Agricultural Growth   95

Investment Note 5.1   **Integrating Land and Water Management in Smallholder Livestock Systems in Sub-Saharan Africa**   **96**

Investment Note 5.2   **Integrated Nutrient Management in the Semiarid Tropics**   **103**

Investment Note 5.3   **Integrated Natural Resource Management for Enhanced Watershed Function and Improved Livelihoods in the Semiarid Tropics**   **108**

Investment Note 5.4   **Enhancing Mobility of Pastoral Systems in Arid and Semiarid Regions of Sub-Saharan Africa to Combat Desertification**   **114**

Investment Note 5.5   **Sustainable Land Management in Marginal Dry Areas of the Middle East and North Africa: An Integrated Natural Resource Management Approach**   **120**

Investment Note 5.6   **Adaptation and Mitigation Strategies in Sustainable Land Management Approaches to Combat the Impacts of Climate Change**   **126**

Innovative Activity Profile 5.1   **High-Value Cash Crops for Semiarid Regions: Cumin Production in Khanasser, Syrian Arab Republic**   **131**

Innovative Activity Profile 5.2   **Economic and Sustainable Land Management Benefits of the Forage Legume: Vetch**   **133**

Innovative Activity Profile 5.3   **Participatory Barley-Breeding Program for Semiarid Regions**   **134**

Innovative Activity Profile 5.4   **Climate Risk Management in Support of Sustainable Land Management**   **136**

Innovative Activity Profile 5.5   **Land Degradation Surveillance: Quantifying and Monitoring Land Degradation**   **141**

PART III
WEB-BASED RESOURCES 149

Chapter 6   **Web-Based Tools and Methods for Sustainable Land Management** 151

Global Field and Market Intelligence on Cereal and Oilseeds 151

Remote-Sensing Tool for Water Resources Management 151

Hydrological Data and Digital Watershed Maps 151

Basin and Watershed Scale Hydrological Modeling 153

River Basin Development and Management 153

Tracking Floods Globally: The Dartmouth Flood Observatory 154

The Carnegie Landsat Analysis System 154

Plant Biodiversity: Rapid Survey, Classification, and Mapping 156

Agricultural Production Regions and MODIS: NASA's Moderate Resolution Imaging Spectroradiometer 157

Integrated Global Observations for Land 157

Glossary 161

Index 167

BOXES

1.1   Ecosystem Services 4

1.2   Historical Perspective on Landscapes, Land Management, and Land Degradation 6

1.3   Pressure-State-Response Framework 14

1.4   Household Strategies to Improve Livelihoods 16

1.5   Key Safeguard Policy Issues for SLM and Natural Resource Management Investments 18

3.1   Example of Pasture Rehabilitation and Intensification from Honduras 30

3.2   Examining Hydrological Contradictions in the North China Plain 46

3.3   Types of Environmental Services Generated by Good Land-Use Practices 52

5.1   Steps in the Diagnostic Surveillance Framework 143

5.2   Steps in the Land Degradation Surveillance Framework 145

FIGURES

1.1   Global Food Production, Food Prices, and Undernourishment in Developing Countries, 1961–2003 6

1.2   Typical Set of Production Activities (Forestry, Crop and Livestock Production, Hydropower, and Coastal Fisheries) Encountered in a Production Landscape 7

1.3   World Comparisons of Food Production and Consumption 2003 10

3.1   Months of Consecutive Dry Season 28

3.2   Nigerian Soybean Production (1988–2006) and Markets in Ibadan (1987–2000) 35

3.3   Irrigation History of Luancheng County: Estimated Pumping for Irrigation, 1949–99 46

3.4   General Relationships between Precipitation and Evapotranspiration for Cropland in Luancheng County, 1947–2000 47

3.5   Hydronomic Zones in a River Basin 48

3.6   Schematic Trade-off between Reduced GHG Emissions through Avoided Deforestation and National Economic Development Opportunities 68

3.7   Area and Production Increases in Freshwater Aquaculture in Vietnam, 1999–2005 72

3.8   Bioresource Flows of an IAA Pond with Medium-Input Fish Farming in the Mekong Delta 74

5.1   Effect of Watershed Interventions on Groundwater Levels at Two Benchmark Sites in India 111

5.2   Application of the Multilevel Analytical Framework to the Management of Olive Orchards on Hill Slopes at Khanasser Valley 124

5.3   Successive Samples of Land Degradation Problem Domains at a Hierarchy of Scales Using Satellite Imagery, Ground Sampling, and Laboratory Analysis of Soils by Infrared Spectroscopy 144

6.1   USDA-FAS Crop Explorer 152

6.2   USDA-FAS Global Reservoir and Lake Monitor 152

6.3   HydroSHEDS Database 153

6.4	The Distributed Hydrology Soil Vegetation Model	154
6.5	River Basin Development and Management Comparative Study	155
6.6	Dartmouth Flood Observatory Map	155
6.7	Comparison of CLAS High-Resolution Processing with Standard Landsat Processing	156
6.8	MODIS Image Gallery	158
6.9	Integrated and Operational Land Observation System	159

TABLES

1.1	Comparison of Farming Systems by Category	15
3.1	Forage Use and Production Criteria	29
3.2	ASB Summary Matrix: Forest Margins of Sumatra	40
3.3	Incidence of Costs and Benefits for Environmental Services	52
3.4	Total Number of Plant Species Recorded in Three Fallow Types in the Humid Forest Zone of Southern Cameroon	58
3.5	List of the Four Most Preferred Priority Indigenous Fruit Tree Species in Selected Regions	61
3.6	Percentage of Farm Households Practicing Freshwater Aquaculture in 2000 and 2004 by Wealth Groups	73
4.1	Farmers Planting Fodder Shrubs in Kenya, Northern Tanzania, Rwanda, and Uganda	91
5.1	Chemical Characteristics of 924 Soil Samples Collected from Farmers' Fields in Three Districts of Andhra Pradesh, India, 2002–04	104
5.2	Biological and Chemical Properties of Semiarid Tropical Vertisols	105
5.3	Nutrient Composition of Vermicompost	106
5.4	Seasonal Rainfall, Runoff, and Soil Loss from Different Benchmark Watersheds in India and Thailand	110
5.5	Major Strengths, Weaknesses, Opportunities, and Threats for the Khanasser Valley as an Example of Marginal Drylands	121
5.6	Technological Interventions Introduced in the Khanasser Valley	123

PREFACE

The World Bank's Rural Strategy, *Reaching the Rural Poor,* commits the Bank to five core areas of rural development:

- fostering an enabling environment for broad-based and sustainable rural growth
- enhancing agricultural productivity and competitiveness
- encouraging nonfarm economic growth
- improving social well-being, managing and mitigating risk, and reducing vulnerability
- enhancing sustainability of natural resource management.

A key goal of the Rural Strategy is support to agricultural growth that benefits the poor, for without a renewed effort to accelerate growth in the agricultural sector, few countries will be able to reach the Millennium Development Goals—especially the goal of halving poverty and hunger—by 2015. Furthermore, the *World Development Report 2007*: *Agriculture for Development* (WDR 2007) calls for greater investment in agriculture in developing countries. *WDR 2007* warns that the sector must be placed at the center of the development agenda because, while 75 percent of the world's poor live in rural areas, a mere 4 percent of official development assistance goes to agriculture in developing countries. In Sub-Saharan Africa, a region heavily reliant on agriculture for overall growth, public spending for farming is also only 4 percent of total government spending, and the sector is still taxed at relatively high levels.

Increasing demands for food, feed, and bio-energy challenge an already dwindling land, water, and forest base. To address these demands for natural resources and the accompanying challenges, the Bank's work emphasizes sustainable land, fisheries, forest, and livestock and water management, including governance issues. Until recently, increases in agricultural productivity—particularly in industrial regions of the world—have, with the help of both science and subsidy, pushed world agricultural commodity prices down, making it increasingly difficult for marginal land farmers to operate profitably within existing technical and economic parameters. In the first few months of 2008, however, a combination of high oil prices, poor crop yields caused by unfavorable weather in major producer countries such as Australia, skyrocketing demand for grains for biofuels (ethanol), and market speculation have all combined to push commodity prices to all-time highs. This price trend is projected to continue for the foreseeable future and will stimulate rapid expansion or intensification of agricultural land use—or both. Good land management practices will be essential to sustain high agricultural productivity without degrading land and the associated natural resource base and ecosystem services essential for sustaining land productivity.

The *Sustainable Land Management Sourcebook* is intended to be a ready reference for practitioners (including World Bank stakeholders, clients in borrowing countries, and World Bank project leaders) seeking state-of-the-art information about good land management approaches, innovations for investments, and close monitoring for potential scaling up. The *Sourcebook* provides introductions to topics, but not detailed guidelines on how to design and implement investments. The Investment Notes and Innovative Activity Profiles include research contacts, a list of references, and Web resources for readers who seek more in-depth information and examples of practical experience.

WHAT IS NOT COVERED

Thematic topic coverage is not always comprehensive, as materials were assembled on a pragmatic basis, depending on available materials and on specialists willing to contribute original notes. The modules generally address the priority issues within a thematic area or areas in which operational guidance is needed, but there are important gaps that should be filled in future editions.

This edition of the *Sourcebook* includes the three major rainfed systems out of the eight system types for development of detailed investment notes:

- rainfed farming systems in humid and subhumid areas
- rainfed farming systems in highland and sloping areas
- rainfed farming systems in dry (semiarid and arid) areas.

The decision to start with three rainfed systems was based on the level of available resources (funds and time) and also on the fact that these rainfed systems occupy over 540 million hectares of cultivated land globally and involve approximately 1.4 billion people, who, in turn, practice about 40 different land management and cropping arrangements. Future editions will systematically cover the remaining farming systems that include the following:

- irrigated farming systems with a broad range of food and cash crop production
- wetland rice-based farming systems dependent on monsoon rains supplemented by irrigation
- dualistic farming systems with both large-scale commercial and smallholder farms across a variety of ecologies and with diverse production patterns.

THE *SOURCEBOOK* AS A LIVING DOCUMENT

This first edition draws on the experiences of various institutional partners that work alongside the World Bank in the agriculture and natural resource management sectors. Major contributors are research and development experts from the Consultative Group on International Agriculture Research (CGIAR) centers, together with their national partners from government and nongovernmental agencies. The diverse menu of options for profitably investing in sustainable land management that is presented is still a work in progress. Important gaps still need to be filled, and good practices are constantly evolving as knowledge and experience accumulate. The intention of this *Sourcebook* is to continue to harness the experience of the many World Bank projects in all regions as well as those of partners in other multilateral and bilateral institutions, national organizations, and civil society organizations.

The *Sourcebook* will be updated and expanded, as experience is gained with new investment initiatives. The current chapters and investment notes should be valid for a number of years. The useful life of an IAP will be less, as most are based on recent experience and have been subjected to limited evaluation. Readers are encouraged to check on current status by contacting the person named in each profile.

ACKNOWLEDGMENTS

The preparation of this *Sourcebook* involved a large number of people from within units of the World Bank working on agriculture, as well as from a variety of partner organizations. The design and day-to-day coordination of the *Sourcebook* was carried out by Erick Fernandes (ARD), Erika Styger, and Gary Costello (ARD consultants).

The following individuals made written contributions to module overviews and good practice notes:

M. Peters and D. White, Centro Internacional de Agricultura Tropical (CIAT), Cali, Colombia, and F. Holmann, CIAT and the International Livestock Research Institute (ILRI), Cali, Colombia; J. N. Chianu, O. Ohiokpehai, B. Vanlauwe, and N. Sanginga, Tropical Soil Biology and Fertility Institute (TSBF) and the World Agroforestry Centre (ICRAF), Nairobi, and A. Adesina, Rockefeller Foundation, Nairobi, Kenya; T. Tomich, J. Lewis, and J. Kasyoki, ICRAF; J. Valentim, Empresa Brasileira de Pesquisa Agropecuária (EMBRAPA); S. Vosti and J.Witcover, University of California–Davis, California; E. Kendy, The Nature Conservancy, Washington, DC, United States; P. H. May, Department of Agriculture, Development and Society, Federal Rural University, Rio de Janeiro, Brazil; M. Ngobo and S.Weise, International Institute of Tropical Agriculture (IITA), Yaoundé, Cameroon; F. K. Akinnifesi, O. C. Ajayi, and G. Sileshi, ICRAF, Makoka, Malawi; M. van Noordwijk, B. Swallow, L. Verchot, and J. Kasyoki, ICRAF, Indonesia and Kenya; D. K. Nhan, D. N. Thanh, and Le T. Duong, Mekong Delta Development Research Institute, Can Tho University, Can Tho, Vietnam, and M. J. C. Verdegem and R. H. Bosma, Aquaculture and Fisheries Group, Department of Animal Sciences, Wageningen University, Wageningen, Netherlands; L. A.Welchez, Consortium for Integrated Soil Management, Tegucigalpa, Honduras; M. Ayarza, TSBF and CIAT, Tegucigalpa, Honduras; E. Amezquita, E. Barrios, M. Rondon, A. Castro, M. Rivera, and I. Rao, CIAT, Cali, Colombia; J. Pavon, Instituto Nacional de Tecnologia Agropecuaria, Managua, Nicaragua; and O. Ferreira, D.Valladares, and N. Sanchez, Escuela Nacional de Ciencias Forestales, Siguatepeque, Honduras; D. White, CIAT and Pan-African Bean Research Alliance; S. Franzel, C.Wambugu, H. Arimi, and J. Stewart, ICRAF, Nairobi, Kenya; T. Amede, ILRI, Addis Ababa, Ethiopia, and International Water Management Institute (IWMI), Addis Ababa, Ethiopia; A. Haileslasie and D. Peden, ILRI, Addis Ababa, Ethiopia; S. Bekele, IWMI, Addis Ababa, Ethiopia, and M. Blümmel, ILRI, Addis Ababa, Ethiopia, and Hyderabad, India; S. P. Wani, K. L. Sahrawat, and C. Srinivasan Rao, International Crops Research Institute for the Semi-Arid Tropics (ICRISAT), Hyderabad, India; T. K. Sreedevi, P. Pathak, Piara Singh, and T. J. Rego, ICRISAT, Patancheru, Andhra Pradesh, India; Y. S. Ramakrishna, Central Research Institute for Dryland Agriculture, Santoshnagar, Hyderabad, Andhra Pradesh, India; Thawilkal Wangkahart, Agricultural Research and Development, Muang, Khon Kaen, Thailand; Yin Dixin, Guizhou Academy of Agricultural Sciences, Integrated Rural Development Center, Guiyang, Guizhou, China, and Zhong Li, Yunnan Academy of Agricultural Sciences, Kunming, Yunnan, China; S. Leloup, ARD consultant; R. Thomas, F. Turkelboom, R. La Rovere, A. Aw-Hassan, and A. Bruggeman, International Center for Agricultural Research in the Dry Areas (ICARDA), Aleppo, Syrian Arab Republic; J. Padgham, U.S. Agency for International Development (USAID); S. Ceccarelli and S. Grando, ICARDA, Aleppo, Syrian Arab Republic; A. Lotsch, ARD; K. D. Shepherd, T.-G. Vågen, and T. Gumbricht, ICRAF, Nairobi, Kenya, and M. G. Walsh, Earth Institute, Columbia University, New York; J. Richey, University of Washington, Seattle; G. Asner, Stanford University and Carnegie Institution of Washington, California, United States; A. Gillison, Center for Biodiversity Management (CBM), Australia; R. Brakenridge, Dartmouth Flood Observatory, Dartmouth College, New Hampshire, United States.

Many Bank staff contributed and/or peer reviewed the concept note, early drafts, and final chapters or the *Sourcebook*: Sushma Ganguly (ARD), Mark Cackler (ARD), Eija Pehu (ARD), Nwanze Okidegbe (ARD), Paola Agostini (AFR), Jessica Mott (ECA), Daniel Sellen (AFR), Nadim Khouri (LAC), Idah Pswarayi-Riddihough (EAP), Grant Milne (SAR), and Robert Ragland Davis (LCR).

Sarian Akibo-Betts (ARD) assisted with logistics and managing the consultant hiring process, Regina Vasko, Felicitas Doroteo-Gomez (ARD), and Rebecca Oh (ARD) were extremely supportive in managing finances and contracts. Melissa Williams (ARD), Lisa Li Xi Lau (ARD), and Gunnar Larson (ARD) managed the publication production and electronic version.

While this list is comprehensive, it is likely that we have overlooked important contributors. Our apologies for this oversight, but thank you all the same.

ABBREVIATIONS

AFOLU	agriculture, forestry, and other land use
AgREN	Agricultural Research and Extension Network
AMSR-E	Advanced Microwave Scanning Radiometer for the Earth Observing System
ASB	Alternatives to Slash-and-Burn (program)
BNF	biological nitrogen fixation
C	carbon
CAF	crop agrobiodiversity factor
CaNaSTA	Crop Niche Selection in Tropical Agriculture (spatial analysis tool)
CBM	Center for Biodiversity Management
CDM	clean development mechanism
CGIAR	Consultative Group on International Agricultural Research
CH4	methane
CIAT	Centro Internacional de Agricultura Tropical, or International Center for Tropical Agriculture
CLAS	Carnegie Landsat Analysis System
CO_2	carbon dioxide
CO_{2e}	carbon dioxide equivalent
D-PPB	Decentralized-Participatory Plant Breeding (approach)
DHSVM	Distributed Hydrology Soil Vegetation Model
DM	dry matter
DTPA	diethylene triamine pentaacetic acid
FAO	Food and Agriculture Organization
FAS	Foreign Agricultural Service (United States)
FONAFIFO	Fondo Nacional de Financiamiento Forestal, or National Forestry Financing Fund (Costa Rica)
GDP	gross domestic product
GEF	Global Environment Facility
GHG	greenhouse gas
GLASOD	Global Assessment of Human Induced Soil Degradation (database)
HFC	hydrofluorocarbon
IAA	integrated agriculture-aquaculture (system)
ICAR	Indian Council for Agricultural Research
ICARDA	International Center for Agricultural Research in the Dry Areas
ICRAF	International Centre for Research in Agroforestry
ICRISAT	International Crops Research Institute for the Semi-Arid Tropics
IFT	indigenous fruit tree

IGNRM	integrated genetic and natural resource management
IGOL	Integrated Global Observations for Land
IGOS	Integrated Global Observing Strategy
IITA	International Institute of Tropical Agriculture
ILRI	International Institute for Land Reclamation and Improvement
INM	integrated nutrient management
INRM	integrated natural resources management
IPAD	impact assessment of policy reforms to agricultural development
IPCC	Intergovernmental Panel on Climate Change
IPDM	integrated pest and disease management
IPM	integrated pest management
ISI	Indian Standards Institution
IWMI	International Water Management Institute
LBS	little bag silage
LEAD	Livestock, Environment, and Development
LULUCF	land use, land-use change, and forestry
MODIS	Moderate-Resolution Imaging Spectroradiometer
MPCI	multiperil crop insurance
NARS	national agricultural research system
NASA	National Aeronautics and Space Administration
NEPAD	New Partnership for Africa's Development
NGGIP	National Greenhouse Gas Inventories Programme (Japan)
NGO	nongovernmental organization
NO_2	nitrous oxide
NRM	natural resource management
O_3	tropospheric ozone
PABRA	Pan-African Bean Research Alliance
PES	payment for environmental services
PFC	perfluorocarbon
PRODES	Program for the Estimation of Deforestation in the Brazilian Amazon
PUA	peri-urban and urban agriculture
QSMAS	Quesungual Slash-and-Mulch Agroforestry System
REDD	reduction of emissions from deforestation and degradation
RUPES	Rewarding Upland Poor for Environmental Services (program)
SCALE	Systemwide Collaborative Action for Livelihoods and the Environment (methodology)
SF6	sulfur hexafluoride
SHG	self-help group
SLM	sustainable land management
SoFT	Selection of Forages for the Tropics (knowledge management tool)
SOM	soil organic matter
TLU	tropical livestock unit
TSBF	Tropical Soil Biology and Fertility Institute
UNEP	United Nations Environment Programme
UNFCCC	United Nations Framework Convention on Climate Change
USDA	U.S. Department of Agriculture
UTA	University of Tropical Agriculture Foundation
VGGR	Voluntary greenhouse gas reporting
VIC	variable infiltration capacity model
WHS	water-harvesting structure
WWF	World Wildlife Fund

PART I

Sustainable Land Management:
Challenges and Opportunities

CHAPTER I

Overview

Increased investment to promote agricultural growth and poverty reduction is a key objective of the World Bank's (2003) rural strategy, *Reaching the Rural Poor*. A major component of the strategy outlines the priorities and the approaches that the public sector, private sector, and civil society can use to enhance productivity and competitiveness of the agricultural sector in ways that reduce rural poverty and sustain the natural resource base. The pathways and possible actions involve participation by rural communities, science and technology, knowledge generation and further learning, capacity enhancement, and institution building.

The strategy commits the World Bank to five core areas of rural development:

- Foster an enabling environment for broad-based and sustainable rural growth.
- Promote agricultural productivity and competitiveness.
- Encourage nonfarm economic growth.
- Improve social well-being, manage and mitigate risk, and reduce vulnerability.
- Enhance sustainability of natural resource management.

Underlying all of the investments and actions is pro-poor agricultural growth, with the specific aim of helping client countries reach the Millennium Development Goals—especially the goal of halving poverty and hunger by 2015.

While the new rural strategy was being developed, the need to better articulate good practice in agricultural poli-

cies and investments became clear. To support the rural strategy, the Agriculture and Rural Development Department compiled and launched the *Agriculture Investment Sourcebook* (World Bank 2004) and *Shaping the Future of Water for Agriculture: A Sourcebook for Investment in Agricultural Water Management* (World Bank 2005a). Those two sourcebooks document and highlight a wide range of emerging good practices and innovative approaches to investing in the agricultural and rural sector. Good land management is essential for sustaining the productivity of agriculture, forestry, fisheries, and hydrology (water), and it affects a range of ecosystem services on which the sustainability of agriculture depends. Hence, this sourcebook has been produced to complement the previous sourcebooks. The focus is on land management for enhanced production as well as ecosystem services (box 1.1).

Until recently, increases in agricultural productivity—particularly in industrial regions of the world—have, with the help of both science and subsidy, pushed world agricultural commodity prices down, thereby making it increasingly difficult for marginal land farmers to operate profitably within existing technical and economic parameters (Sachs 2005). In the first few months of 2008, however, a combination of high oil prices, poor crop yields caused by unfavorable weather in major producer countries such as Australia, skyrocketing demand for grains for biofuels (ethanol), and market speculation has pushed commodity prices to all-time highs. This price trend is projected to continue for the foreseeable future and will stimulate rapid expansion or intensification of agricultural land use—or both. Good land management practices will be essential to sustain high productivity without degrading land and the associated natural resource base.

STRUCTURE OF THE SOURCEBOOK AND GUIDE FOR USERS

This sourcebook is intended to be a ready reference for practitioners (including World Bank stakeholders, clients in borrowing countries, and World Bank project leaders) seeking state-of-the-art information about good land management approaches, innovations for investments, and close monitoring for potential scaling up.

This sourcebook is divided into three parts:

- Part I identifies the need and scope for sustainable land management (SLM) and food production in relation to cross-sector issues such as freshwater and forest resources, regional climate and air quality, and interactions with existing and emerging infectious diseases. It

introduces the concept of production landscapes and analysis of trade-offs and establishes a framework for linking indicators that provide a measure of the outcomes of SLM. It then categorizes the diversity of land management (that is, farming) systems globally and the strategies for improving household livelihoods in each type of system. For the farming system types, a set of SLM principles and common but important issues for future investments are identified.

- Part II focuses on three major farming system types and presents a range of Investment Notes and Innovative Activity Profiles:
  - *Investment Notes* summarize good practices and lessons learned in specific investment areas. They provide a brief, but technically sound, overview for the nonspecialist. For each Investment Note, the investments have been evaluated in different settings for effectiveness and sustainability, and they have been broadly endorsed by a community of practitioners operating both within and outside the World Bank.
  - *Innovative Activity Profiles* highlight the design of successful or innovative investments. They provide a short description of an activity that is found in the World Bank's portfolio or that of a partner agency and that focuses on potential effectiveness in poverty reduction, empowerment, or sustainability. Activities profiled often have not been sufficiently tested and evaluated in a range of settings to be considered good practice, but they should be closely monitored for potential scaling up.
- Part III provides users of the source book with easy-to-access, Web-based resources relevant for land and natural resource managers. The resources are available in the public domain, and readers can access the Web sites of various international and national agencies.

This sourcebook provides introductions to topics, but not detailed guidelines on how to design and implement investments. The Investment Notes and Innovative Activity Profiles include a list of references and Web resources for readers who seek more in-depth information and examples of practical experience.

This first edition draws on the experiences of various institutional partners that work alongside the World Bank in the agriculture and natural resource management sectors. Major contributors are research and development experts from the Consultative Group on International Agriculture Research centers, together with their national partners from government and nongovernmental agencies. The diverse menu of options for profitably investing in SLM that is presented is still a work in progress. Important gaps still need to be filled, and good practices are constantly evolving as knowledge and experience accumulate. The intention of this sourcebook is to continue to harness the experience of the many World Bank projects in all regions as well as those of partners in other multilateral and bilateral institutions, national organizations, and civil society organizations. The sourcebook will be updated annually.

THE NEED FOR SUSTAINABLE LAND MANAGEMENT

Land-use activities—whether converting natural landscapes for human use or changing management practices on human-dominated lands—have transformed a large proportion of the planet's land surface. By clearing tropical forests, practicing subsistence agriculture, intensifying farmland production, or expanding urban centers, humans are changing the world's landscapes. Although land-use practices vary greatly across the world, their ultimate outcome is generally the same: (a) to produce food and fiber and (b) to acquire natural resources for immediate human needs.

The sections that follow present the rationale for why SLM is a critical cross-sector driver for maintaining production and services from human-dominated landscapes. The challenges identified are also entry points for carefully targeted interventions and represent opportunities for pro-poor investments.

DEFINITION OF SUSTAINABLE LAND MANAGEMENT

Sustainable land management is a knowledge-based procedure that helps integrate land, water, biodiversity, and environmental management (including input and output externalities) to meet rising food and fiber demands while sustaining ecosystem services and livelihoods. SLM is necessary to meet the requirements of a growing population. Improper land management can lead to land degradation and a significant reduction in the productive and service functions (World Bank 2006).

In lay terms, SLM involves these activities:

- Preserving and enhancing the productive capabilities of cropland, forestland, and grazing land (such as upland areas, down-slope areas, flatlands, and bottomlands)
- Sustaining productive forest areas and potentially commercial and noncommercial forest reserves

- Maintaining the integrity of watersheds for water supply and hydropower-generation needs and water conservation zones
- Maintaining the ability of aquifers to serve the needs of farm and other productive activities.

In addition, SLM includes actions to stop and reverse degradation—or at least to mitigate the adverse effects of earlier misuse. Such actions are increasingly important in uplands and watersheds—especially those where pressures from the resident populations are severe and where the destructive consequences of upland degradation are being felt in far more densely populated areas downstream.

Fortunately, in the past four decades, scientific advances and the application of improved knowledge and technologies by land managers and some farmers have resulted in significant total and per capita food increases, reduced food prices (figure 1.1), and the sparing of new land that otherwise would have been needed to achieve the same level of production (Evenson and Gollin 2003). For example, if yields of the six major crop groups that are cultivated on 80 percent of the total cultivated land area had remained at 1961 levels, an additional 1.4 billion hectares of farmland (more than double the amount of land currently being used) would have been required by 2004 to serve an expanding population. Asia alone would have required an additional 600 million hectares, which represents 25 percent more land area than is suitable for cultivation on that continent. Rather than enjoying surpluses of grains, Asia would now depend heavily on food imports (Cassman and Wood 2005). Nevertheless, those gains have some medium- to long-term costs (figure 1.1).

Until recently, increases in agricultural productivity—particularly in developed regions of the world, where they are facilitated by both science and subsidy—have pushed world agricultural commodity prices down, making it increasingly difficult for marginal land farmers to operate profitably within existing technical and economic parameters. These trends may not be reliable pointers to the future.

In the 21st century, food and fiber production systems will need to meet three major requirements:

1. They must adequately supply safe, nutritious, and sufficient food for the world's growing population.
2. They must significantly reduce rural poverty by sustaining the farming-derived component of rural household incomes.
3. They must reduce and reverse the degradation of natural resources and the ecosystem services essential to sustaining healthy societies and land productivity.

Figure 1.1   Global Food Production, Food Prices, and Undernourishment in Developing Countries, 1961–2003

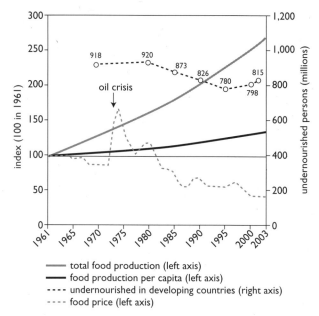

Source: Millennium Ecosystem Assessment 2005.
Note: The spike in the food price index in 1974 was caused by the oil crisis.

DRIVERS AND IMPACTS OF GLOBAL CHANGE

It is now known that the challenges to sustaining land productivity will need to be resolved in the face of significant but highly unpredictable changes in global climate—a key factor in natural and agro-ecosystem productivity. Other major issues that will influence how land use evolves to meet the challenge of food security include globalization of markets and trade, increasing market orientation of agriculture, significant technological changes, and increasing public concern about the effects of unsustainable natural resource management.

Several decades of research have revealed the environmental impacts of land use throughout the globe. These impacts range from changes in atmospheric composition to the extensive modification of Earth's ecosystems. For example, land-use practices have played a role in changing the global carbon cycle and, possibly, the global climate: Since 1850, roughly 35 percent of anthropogenic carbon dioxide emissions resulted directly from land use. Changes in land cover also affect regional climates by affecting surface energy and water balance (box 1.2).

Humans have also transformed the hydrologic cycle to provide freshwater for irrigation, industry, and domestic consumption. Furthermore, anthropogenic nutrient inputs

to the biosphere from fertilizers and atmospheric pollutants now exceed natural sources and have widespread effects on water quality and coastal and freshwater ecosystems. Land use has also caused declines in biodiversity through the loss, modification, and fragmentation of habitats; degradation of soil and water; and overexploitation of native species. Figure 1.2 shows some of the watershed- and landscape-level interactions and potential consequences of

Figure 1.2   Typical Set of Production Activities (Forestry, Crop and Livestock Production, Hydropower, and Coastal Fisheries) Encountered in a Production Landscape

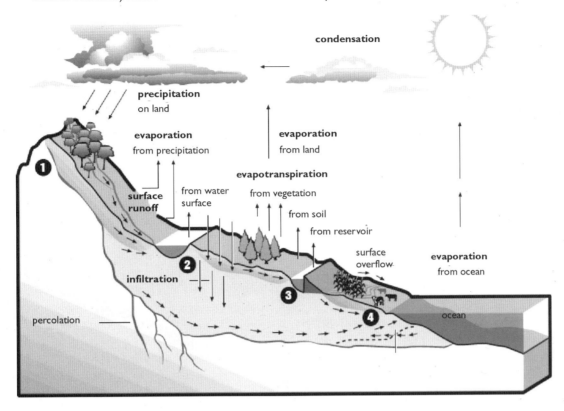

Source: World Bank 2006.

Note: The land management interventions depicted at various points in the landscape all have an impact on surface and subsurface water and nutrient flows and energy balances. Understanding how these interrelated but spatially separated interactions occur is very important for sustainable land management for enhanced productivity and ecosystem functions. ❶ = Forested catchments, ❷ = dams and reservoirs, ❸ = irrigation canals, and ❹ = coastal settlements.

individual land management decisions on water uptake and loss to the atmosphere (*evapotranspiration*) and hydrology.

Human activities now appropriate nearly one-third to one-half of global ecosystem production, and as development and population pressures continue to mount, so could the pressures on the biosphere. As a result, the scientific community is increasingly concerned about the condition of global ecosystems and ecosystem services.

Thus, land use presents a dilemma. On one hand, many land-use practices are absolutely essential for humanity because they provide critical natural resources and ecosystem services, such as food, fiber, shelter, and freshwater. On the other hand, some forms of land use are degrading the ecosystems and services on which we depend. A natural question arises: are land-use activities degrading the global environment in ways that may ultimately undermine ecosystem services, human welfare, and long-term sustainability of human societies?

The subsections that follow examine this question and focus on a subset of global ecosystem conditions that are most affected by land use. They also consider the challenge of reducing the negative environmental impacts of land use while maintaining economic and social benefits.

Food Production

Together, croplands and pastures have become one of the largest terrestrial biomes on the planet, rivaling forest cover in extent and occupying approximately 40 percent of the land surface (figure 1.3). Changes in land-use practices have enabled world grain harvests to double in the past four decades, so they now exceed 2 billion tons per year. Some of this increase can be attributed to a 12 percent increase in world cropland area, but most of these production gains resulted from "Green Revolution" technologies, which include (a) high-yielding cultivars, (b) chemical fertilizers and pesticides, and (c) mechanization and irrigation. During the past 40 years, global fertilizer use has increased about 700 percent, and irrigated cropland area has increased approximately 70 percent.

Although modern agriculture has been successful in increasing food production, it has also caused extensive environmental damage. For example, increasing fertilizer use has led to the degradation of water quality in many regions. In addition, some irrigated lands have become heavily salinized, causing the worldwide loss of approximately 1.5 million hectares of arable land per year, along with an estimated US$11 billion in lost production. Up to 40 percent of global croplands may also be experiencing some degree of soil erosion, reduced fertility, or overgrazing.

The loss of native habitats also affects agricultural production by degrading the services of pollinators, especially bees. In short, modern agricultural land-use practices may be trading short-term increases in food production for long-term losses in ecosystem services, which include many that are important to agriculture.

Freshwater Resources

Land use can disrupt the surface water balance and the partitioning of precipitation into evapotranspiration, runoff, and groundwater flow. Surface runoff and river discharge generally increase when natural vegetation (especially forestland) is cleared. For instance, the Tocantins River Basin in Brazil showed a 25 percent increase in river discharge between 1960 and 1995, coincident with expanding agriculture but no major change in precipitation.

Water demands associated with land-use practices, especially irrigation, directly affect freshwater supplies through water withdrawals and diversions. Global water withdrawals now total approximately 3,900 cubic kilometers per year, or about 10 percent of the total global renewable resource. The consumptive use of water (not returned to the watershed) is estimated to be between 1,800 and 2,300 cubic kilometers per year.

Agriculture alone accounts for approximately 75 percent of global consumptive use. As a result, many large rivers—especially in semiarid regions—have greatly reduced flows, and some routinely dry up. In addition, the extraction of groundwater reserves is almost universally unsustainable and has resulted in declining water tables in many regions.

Land use often degrades water quality. Intensive agriculture increases erosion and sediment load and leaches nutrients and agricultural chemicals to groundwater, streams, and rivers. In fact, agriculture has become the largest source of excess nitrogen and phosphorus to waterways and coastal zones. Urbanization also substantially degrades water quality, especially where wastewater treatment is absent. The resulting degradation of inland and coastal waters impairs water supplies, causes oxygen depletion and fish kills, increases blooms of cyanobacteria (including toxic varieties), and contributes to water-borne disease.

Forest Resources

Land-use activities, primarily for agricultural expansion and timber extraction, have caused a net loss of 7 million to 11 million square kilometers of forest in the past 300 years. Highly managed forests, such as timber plantations in North America and oil palm plantations in Southeast Asia, have also replaced many natural forests and now cover 1.9 million square kilometers worldwide. Many land-use practices (such as fuelwood collection, forest grazing, and road expansion) can degrade forest ecosystem conditions—in terms of productivity, biomass, stand structure, and species composition—even without changing forest area. Land use can also degrade forest conditions indirectly by introducing pests and pathogens, changing fire fuel loads, changing patterns and frequency of ignition sources, and changing local meteorological conditions.

Regional Climate and Air Quality

Land conversion can alter regional climates through its effects on net radiation, the division of energy into sensible and latent heat, and the partitioning of precipitation into soil water, evapotranspiration, and runoff. Modeling studies demonstrate that changes in land cover in the tropics affect the climate largely through water-balance changes, but changes in temperate and boreal vegetation influence the climate primarily through changes in the surface radiation balance. Large-scale clearing of tropical forests may create a warmer, drier climate, whereas clearing temperate and boreal forest is generally thought to cool the climate, primarily through increased albedo.

Urban "heat islands" are an extreme case of how land use modifies the regional climate. The reduced vegetation cover, impervious surface area, and morphology of buildings in cityscapes combine to lower evaporative cooling, store heat, and warm the surface air. A recent analysis of climate records in the United States suggests that a major portion of the temperature increase during the past several decades resulted from urbanization and other land-use changes. Changes in land cover have also been implicated in changing the regional climate in China; recent analyses suggest that the daily diurnal temperature range has decreased as a result of urbanization.

Land-use practices also change air quality by altering emissions and changing the atmospheric conditions that affect reaction rates, transportation, and deposition. For example, tropospheric ozone (O_3) is particularly sensitive to changes in vegetation cover and biogenic emissions. Land-use practices often determine dust sources, biomass burning, vehicle emission patterns, and other air pollution sources. Furthermore, the effects of land use on local meteorological conditions, primarily in urban heat islands, also affect air quality: higher urban temperatures generally cause O_3 to increase.

Infectious Diseases

Habitat modification, road and dam construction, irrigation, increased proximity of people and livestock, and concentration or expansion of urban environments all modify the transmission of infectious disease and can lead to outbreaks and emergence episodes. For example, increasing tropical deforestation coincides with an upsurge of malaria and its vectors in Africa, Asia, and Latin America, even after accounting for the effects of changing population density.

Disturbing wildlife habitat is also of particular concern, because approximately 75 percent of human diseases have links to wildlife or domestic animals. Land use has been associated with the emergence of bat-borne Nipah virus in Malaysia, cryptosporidiosis in Europe and North America, and a range of food-borne illnesses globally. In addition, road building in the tropics is linked to increased bushmeat hunting, which may have played a key role in the emergence of human immunodeficiency virus types 1 and 2. Simian foamy virus was recently documented in hunters, confirming this mechanism of cross-species transfer.

The combined effects of land use and extreme climatic events can also have serious impacts, both on direct health outcomes (such as heat mortality, injury, and fatalities) and on ecologically mediated diseases. For example, Hurricane Mitch, which hit Central America in 1998, exhibited these combined effects: 9,600 people perished, widespread water- and vector-borne diseases ensued, and 1 million people were left homeless. Areas with extensive deforestation and settlements on degraded hillsides or floodplains suffered the greatest morbidity and mortality.

PRODUCTION LANDSCAPES: THE CONTEXT FOR LAND MANAGEMENT

When one travels on an airplane, the view from the window reveals landscapes below with mountain ranges, forests, grasslands, coastlines, and deserts. As human civilization evolved, people planted crops, reared animals, developed complex irrigation schemes, built cities, and devised technologies to make life more comfortable and less vulnerable to droughts, floods, and other potentially damaging climatic events. The outcomes of this human occupation are transformed landscapes over 40 percent of the Earth's ice-free land surface. Only places that are extremely cold, extremely hot, very mountainous, or as yet inaccessible remain free from human use (figure 1.3).

Landscapes also reveal how people obtain their food and pursue their livelihoods. In the industrial world of North America and Western Europe, a majority of people live in urban areas (77 percent in 2003) and obtain food transported from land devoted to high-yield agriculture. Diets are relatively high in animal products. Agricultural production is highly mechanized, with only 15 percent of people living in rural areas engaged in farming or ranching. The pattern is markedly different in parts of the world that are still in agrarian stages of development (figure 1.3).

Although overall global food production has increased 168 percent over approximately the past 40 years and is ample to feed all 6.5 billion people on the planet today, 13 percent of the world's people still suffered from malnutrition between 2000 and 2002 because they were too poor to purchase adequate food. The imprint of this paradox is seen throughout the rural landscape of the developing world in crops grown on infertile soils and steep slopes, mosaics of shifting cultivation, forests scavenged for fuelwood, and seasonal migrations pursuing fodder for livestock. Most people in the developing world live in rural areas, with South Asia having the highest percentage at more than 70 percent (Latin America and the Caribbean is the most urbanized developing region.) Of the rural population throughout all developing regions, the vast majority is engaged in agriculture. These rural farmers grow low-yield crops for their own households and local markets. Diets also contrast with those in the industrial world, with consumption of animal products far less than half that in industrial societies and per capita caloric intake at 65 to 80 percent.

Poverty, agriculture, and land use make a complex and challenging system with many flaws and interacting elements. Poor farmers do not want to be poor, and few choose actively to damage their environments. The reason so many are living on the edge of survival is that too many of their traditional approaches to agricultural production are breaking down. Economic growth has been insufficient to offer alternative means of employment for the rural poor. Profits from farming at low levels of productivity have been too small to allow farmers to reinvest in their farms and maintain productivity at acceptable levels (Eicher and Staatz

Figure 1.3   World Comparisons of Food Production and Consumption 2003

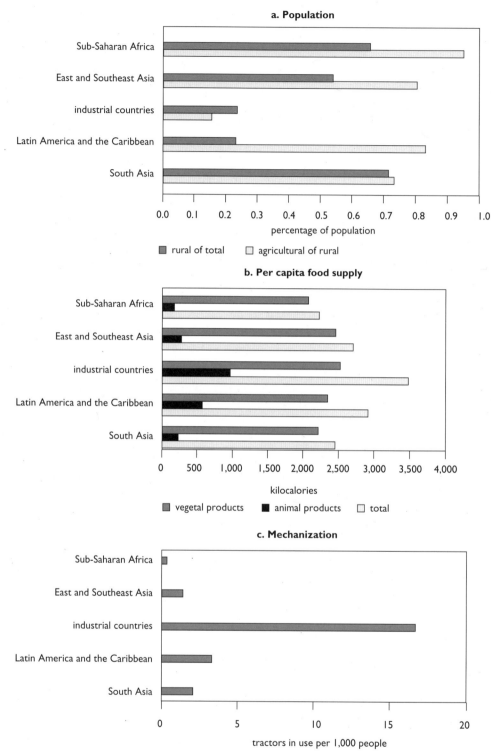

Source: Food and Agriculture Organization statistical databases (FAOSTAT), http://www.faostat.fao.org.
Note: In panel a, the percentage of total population living in rural areas is highest in South Asia and lowest in industrial countries, while agricultural populations (defined as all persons depending for their livelihood on agriculture, hunting, fishing, or forestry) constitute more than 70 percent of the rural population in all developing regions but only 15 percent in industrial countries. In panel b, per capita food supply per day and proportion of total in animal products
is highest in industrial countries. In panel c, food production is more mechanized in industrial countries, as illustrated by the number of tractors in use.

1990). Meanwhile, continual increases in population have depleted both the available resource base and social entitlements that hitherto provided a state of equilibrium in rural areas of Africa (Lele 1989).

Those who are most in need of new livelihood options are the least able to pay for them. Furthermore, the advice that they receive on the choices open to them is disgraceful—what the farmer needs is reliability and consistency of performance. A single mother hoping to harvest a metric ton of rice on a hectare of depleted upland soil can ill afford to lose 100 kilograms of her harvest to a crop pest or disease in a single season, even if, under some conditions (which she may not be able to achieve), she can potentially get a higher yield from a new variety. She needs to move to a higher level of productivity but cannot afford the means to lift herself there. Although group savings and credit schemes (such as savings and credit cooperative societies, household income security associations, and self-help groups) can help poor families to access inputs to get out of the poverty spiral, the effectiveness of such interventions is badly blunted when the inputs themselves are inadequately tailored to the needs of the poor. SLM practices are often complex, are difficult to implement, and have payoffs that may be beyond the horizon of the poor. But as the cases in this sourcebook will show, those constraints do not mean that SLM practices are impractical or impossible for the poor to adopt.

Much of the debate on poverty revolves around the low prices that farmers get for their produce. Remember, though, that the first priority for the rural poor is to grow their own food. Many of the rural poor do not even produce enough to feed themselves all year round, so they buy food when supplies are short and prices are high. Poor people do not need expensive food. Thus, an evident priority in the struggle against poverty is to bring food prices down. The costs of many of the improved technologies (such as improved seeds, fertilizer, and livestock breeds) needed by smallholders—despite ongoing efforts at market development—will remain high. Low-cost technologies (such as home-produced seed and household composts) often have a substantial cost in terms of labor—which is also a scarce resource in many poor households.

The advice given to many poor farmers regarding the use of essential inputs (both those purchased from outside and those that the farmer may generate from homestead resources, such as manures and home-produced seed) serves actively to discourage their use. In large part, this outcome occurs because of inadequate incorporation of basic economic parameters into recommendations to farmers (Blackie 2006). The information provided frequently overlooks the obvious fact that an expensive input (whether in cash or labor) can be profitable if it is used efficiently. The knowledge the poor seek is how to make best use of the limited amounts that they are able to purchase. So poverty alleviation and food security have to be arranged around low food prices and efficient production methods. With low food prices, the poor can use their limited cash to invest in better housing, education, and health care. With high food prices, they are further trapped in poverty, and the opportunities for livelihood diversification are few.

The human imprint on the landscape emerges from millions of individual decisions in pursuit of food and livelihoods. Through time, as societies evolve from agrarian to industrial and information-based economies, the landscape mirrors accompanying shifts in how people obtain food, what they eat, and where they work. Historical examples in Europe and North America follow a general pattern, and similar patterns are emerging in some developing regions, but with one major caveat: the early stages of agricultural transformation and industrialization in Europe and North America were supported by significant shifts of populations to new lands through colonization and settlement. In today's crowded world, that safety valve is no longer an option.

Instead a "Green Evolution" strategy is needed to help people transform their own landscapes rather than seeking to escape to fresh pastures. Local knowledge (of soils, landscapes, markets, and climate) is linked to the best of national and international expertise in a focused, problem-solving effort. The focus is on quality and results, facilitated through enhanced networking and coordination among the various sector stakeholders and international organizations. The best options are pulled together and then promoted through large-scale initiatives. The poor influence the choice of recommendations, while the private sector contributes toward sector needs such as seed and market systems. In that way, the power of millions of individuals' decisions can be tapped to create a more benign and sustainable human imprint on the landscape. The Green Evolution strategy encourages the efficient and swift transformation of practices leading to SLM by harnessing the best skills in a collaborative, learning-by-doing manner in which all people feel ownership and pride. Existing structures are improved and enhanced to build change through an evolutionary, rather than a revolutionary, approach. This approach is cost-effective and brings the best expertise of both developing countries and the international community together in a problem-solving format that can be rapidly scaled up to reach the poor quickly and effectively.

This process of participatory experimentation empowers the poor through knowledge generation and sharing. Through experimentation, the poor can investigate—and contribute to—the development of practical, affordable, and sustainable practices that are reliable and robust in their circumstances. The poor gain the information they need to select the best technology combinations for their conditions. They then share this knowledge with their fellow farmers through different channels, such as farmer field schools, field tours, and field days. Information from pilot project areas spreads widely and quickly across geographic and socioeconomic gradients. Experimentation is followed by diversification. After experimenting with different crops, farmers choose those that respond favorably to inputs or that perform well in their environments. They use an incremental adoption strategy. As their knowledge about a specific technology increases, as their farm produce increases, and as more profits accrue from the sales, farmers gradually expand their capacity to diversify into other production activities.

The key element is building the trust and respect of the poor. Trust and respect are gained through a continuing exercise of discussing and coming to a consensus on options, together with obtaining routine and informed feedback on results. Some tools are already in use. Researchers have been highly innovative in developing the necessary tools to meet the challenge of conducting participatory activities with many clients over an extended geographic area in a cost- and time-effective manner. See, for example, Snapp, Blackie, and Donovan's (2003) "mother and baby" trial design, which collects quantitative data from mother trials that are managed by researchers and systematically cross-checks them against baby trials that are managed by farmers. This approach quickly generates best bet options that are owned by the participating communities. Moreover, it creates a fertile environment for developing new insights and priorities. The eventual product has several advantages:

- It is owned by those who need to adopt it, so they have a genuine belief that it actually is useful.
- It builds bridges of communication between target communities and the agencies working to assist them (the chronic research-extension linkage problem).
- It creates a confidence among the target population that they can solve their own problems, leading to quicker innovation and also spread of innovation across communities.

In many of the success stories developed in the subsequent Investment Notes, the path was laid through skillful building of partnerships with farmers, communities, and institutions in the countryside.

LAND MANAGEMENT TRADE-OFFS

Land-use change has allowed civilizations to grow crops, feed livestock, obtain energy, build cities, and carry out myriad other activities that underlie material advancement of any society and progression through the other major societal transitions. Land-use change also profoundly alters ecosystems as vegetation is cleared and biomass is diverted for human consumption. Unintended environmental consequences potentially undermine future land-use options.

Since publication of the Brundtland report (WCED 1987), the concept of sustainability has received increasing attention in agriculture, yet researchers have struggled to operationalize the concept. Smyth and Dumanski (1993) subdivided the general concept of sustainability into four main pillars: (a) productivity, (b) stability of production, (c) soil and water quality, and (d) socioeconomic feasibility. A slightly different approach for using the concept of sustainability has been to define various indicators (see, for example, Bockstaller, Girardin, and van der Werf 1997; Pieri and others 1995).

Several practical problems arise in implementing this strategy, including the large amount of data needed to quantify a large number of different sustainability indicators and the challenge of understanding the complex interactions among such indicators. Some researchers have combined indicators into indexes (for example, Farrow and Winograd 2001; Sands and Podmore 2000). This procedure raises the question of how indexes measured in different units can be meaningfully aggregated. The choice of "weights" used for such aggregation is often arbitrary and lacks adequate rigor. One well-known strategy for weighting different indexes was developed by economists for cost-benefit analysis, wherein systematic methods have been created to ascertain monetary values to attribute to both market and nonmarket goods and services, including services of natural capital. Yet even those systematic attempts to value and aggregate market and nonmarket goods have proved controversial and have not been widely accepted within and outside the economics profession (Belzer 1999; Portney 1994).

The alternative approach taken in trade-off analysis is to work with decision makers to identify a limited set of high-priority indicators and then to provide decision makers with quantitative estimates of the relationships among those indicators, leaving to the decision makers the task of subjectively assessing the implied trade-offs or win-win options. Trade-off curves are used to communicate information about trade-offs to decision makers. Trade-off curves are designed to embody the principle of opportunity cost in production systems. They are typically constructed by varying parameters in the production system that affect the economic incentives perceived by farmers in their land-use and input-use decisions.

A key potential benefit of the trade-off approach is the ability to model the desirability and likely effects of scaling up good practice. Most often, the scaling-up approach used is based on the simplistic assumption of additive economic and ecological benefits as one scales up good practice. The goal of trade-off analysis is to support decision making related to public policy issues associated with agricultural production systems. Thus, the focus of trade-off analysis is to provide information at a spatial scale relevant to such policy questions—typically at a level of analysis such as a watershed, a political unit, or a region, or even at the national level. Yet the environmental effects of production systems are generally site specific. A critical question, therefore, is how to bridge the gap between the site-specific effects of agricultural production systems and the scale relevant for policy decisions. The trade-off analysis model is designed to solve this problem by characterizing the population of biophysical and economic decision-making units in a region, simulating their behavior at the field scale, and then aggregating outcomes to a regional scale that is relevant for policy analysis by using trade-off curves and other means of communicating results.

CONFRONTING THE EFFECTS OF LAND USE

Current trends in land use allow humans to appropriate an ever-larger fraction of the biosphere's goods and services while simultaneously diminishing the capacity of global ecosystems to sustain food production, maintain freshwater and forest resources, regulate climate and air quality, and mediate infectious diseases. This assertion is supported across a broad range of environmental conditions worldwide, although some (for example, alpine and marine areas) are not considered in this sourcebook. Nevertheless, the conclusion is clear: modern land-use practices, while increasing the short-term supplies of material goods, may undermine many ecosystem services in the long run, even on regional and global scales.

Confronting the global environmental challenges of land use requires assessing and managing inherent trade-offs between meeting immediate human needs and maintaining the capacity of ecosystems to provide goods and services in the future. Assessments of trade-offs must recognize that land use provides crucial social and economic benefits, even while leading to possible long-term declines in human welfare through altered ecosystem functioning.

SELECTING AND USING APPROPRIATE INDICATORS FOR SLM AND LANDSCAPE RESILIENCE

SLM policies must also assess and enhance the resilience of different land-use practices. Managed ecosystems—and the services they provide—are often vulnerable to diseases, climatic extremes, invasive species, toxic releases, and the like. Increasing the resilience of managed landscapes requires practices that are more robust to disturbance and that can recover from unanticipated surprises. The need for decision-making and policy actions across multiple geographic scales and multiple ecological dimensions is increasing. The very nature of the issue requires such actions: land use occurs in local places, with real-world social and economic benefits, while potentially causing ecological degradation across local, regional, and global scales. Society faces the challenge of reliably assessing outcomes and developing strategies that reduce the negative environmental impacts of land use across multiple services and scales while sustaining social and economic benefits.

Indicators are interlinked components and processes in one land management system, not a group of separate variables. Although each indicator could be interpreted independently, SLM as a whole can be assessed only if its indicators are linked in a meaningful way. In the context of SLM, different biophysical and socioeconomic indicators of both a quantitative and a qualitative nature are selected, measured, and evaluated. This heterogeneous mix of indicators requires a qualitative frame or structural model for a meaningful analysis of the links between and causal effects of the indicators (box 1.3).

DIVERSITY OF LAND MANAGEMENT SYSTEMS AND POVERTY ALLEVIATION

For structure, the sourcebook follows the comprehensive 2001 Food and Agriculture Organization (FAO)–World Bank study, *Farming Systems and Poverty: Improving Farm-*

Box 1.3   Pressure-State-Response Framework

The framework shown in the accompanying figure can be used as a structural model for identifying core issues, formulating impact hypotheses, and selecting a meaningful set of indicators. The indicators are related to the components of the model.

The Sahara and Sahel Observatory in Tunisia identified four topics for coverage when developing impact indicators using the Pressure-State-Response framework:

1. *Driving forces causing pressure on natural resources.* These forces include population pressure, economic growth, and urbanization; policy failures or distortions (such as stagnant technology and delayed intensification); imperfect markets (including lack of markets and poor market access); transaction costs and imperfect information (including limited access to information about market opportunities); social inequity and poverty; and political and social instability.

2. *Pressure indicators.* These indicators include changes in cropping techniques, financial position of holdings, fuelwood and charcoal consumption, use of crop residues, use of animal dung for fuel, and price of fuelwood and charcoal.

3. *State indicators.* These indicators include rate of deforestation, rate of soil erosion, degree of salinization, soil crusting and compaction, crop productivity, livestock productivity, and nutrient balance (on-farm organic matter recycling).

4. *Response indicators.* These indicators include legislative change, investment, tree planting, state conservation programs, farmer conservation groups, and farmer adoption of tree planting and soil and water conservation.

Pressure-State-Response Framework

Source: Herweg, Steiner, and Slaats 1999.

ers' Livelihoods in a Changing World (Dixon and Gulliver with Gibbon 2001). The study adopted a farming systems approach to provide an agricultural perspective to the revision of the World Bank's rural development strategy. It drew on many years of experience in the FAO and the World Bank, as well as in a number of other national and international institutions. More than 70 major farming systems were defined throughout the six developing regions of the world. Findings were supported by more than 20 case studies from around the world that analyzed innovative approaches to small farm or pastoral development. Although recognizing the heterogeneity that inevitably exists within such broad systems, the farming systems approach provides a framework for understanding the needs of those living within a system, the likely challenges and opportunities that they will face over the next 30 years, and the relative importance of different strategies for escaping from poverty and hunger.

The key farming system types identified and described by the study (Dixon and Gulliver with Gibbon 2001) are briefly summarized here to guide and focus the interventions and investment examples and guidelines.

Overview of Farming Systems as a Baseline for Targeting Investments

A *farming system* is defined as a population of individual farm systems that have broadly similar resource bases, enterprise patterns, household livelihoods, and constraints and for which similar development strategies and interventions would be appropriate. Depending on the scale of the analysis, a farming system can encompass a few dozen or many millions of households.

The delineation of the major farming systems provides a useful framework within which appropriate agricultural development strategies and interventions can be determined. The classification of the farming systems of developing regions has been based on the following criteria:

- *Available natural resource base.* Classification takes into account water, land, grazing areas, and forest; the climate (altitude is an important determinant); the landscape (slope is considered); and farm size, tenure, and organization.
- *Dominant pattern of farm activities and household livelihoods.* Classification takes into account such factors as field crops, livestock, trees, aquaculture, hunting and gathering, processing, and off-farm activities. The main technologies used determine the intensity of production and integration of crops, livestock, and other activities.

On the basis of those criteria, 8 broad categories of farming system and 72 farming systems have been identified:

1. Irrigated farming systems (3), embracing a broad range of food and cash crop production
2. Wetland rice-based farming systems (3), dependent on monsoon rains supplemented by irrigation
3. Rainfed farming systems in humid and subhumid areas of high resource potential (11), characterized by crop activity (notably root crops, cereals, industrial tree crops—both small scale and plantation—and commercial horticulture) or mixed crop-livestock systems
4. Rainfed farming systems in steep and highland areas (10), often characterized by mixed crop-livestock systems
5. Rainfed farming systems in dry and cold areas (19), characterized by mixed crop-livestock and pastoral systems merging into sparse and often dispersed systems with very low current productivity or potential because of extreme aridity or cold
6. Dualistic farming systems with both large-scale commercial and smallholder farms (16) across a variety of ecologies and with diverse production patterns
7. Coastal artisanal fishing and farming systems (4)
8. Urban-based farming systems (6), typically focused on horticultural and livestock production.

The eight categories of farming system are further compared in table 1.1, which shows the areas of total land, cultivated land, and irrigated land; agricultural population; and market surplus. A recent study investigating alternative household strategies for land management (farming) systems in developing countries reinforced the need for greater development attention to diversification and intensification (box 1.4). In the relatively constrained circumstances of rainfed highlands and rainfed dry or cold climates, however, off-farm employment and exit from

Table 1.1 Comparison of Farming Systems by Category

Category characteristic	Irrigated systems	Wetland rice-based	Rainfed humid	Rainfed highlands	Rainfed dry and cold	Dualistic (large and small)	Coastal artisanal fishing	Urban-based
Number of systems	3	3	11	10	19	16	4	6
Total land (million hectares)	219	330	2,013	842	3,478	3,116	70	—
Cultivated area (million hectares)	15	155	160	150	231	414	11	—
Cultivated area/total area (%)	7	47	8	18	7	13	16	—
Irrigated area (million hectares)	15	90	17	30	41	36	2	—
Irrigated area/cultivated area (%)	99	58	11	20	18	9	19	—
Agricultural population (million)	30	860	400	520	490	190	60	40
Agricultural persons/cultivated area (person/hectare)	2.1	5.5	2.5	3.5	2.1	0.4	5.5	—
Market surplus	High	Medium	Medium	Low	Low	Medium	High	High

Source: FAO data and expert knowledge.

Note: — = not available. *Cultivated area* refers to both annual and perennial crops.

Several strategies can help households improve their livelihoods:

- Intensify existing farm production patterns through increased use of inputs or better-quality inputs.
- Diversify production, with emphasis on greater market orientation and added value, involving a shift to new, generally higher-value products.
- Increase farm size (an option limited to a few areas where additional land resources are still available).
- Increase off-farm income to supplement farm activities and provide financing for additional input use.
- Exit from agriculture, in many cases by migrating from rural areas.

Source: Dixon and Gulliver with Gibbon 2001.

agriculture are important (though not always easy to achieve).

Principles for Sustainable Land Management in Rainfed Farming Systems

For rainfed systems, a number of studies (including Dixon and Gulliver with Gibbon 2001) have identified a set of principles. According to these studies, good land management requires an integrated and synergistic resource management approach that embraces locally appropriate combinations of the following technical options:

- Buildup of soil organic matter and related biological activity to optimum sustainable levels for improved moisture, infiltration and storage, nutrient supply, and soil structure through the use of compost, farmyard manure, green manures, surface mulch, enriched fallows, agroforestry, cover crops, and crop residue management
- Integrated plant nutrition management with locally appropriate and cost-effective combinations of organic or inorganic and on-farm or off-farm sources of plant nutrients (such as use of organic manures, crop residues, and rhizobial nitrogen fixation; transfer of nutrients released by weathering in the deeper soil layers to the surface by way of tree roots and leaf litter; and use of rock phosphate, lime, and mineral fertilizer)

- Better crop management using improved seeds of appropriate varieties; improved crop establishment at the beginning of the rains (to increase protective ground cover, thereby reducing water loss and soil erosion); effective weed control; and integrated pest management
- Better rainwater management to increase infiltration and eliminate or reduce runoff so as to improve soil moisture conditions within the rooting zone, thereby lessening the risk of moisture stress during dry spells, while reducing erosion
- Improvement of soil rooting depth and permeability through breaking of cultivation-induced compacted soil layers (hoe or plow pan) by means of conservation tillage practices (using tractor-drawn subsoilers, ox-drawn chisel plows, or hand-hoe planting pits or double-dug beds or interplanting deep-rooted perennial crops, trees, and shrubs)
- Reclamation, where appropriate (that is, if technically feasible and cost-effective), of cultivated land that has been severely degraded by such processes as gullying, loss of topsoil from sheet erosion, soil compaction, acidification, or salinization.

These good SLM principles are used to derive the lending directions suggested in the next section. They are also a basis for the Investment Notes and Innovative Activity Profiles presented for potential application in areas with rainfed farming systems.

FUTURE DIRECTIONS FOR INVESTMENTS

Public and private investments to intensify sustainable production systems are generally best focused on the following:

- Facilitating the capacity of farmers, the government, and the private sector to make decisions about the appropriate technological and resource allocation
- Providing the necessary social, organizational, and physical infrastructure.

It is critical that agricultural production systems be sufficiently flexible to adapt to changing environmental and economic conditions.

New technologies will be developed, and variations on established production systems are likely to continue. At present, options that may warrant public sector support include the following:

- Improvement of plant varieties will remain crucial as it becomes increasingly difficult to adjust the environment to the plant. Plant varieties that are adapted to specific production environments and sustainable agricultural practices and that are resistant to specific pests and diseases will become increasingly important. Livestock improvement will increase productivity and make more efficient use of scarce land and water. Biotechnology's potential as a tool for sustainable production systems should be evaluated and supported on a case-by-case basis.

■ Conservation farming practices can reduce unnecessary input use. Minimum tillage or no-till crop production reduces labor and equipment costs, enhances soil fertility, reduces erosion, and improves water infiltration, thereby reducing unit costs and conserving land resources. Improved crop residue management, including mulching, is often a necessary component of these systems. No-till systems of conservation farming have proved a major success in Latin America and are being used in South Asia and Africa.

■ Organic farming eliminates use of chemical inputs and can be sustainable as long as practices maintain productivity at a reasonable level, consistent with price incentives provided by growing market opportunities for organic produce. Organic farming depends mainly on the development of niche markets with reliable standards and certification systems for production.

■ Integrated pest management (IPM) systems have been developed for many crops to control pests, weeds, and diseases while reducing potential environmental damage from excessive use of chemicals. Scaling up IPM technologies is a challenge, as these management systems rely on farmers' understanding of complex pest ecologies and crop-pest relationships. Thus, although IPM messages need to be simplified, IPM systems require continuous research and technical support and intensive farmer education and training along with policy-level support.

■ Precision agriculture improves productivity by better matching management practices to local crop and soil conditions. Relatively sophisticated technologies are used to vary input applications and production practices, according to seasonal conditions, soil and land characteristics, and production potential. However, with help from extension and other services, resource-poor farmers can also apply principles of precision agriculture for differential input application and management on dispersed small plots. Appropriate technologies suitable for use by small-scale farmers include simple color charts to guide decisions on fertilizer application and laser leveling of fields for irrigation.

■ Fertilizer use is relatively low, especially in Africa, and soil fertility is declining, which explains much of the lagging agricultural productivity growth in Africa relative to other regions. Fertilizer use is resurfacing on the African development agenda, and policy makers face a major challenge in deciding how to promote increased use of mineral fertilizers. Several obstacles must be overcome to avoid fertilizer market failure, however. They include the strong seasonality in demand for fertilizer, the risk of using fertilizer stemming from weather-related production variability and uncertain crop prices, the highly dispersed demand for fertilizer, a lack of purchasing power on the part of many potential users, the bulkiness and perishability of most fertilizer products, and the need to achieve large volumes of throughput in fertilizer procurement and distribution to capture economies of scale.

Agricultural intensification is a key and desirable way to increase the productivity of existing land and water resources in the production of food and cash crops, livestock, forestry, and aquaculture. Generally associated with increased use of external inputs, *intensification* is now defined as the more efficient use of production inputs. Increased productivity comes from the use of improved varieties and breeds, more efficient use of labor, and better farm management (Dixon and Gulliver with Gibbon 2001). Although intensification of production systems is an important goal, these land management systems need to be sustainable to provide for current needs without compromising the ability of future generations to meet their needs.

Some of the system adaptations that are options for sustainable intensification of production include the following:

■ Integrated crop-livestock production can enhance environmental sustainability by feeding crop residues to animals, thus improving nutrient cycling. This crop-livestock approach is likely to become increasingly profitable given the large, worldwide increase in demand for meat, milk, and other products derived from animals. The suitability of many livestock enterprises to the production systems of small farms holds considerable potential for poverty reduction.

■ Agricultural diversification must be pursued where existing farming systems are not environmentally sustainable or economically viable. Diversification into high-value, nontraditional crop and livestock systems (for example, horticultural crops) is attractive because of the growing market demand for these products, their high labor intensity, and the high returns to labor and management. In contrast to other low-input strategies for sustainable intensification, diversification to high-value products frequently requires the use of relatively high levels of inputs, which must be monitored and managed carefully.

- Tree crops, including fruit, beverage, timber, and specialty crops, offer opportunities for environmentally sound production systems because they maintain vegetative cover and can reduce soil erosion. Tree crops, especially when multiple species are planted, help maintain a relatively high level of biodiversity. They are important for export earnings in many countries and, although often suited to large-scale plantations, are also important to smallholders with mixed cropping systems.

Both public and private investments are needed to support the transition to more profitable and sustainable farming systems. Sustainable intensification will frequently require activities that provide an enabling environment and support services for the market-led changes or component technologies, including management practices. Much investment will come from market supply chains based in the private sector, including input supply and output marketing and processing enterprises and farmers. Public investment will need to focus on (a) new knowledge and information services, (b) public policy and regulatory systems, and (c) market and private sector development.

A key investment area is in technology associated with management innovations to improve overall productivity and sustainability of agricultural systems. Much research will focus on developing improved management systems, with an emphasis on understanding agricultural ecology, farm management, and social systems. Biotechnology offers opportunities to diversify and intensify agricultural production systems: tissue culture for production of virus-free planting stock (such as bananas) and transgenic crops with pest resistance or other beneficial characteristics.

Because of the larger spatial and temporal scales of operations and likely effects of landscape and watershed investments relative to a single site or community project, certain difficulties must be overcome. For example, successfully scaling up site-specific SLM innovations invariably requires negotiated implementation arrangements suited to local power structures and institutions. Safeguard policies are often critical to SLM and natural resource management investments. The key policies of the World Bank are identified in box 1.5.

Box 1.5   Key Safeguard Policy Issues for SLM and Natural Resource Management Investments

The World Bank has implemented the following policies with respect to SLM and natural resource management investments:

- *Environmental assessment (Operational Policy/Bank Procedure 4.01).* An environmental assessment is required if a natural resource management project has potential for adverse environmental risks or impacts.
- *Natural habitats (Operational Policy 4.04).* Protection of natural habitats (land and water areas where most of the original plant and animal species are still present) is required for any natural resource management investment that may cause degradation of the habitat.
- *Projects in international waterways (Operational Policy 7.50).* The borrower must notify other riparian countries of any proposed natural resource management investment involving a body of water that flows through or forms part of the boundary of two or more countries.

- *Involuntary resettlement (Operational Policy/Bank Procedure 4.12).* A resettlement action plan is required if a natural resource management investment results in physical relocation, results in loss of land or access to land or other assets, or impacts on livelihoods arising from restrictions on access to parks or protected areas.
- *Indigenous peoples (Operational Directive 4.20).* An indigenous peoples action plan is required if a natural resource management investment affects indigenous people.
- *Forestry (Operational Policy 4.36).* Government commitment to undertake sustainable management and conservation-oriented forestry is required for any investment with potential to have a significant impact on forested areas. (Investment with exclusive focus on environmental protection or supportive of small-scale farmers may be appraised on its own merits.)

Source: World Bank 2005b.

REFERENCES

Belzer, R. B. 1999. "HACCP Principles for Regulatory Analysis." In *The Economics of HACCP: Studies of Costs and Benefits*, ed. L. Unnevehr, 97–124. St. Paul, MN: Eagan Press.

Blackie, M. J. 2006. "Are Fertiliser Subsidies Necessary?" ID21 Insights 61, Institute of Development Studies, Brighton, U.K.

Bockstaller, C., P. Girardin, and H. M. G. van der Werf. 1997. "Use of Agro-ecological Indicators for the Evaluation of Farming Systems." *European Journal of Agronomy* 7 (1–3): 261–70.

Cassman, K. G., and S. Wood. 2005. "Cultivated Systems." In *Ecosystems and Human Well-Being: Current States and Trends*, vol. 1 Millennium Ecosystem Assessment series, 745–94. Washington, DC: Millennium Ecosystem Assessment.

DeFries, R., G. P. Asner. amd J. Foley. 2006. "A Glimpse Out the Window: What Landscapes Reveal about Livelihoods, Land Use, and Environmental Consequences." *Environment* 48(8): 22–36.

Dixon, J., and A. Gulliver, with D. Gibbon. 2001. *Farming Systems and Poverty: Improving Farmers' Livelihoods in a Changing World*. Rome: Food and Agriculture Organization and World Bank. http://www.fao.org/farmingsystems/.

Eicher, C. K, and J. M. Staatz, ed. 1990. *Agricultural Development in the Third World*. Baltimore, MD: Johns Hopkins University Press.

Evenson, R. E., and D. Gollin. 2003. "Assessing the Impact of the Green Revolution, 1960 to 2000." *Science* 300 (5620): 758–62.

Farrow, A., and M. Winograd. 2001. "Land Use Modelling at the Regional Scale: An Input to Rural Sustainability Indicators for Central America." *Agricultural Ecosystems and Environment* 85 (1): 249–68.

Foley, J. A., R. DeFries, G. P. Asner, C. Barford, G. Bonan, S. R. Carpenter, F. S. Chapin, M. T. Coe, G. C. Daily, H. K. Gibbs, J. H. Helkowski, T. Holloway, E. A. Howard, C. J. Kucharik, C. Monfreda, J. A. Patz, I. C. Prentice, N. Ramankutty, and P. K. Snyder. 2005. "Global Consequences of Land Use." *Science* 309 (5734): 570–74.

Herweg, K., K. Steiner, and J. Slaats. 1999. *Sustainable Land Management: Guidelines for Impact Monitoring—Tool Kit Module*. Berne, Switzerland: Centre for Development and Environment.

Lele, U. J. 1989. "Managing Agricultural Development in Africa: Three Articles on Lessons from Experience." MADIA Discussion Paper 2, World Bank, Washington, DC.

Millennium Ecosystem Assessment. 2005. *Millennium Ecosystem Assessment Report, 2005*. Washington, DC: Island Press.

Pieri, C., J. Dumanski, A. Hamblin, and A. Young. 1995. "Land Quality Indicators." World Bank Discussion Paper 315, World Bank, Washington, DC.

Plato. 2003. *The Timaeus and Critias of Plato*. Whitefish, MT: Kessinger.

Portney, P. R. 1994. "The Contingent Valuation Debate: Why Economists Should Care." *Journal of Economic Perspectives* 8 (4):3–17.

Sachs, J. D., ed. 2005. *Investing in Development: A Practical Plan to Achieve the Millennium Development Goals*. London: United Nations Development Programme.

Sands, G. R., and T. H. Podmore. 2000. "A Generalized Environmental Sustainability Index for Agricultural Systems." *Agriculture, Ecosystems, and Environment* 79 (1): 29–41.

Smyth, A. J., and J. Dumanski. 1993. "FESLM: An International Framework for Evaluating Sustainable Land Management." World Soil Resources Report 73. Food and Agriculture Organization, Rome.

Snapp, S. S., M. J. Blackie, and C. Donovan. 2003. "Realigning Research and Extension Services: Experiences from Southern Africa." *Food Policy* 28: 349–63.

WCED (World Commission on Environment and Development). 1987. *Our Common Future*. Oxford, U.K.: Oxford University Press.

World Bank. 2003. *Reaching the Rural Poor: A Renewed Strategy for Rural Development*. Washington, DC: World Bank.

———. 2004. *Agriculture Investment Sourcebook*. Washington, DC: World Bank.

———. 2005a. *Shaping the Future of Water for Agriculture: A Sourcebook for Investment in Agricultural Water Management*. Washington, DC: World Bank.

———. 2005b. *The World Bank Operational Manual*. Washington, DC: World Bank.

———. 2006. *Sustainable Land Management*. Washington, DC: World Bank.

PART II

Major Farming Systems: Investment Options and Innovations

CHAPTER 2

Introduction

This edition of the sourcebook includes the three major rainfed systems out of the eight system types identified by Dixon and Gulliver with Gibbon (2001) for development of detailed investment notes:

1. Rainfed farming systems in humid and subhumid areas are covered in chapter 3.
2. Rainfed farming systems in highlands and sloping areas are covered in chapter 4.
3. Rainfed farming systems in dry and cold (semiarid and arid) areas are covered in chapter 5.

The decision to start with three rainfed systems was based on the level of available resources (funds and time) and also on the fact that these rainfed systems occupy more than 540 million hectares of cultivated land globally and involve approximately 1.4 billion people, who, in turn, practice about 40 different land management and cropping arrangements. Selected readings and Web links are provided for readers who seek more in-depth information and examples of practical experience. Future editions will systematically cover the remaining farming systems.

For each farming system type, good practice examples are identified and summarized as follows:

- *Investment Notes* summarize good practice and lessons learned in specific investment areas. They provide a brief, but technically sound, overview for the nonspecialist. For each Investment Note, the investments have been evaluated in different settings for effectiveness and sustainability, and they can be broadly endorsed by the community of practitioners from within and outside the World Bank.
- *Innovative Activity Profiles* highlight the design of successful or innovative investments. These profiles provide a short description of an activity in the World Bank's portfolio or that of a partner agency, focusing on potential effectiveness in poverty reduction, empowerment, or sustainability. Activities profiled have often not been sufficiently tested and evaluated in a range of settings to be considered "good practice," but they should be closely monitored for potential scaling up.

REFERENCE

Dixon, J., and A. Gulliver, with D. Gibbon. 2001. *Farming Systems and Poverty: Improving Farmers' Livelihoods in a Changing World.* Rome: Food and Agriculture Organization and World Bank. http://www.fao.org/farmingsystems/.

CHAPTER 3

Rainfed Farming and Land Management Systems in Humid Areas

OVERVIEW

The 11 systems covered in this chapter are found in the humid and subhumid zones of Africa, Asia, and Latin America. They support an agricultural population of approximately 400 million on about 160 million hectares of cultivated land, of which only 11 percent is irrigated. Pressure on land is typically moderate—only 2.5 persons per cultivated hectare on average—although some areas of intense pressure exist.

These systems depend on slash-and-burn agriculture, where forest is cleared to cultivate root crops, cereals, and groundnuts, among other crops. The number of cattle and small ruminants is low. Cash income is based on forest products and wild game rather than on cash crops. Rainfed farming and land management systems in humid areas are characterized by their physical isolation; a lack of roads and markets hinders their economic development. Deforestation and consequent loss of biodiversity is a serious issue that affects the local to global levels. Because of locally increasing population pressure, fallow periods are shortened, resulting in soil fertility loss and yield decline, which can drive further deforestation. The agricultural growth potential is moderate. Despite the existence of large uncultivated areas and high rainfall, only modest yield increases are expected in the near future. The fragility of the soils and the call for rainforest protection, with its associated biodiversity and multiple environmental services, represent strong arguments against further extension of the agricultural system.

Eight of the 11 systems presented here can be characterized as *mixed farming systems*. Cereals, root crops, and tree crops are cultivated for food and cash. They use little irrigation. These systems often have an important livestock component. The degree of market development is moderate but varying and has substantial opportunities for further development. Because of their diversity, these systems differ considerably in constraints and potentials. Where population densities are low, the systems have significant potential for agricultural growth and poverty reduction. For instance, the cereal and root crop farming systems could become a breadbasket of Africa and an important source of export earnings. The mixed-maize system in eastern and southern Africa also has good potential, but it is currently in crisis because shortages of seed, fertilizer, and agrochemicals and the high prices of fertilizer relative to the maize prices have sharply curtailed agricultural investment. As a result, yields have fallen and soil fertility is declining, while smallholders are reverting to extensive production practices. In these systems, the main sources of vulnerability are market volatility, lack of improved and appropriate farming technologies, lack of off-farm opportunities, and drought (in the drier areas). The prevalence of poverty is limited to moderate, although it can be extensive in the forest-based farming systems.

POTENTIALS FOR POVERTY REDUCTION AND AGRICULTURAL GROWTH

In broad terms, there are five main farm household strategies to improve livelihoods (Dixon and others 2001):

1. Intensification of existing production patterns
2. Diversification of production and processing
3. Expanded farm or herd size
4. Increased off-farm income, both agricultural and non-agricultural
5. Complete exit from the agricultural sector within a particular farming system.

Rainfed farming systems in humid areas depend on all of these five household strategies for the halving of poverty. Among these strategies, diversification is the most significant. Livestock plays a major role in diversification. Opportunities for system development lie in improved crop-livestock integration, integrated pest management, and improved land management techniques, such as conservation farming. Sustainable land management and soil nutrient capitalization depend on secure and equitable access to resources, especially for land and water. The development of small-scale and farmer-managed irrigation will contribute to both intensification and diversification.

REFERENCE

Dixon, J., and A. Gulliver. 2001. *Farming Systems and Poverty: Improving Farmers' Livelihoods in a Changing World.* Rome: Food and Agriculture Organization and World Bank. http://www.fao.org/farmingsystems.

Science and Local Innovation Make Livestock More Profitable and Friendlier to the Environment in Central America

Forage production and conservation are promising measures to alleviate livestock pressures on the environment. Improved forages can be economically profitable and a good option for improving the livelihoods of livestock producers. They also generate social gains because the adoption of new technologies that are based on improved forages generates more rural employment and increases the availability of staple foods. In a dual-purpose system, employment can be increased from one and one-half to four times. However, because few producers have the cash flow necessary to finance the required investments, farmers need to improve their farms gradually, as funds are available. Fast, large-scale adoption needs to be coordinated with financial organizations.

A potential danger exists that farmers may wish to cut more trees to expand pastures for more cattle and profits. Further research should focus on the role of forages in matching economic and environmental sustainability through intensification and in linking smallholders to markets. Research and development efforts need to proactively find ways to provide alternatives so that land degradation is no longer the most attractive land-use option. Collaborative technical research with farmers that improves productivity and prevents degradation must go hand in hand with policies (such as tax policies, payments for carbon, market development, and media campaigns). Such linked efforts can generate incentives to change traditions and to improve land management practices.

KEY SUSTAINABLE LAND MANAGEMENT ISSUES

Changing old traditions about livestock is not easy. For generations, livestock have made money for their owners, who often have little more than a pasture. Can earnings be increased and sustained? Livestock can cause environmental damage (Steinfield and others 2006). Cattle, horses, and donkeys graze not only farm pastures but also, in many cases, the larger landscape. What are the environmental consequences? This Investment Note explains how the International Center for Tropical Agriculture (Centro Internacional de Agricultura Tropical, or CIAT) and its partners combine science and local knowledge to profitably feed animals while benefiting the environment.

Many parts of the tropics have high annual rainfall, but no rain falls for four to seven months of the year. The landscape turns brown. During those months, livestock overgraze pastures as scarce water causes a severe shortage of livestock feed on the farm. Farmers in many areas of Africa, Asia, and Latin America confront these water and feed challenges (figure 3.1). This note focuses on Central America.

Damage becomes widespread. Many farmers let their livestock free to feed in the landscape. Because most grasses are already dry, the leaves of bushes and young trees are soon gone. These pressures reduce plant health and vitality. Over the years, many plants die, especially the types animals prefer.

As plants disappear, soils become exposed. Annual rains return, washing away soils and further weakening the livestock landscape. With less vegetation comes a reduced ability to absorb water. The landscape is drier for more months of the year. When the rains stop, the water springs stop as well. Unless checked, this trend continues until eroded soils and weeds dominate the landscape.

Damage also occurs to other ecologies downstream. Water flows change. The currents become more dramatic, matching the rains. When the rains stop, the flows trickle.

This note was prepared by M. Peters and D. White, Centro Internacional de Agricultura Tropical, Cali, Colombia, and F. Holmann, Centro Internacional de Agricultura Tropical and the International Livestock Research Institute, Cali, Colombia.

Figure 3.1 Months of Consecutive Dry Season

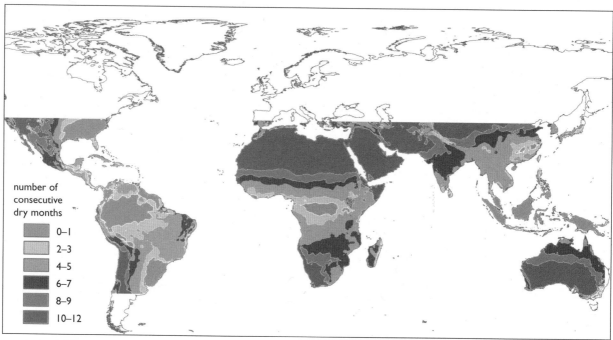

number of
consecutive
dry months

- 0–1
- 2–3
- 4–5
- 6–7
- 8–9
- 10–12

Source: Authors' elaboration.

When the rains pour, the flows can overwhelm. Many people, especially in Central America, remember the pain of Hurricane Mitch in 1999.

About 45 percent of agricultural land in South America is degraded. According to the Global Assessment of Human-Induced Soil Degradation (GLASOD) database, degradation afflicts even larger areas (74 percent) in Central America.[1] Many inhabitants do not even notice land degradation: the story is so old that it is already part of their lives and livelihoods.

LESSONS LEARNED

Despite the potential economic gain (and environmental pain), relatively few farmers see the benefit of investing in forage production for their animals. Those who invest are often pleasantly surprised at the results. They tell their friends. The money is good and worth looking into, as an investor would say.

For decades, CIAT scientists have developed high-yield grasses and legumes that have high nutritional quality and can withstand major climatic and agronomic stresses. By linking science with local perspectives, CIAT is able to apply its extensive germplasm collection of more than 23,000 tropical forage varieties—the largest collection in the world.

With its partners, CIAT advances environmentally friendly and profitable livestock production practices. This process has four components: (a) matching forage germplasm to specific environmental conditions, (b) diagnosing farm and market contexts, (c) fostering innovation and learning processes, and (d) sharing knowledge and scaling out activities, including South-South interactions.

Matching

CIAT and its partners have developed the ability to identify grasses and legumes that thrive in specific ecologic niches. The Selection of Forages for the Tropics (SoFT) knowledge management tool enables not only scientists but also local extensionists and development practitioners to identify likely matches (Cook and others 2005). SoFT is a forage selection tool that includes fact sheets, adaptation maps, and reference lists; it is available to all on the World Wide Web.

The more sophisticated spatial analysis tool, Crop Niche Selection for Tropical Agriculture (CaNaSTA), helps identify suitable forages according to ecological niches, using measures of temperature, rain total, and rainfall seasonal pattern (O'Brien and others 2005). The tool also takes into account both expert knowledge and local knowledge. To improve the accuracy of forage and environment prediction, development workers and extensionists enter their local information

CHAPTER 3: RAINFED FARMING AND LAND MANAGEMENT SYSTEMS IN HUMID AREAS on soils. Precise information on soils is not widely available, particularly in the heterogeneous environments where many smallholders live. Experts can update the model and enhance its prediction accuracy. Inputs of their knowledge improve the adaptation information of specific forage varieties.

Diagnosis

Ecological criteria are not sufficient to ensure that nutritive forages grow on farms and appear on the landscape. Smallholder farmers want to invest in livelihood activities that show good, rapid results. Especially during establishment, forages require scarce farmer resources, such as labor and money. Less wealthy farmers, who are most affected by degradation, want even better payoffs. To better understand farm contexts, CIAT scientists and partners talk with farmers. Those interviews and subsequent analysis generate

additional insights toward identifying a prioritized set of grasses and legumes that farmers would likely prefer (Holmann 1999; Holmann and others 2004). From there, farmers continue the selection process on their farms.

Farmers use a range of criteria to evaluate forages and feed before using them. Table 3.1 summarizes the performance of forage species according to (a) forage and feed characteristics (such as digestibility and energy content), (b) forage management and production requirements (such as soil type), and (c) postharvest considerations (such as processing).

Fostering

Researchers are often surprised how farmers change and adapt recommended technologies and practices. For example, CIAT and its partners introduced *Cratylia* to farmers in Colombia for use as a dry season feed source to be managed

Table 3.1 Forage Use and Production Criteria

Crop	Forage or feed characteristics						Management and production									Postharvest		
	Forage: grain-root-tuber/leaf	In vitro digestibility	Protein and amino acids	Energy	Antinutritive compounds	Voluntary intake	Annual/perennial[a]	Drought tolerance	Adapted to low-fertility soils	Time to plant maturity	Harvest interval grain/leaf (months)	Yield: grain	Yield: leaf	Leaf loss (rot, drop)	Continuity of production	Potential mechanized harvest	Heat treatment (grain)	Grinding and cutting
Maize	G/l						A				5/4							
Sorghum	G/L						A				5/4							
Brachiaria spp.	L						P				1	n.a.						
Vigna unguiculata	G/L		+				A				3/2							
Mucuna pruriens	g/L						A				5/4						?	
Lablab purpureus	g/L						A/p				5/4						?	
Cratylia argentea	L						P				–/2	n.a.					n.a.	
Centrosema brasilianum	L						P				–/4							
Canavalia brasiliensis	g/L						A/p				–/4						n.a.	

Source: Authors' elaboration.

Note: Light-gray shading = superior or preferable; medium-gray shading = medium, acceptable, or required; dark-gray shading = inferior or undesirable; uppercase letter = primary use or product; lowercase letter = secondary use or product; +/– = high amino acid quality/deficiencies in amino acids; ? = unknown; n.a. = not applicable.

a. Requires humidity.

as a cut-and-carry system. Farmers, however, developed several alternatives that reduced labor costs, which included direct grazing of *Cratylia* and *Brachiaria* mixtures and different cut-and-carry systems. In addition, farmers reduced establishment costs by intercropping maize, tomatoes, and cucumbers with *Cratylia*. Most surprising to researchers was the use of *Cratylia* during the wet season, when pastures were waterlogged and difficult to graze.

These farmer innovations generated new research topics, such as the response of *Cratylia* to grazing and trampling, and other suitable forage intercrop combinations. In Central America, the approach of co-researching with farmers has proved effective in technology adoption (White, Labarta, and Leguía 2005). Initial effects of collaborative research can be considered slow, but participation rapidly grows and endures with the proof of concept.

Forage processing also produces benefits to farmers. Hay and silage production enables farmers to feed their animals during the dry season. Despite significant investments in research on silage and hay production, small-scale farmer adoption of "traditional" (first generation) forage conservation methods has been low because of high investment costs, labor requirements, and limited access to technical knowledge ('t Mannetje 2000). To be attractive to smallholders, investments must be low cost, be low risk, and increase profits.

An alternative for ensiling forages is use of plastic bags, named *little bag silage* (LBS) by Lane (2000). LBS conserves small quantities of fodder with reduced risk of fermentation. High-quality legume hay can also be packed and sold in plastic bags. Other technologies include storage in earth silos or larger plastic bags.

Sharing and Scaling

Effective expansion of research results to smallholder farmers requires information exchange and ample seed. Numerous methods enhance dialogue between farmers, including farmer field days, exchange visits, and knowledge sharing between countries. For example, Nicaraguan molds that ease the bag-filling process are now adapted and used by farmers in Colombia and Honduras. Both the private seed sector (for example, the Mexican seed enterprise Papalotla) and small-scale enterprises produce seed for widespread distribution (Chirwa and others 2007).

OPPORTUNITIES FOR SUSTAINABLE LAND MANAGEMENT: PRODUCTS AND SERVICES

Many forages grow well in areas that are prone to drought and have low soil fertility. Leguminous forages are of partic-

ular interest because they fix nitrogen, thereby contributing to system sustainability (Schultze-Kraft and Peters 1997; Shelton, Franzel, and Peters 2005). Improved pasture and forage management enables farmers to change their land uses, thereby generating positive environmental benefits.

System intensification with improved forages and soil conservation technologies increases productivity per animal (box 3.1). Intensification, from the sustainable land management (SLM) perspective, increases the productivity or carrying capacity of land. Other environmental benefits of improved forages include higher organic matter of soils, higher manure quality, and increased agricultural productivity (Giller 2001; Schultze-Kraft and Peters 1997). An emphasis is placed on highly productive and drought-tolerant materials to achieve permanent vegetation cover, thus reducing erosion risks. Cut-and-carry systems can decrease pressure on areas unsuitable for grazing, such as steep slopes and forests (Cruz and others 2003; Schmidt and

---

Box 3.1   Example of Pasture Rehabilitation and Intensification from Honduras

The Nuñezes are smallholder farmers in Yorito, Honduras. For years, they obtained only 35 liters of milk per day from their 12 cows, which fed on low-quality grasses. Pastures included a deforested area in the upper portion of their farm. With help from CIAT and national technicians, the Nuñezes planted *Brachiaria brizantha* Toledo, the hybrid *Brachiaria* Mulato, and the legume shrub *Cratylia argentea*. Management innovations included cut-and-carry forages, pasture rotations, and silage production systems that were appropriate to their smallholder farming system. The changes ensured an ample supply of high-quality fodder during the dry season. The new feeding approach generated both private financial and public environmental benefits. Milk production increased to 75 liters per day on less pasture, animals gained significant weight, and reproductive rates improved. Because their herd increased to 25 head, the Nuñezes planted more forage materials and constructed a 64-cubic-meter brick silo. Increased income from the additional milk has already paid for most of the new investments and will enable the Nuñezes to diversify into new activities. Meanwhile, the more intensive production system let the family allow steeply sloped pastures to revert to forest and thereby protect an important local water source.

Peters 2003). Landscape benefits of forages include both improved quantity and improved quality of water resources. Moreover, intensification through increased productivity can reduce greenhouse gas emissions from deforestation and pasture degradation (Steinfeld and others 2006).

RATIONALE FOR INVESTMENT

Forage production and conservation are promising measures to alleviate livestock pressures on the environment (Peters and others 2001). Especially in Central America, system intensification through improved forages is attractive to farmers. Improved forages are economically profitable and represent a good option for improving the livelihoods of livestock producers (Holmann and Rivas 2005). Adopting *Brachiaria* for direct grazing during the rainy season with the shrub legume *Cratylia argentea* for feeding during the dry season can significantly improve milk and beef productivity. The number of cows can be increased between 2.1 and 3.5 times in the dual-purpose system and between 2.6 and 6.0 times in the specialized beef system. Milk production can increase from 2.3 to 3.5 times in the dual-purpose system. The investments in improved forages bring not only economic benefits for producers but also social gains, because the adoption of new technologies based on improved forages generates more rural employment and increases the availability of staple foods. In the dual-purpose system, it is possible to increase employment from 1.5 to 4.0 times. Investments are economically profitable and represent a good option for improving the livelihoods of livestock producers (Holmann and Rivas 2005).

Nevertheless, investments require ample funds or a line of credit over several years (that is, two to seven years, depending on the production system and macroeconomic conditions). Because few producers have the cash flow necessary to finance the required investments, farmers need to improve their farms gradually, as funds are available. Fast, large-scale adoption needs to be coordinated with financial organizations.

When something works, why not do more? Making livestock production more profitable creates that potential danger. Farmers may wish to cut more trees to expand pastures for more cattle and profits. The SLM challenges continue. Nevertheless, not all farmers do so. CIAT researchers have learned about the positive and negative effects of improved forages.

The environmental effects of improving forage production are mixed but largely predictable (White and others 2001). If land is expensive, intensifying production is cheaper than extending pastures into forest and other areas. Farmers tend to improve their pastures' forages. Problems arise when land is inexpensive. In such areas, land can cost less than a bag of fertilizer. Then, the farmer finds expanding pastures into the forest more logical than improving production of existing pastures. Land becomes expensive when it is scarce, productive, or both. To make land scarce, governments need to put in place policies that restrict access. Policies to protect forests can achieve that aim, again with mixed results (Angelsen and Kaimowitz 2001). Local institutions can be fostered to encourage SLM.

The potential of improved forages to mitigate effects of expanding livestock production and to improve agro-ecosystem health has not yet been fully explored. Thus, further research should focus on the role of forages in matching economic and environmental sustainability through intensification and linking smallholders to markets.

Although the contributions of forages soil resources are many (such as improving nitrogen fixation, building up soil organic matter, enhancing soil biological activity and belowground biodiversity, improving manure quality, and increasing productivity of subsequent crops), the exact quantification and assessment of economic effects require further research. Other challenges include smallholder cut-and-carry systems with very limited external inputs. System nutrient balances are second-generation problems that need to be addressed.

RECOMMENDATIONS FOR PRACTITIONERS

Livestock have been and will continue to be part of the landscape in Central America. Matching forage germplasm with farmer preferences requires coordination among research, development, and policy. Effective efforts contain four components:

1. Targeting according to biophysical conditions
2. Diagnosing farm and market contexts
3. Fostering innovation and learning processes
4. Sharing knowledge and scaling out, including South-South interactions.

Research and development efforts need to proactively find ways to improve the feasibility of adopting forage technologies. Future research should provide alternatives so that land degradation is no longer the most attractive land-use option. To speed adoption processes, collaborative technical research with farmers that improves productivity and prevents degradation must go hand in hand with policies (for example, policies such as taxes, payments for carbon, market development, and media campaigns). Such linked efforts can generate incentives to change traditions and improve land management practices.

NOTE

1. The GLASOD project was funded by the United Nations Environment Programme from 1987 to 1990. The GLASOD project produced a world map of human-induced soil degradation. Data were compiled in cooperation with a large number of soil scientists throughout the world, using uniform guidelines. The status of soil degradation was mapped within loosely defined physiographic units (polygons), on the basis of expert judgment. The type, extent, degree, rate, and main causes of degradation have been printed on a global map, at a scale of 1:10 million and have been documented in a downloadable database at http://www.isric.org/UK/About+ISRIC/Projects/Track+Record/GLASOD.htm

REFERENCES

Angelsen, A., and D. Kaimowitz. 2001. *Agricultural Technologies and Tropical Deforestation.* Wallingford, U.K., and New York: CAB International.

Chirwa, R. M., V. D. Aggarwal, M. A. R. Phiri, and A. R. E. Mwenda. 2007. "Experiences in Implementing the Bean Seed Strategy in Malawi." *Journal of Sustainable Agriculture* 29 (2): 43–69.

Cook, B. G., B. C. Pengelly, S. D. Brown, J. L. Donnelly, D. A. Eagles, M. A. Franco, J. Hanson, B. F. Mullen, I. J. Partridge, M. Peters, and R. Schultze-Kraft. 2005. "Tropical Forages: An Interactive Selection Tool." CD-ROM, jointly developed by CSIRO Sustainable Ecosystems, Queensland Department of Primary Industries and Fisheries, Centro Internacional de Agricultura Tropical, and International Livestock Research Institute, Brisbane, Australia.

Cruz, H., C. Burgos, G. Giraldo, M. Peters, and P. Arge. 2003. "Intensificación y diversificación agropecuaria a través del uso de especies forrajeras multipropósitos: Caso la finca 'La Laguna' de Yorito, Yoro." Presentation to the Programa Cooperativa Centroamericano para el Mejoramiento de Cultivos y Animales, La Ceiba, Honduras, April.

Giller, K. E. 2001. *Nitrogen Fixation in Tropical Cropping Systems.* 2nd ed. Wallingford, U.K.: CAB International.

Holmann, F. 1999. "Ex-ante Economic Analysis of New Forage Alternatives in Dual-Purpose Cattle Farms in Peru, Costa Rica, and Nicaragua." *Pasturas Tropicales* 21 (2): 2–17. http://www.cipav.org.co/lrrd/lrrd11/3/hol113.htm.

Holmann, F., P. Argel, L. Rivas, D. White, R.D. Estrada, C. Burgos, E. Pérez, G. Ramírez, and A. Medina. 2004. "Is It Worth to Recuperate Degraded Pasturelands? An Evaluation of Profits and Costs from the Perspective of Livestock Producers and Extension Agents in Honduras." *Livestock Research for Rural Development* 16 (11). http://www.cipav.org.co/lrrd/lrrd16/11/holm16090.htm.

Holmann, F., and L. Rivas. 2005. "Los forrajes mejorados como promotores del crecimiento económico y la sostenibilidad: El caso de los pequeños ganaderos de Centroamérica." Documento de Trabajo 202, Centro Internacional de Agricultura Tropical, Cali, Colombia.

Lane, I. R. 2000. "Little Bag Silage." In *Silage Making in the Tropics with Particular Emphasis on Smallholders,* ed. L. 't Mannetje, 79–84. Proceedings of the FAO Electronic Conference on Tropical Silage, Rome, September 1–December 15, 1999.

O'Brien, R., M. Peters, R. Corner, and S. Cook. 2005. "CaNaSTA—Crop Niche Selection for Tropical Agriculture, A Spatial Decision Support System." In *XX International Grassland Congress: Offered Papers,* ed. F. P. O'Mara, R. J. Wilkins, L. 't Mannetje, D. K. Lovett, P. A. M. Rogers, and T. M. Boland, 917. Wageningen, Netherlands: Academic Publishers.

Peters, M., P. Horne, A. Schmidt, F. Holmann, F. Kerridge, S. A. Tarawali, R. Schultze-Kraft, C. E. Lascano, P. Argel, W. Stür, S. Fujisaka, K. Müller-Sämann, and C. Wortmann. 2001. "The Role of Forages in Reducing Poverty and Degradation of Natural Resources in Tropical Production Systems." Agricultural Research and Extension Network (AgREN) Network Paper No. 117, Overseas Development Institute's Rural Policy and Environment Group, U.K. Department for International Development.

Schmidt, A., and M. Peters. 2003. "Selection and Strategic Use of Multipurpose Forage Germplasm by Smallholders in Production Systems in the Central American Hillsides." In *Technological and Institutional Innovations for Sustainable Rural Development: Book of Abstracts,* ed. C. Wollny, A. Deininger, N. Bhandari, B. L. Maass, W. Manig, U. Muuss, F. Brodbeck, and I. Howe, 208. Göttingen: Centre for Tropical and Subtropical Agriculture and Forestry. http://www.tropentag.de/2003/pdf/proceedings.pdf.

Schultze-Kraft, R., and M. Peters. 1997. "Tropical Legumes in Agricultural Production and Resource Management: An Overview." Presented at the Tropentag JLU Giessen 22-23.5.1997. *GiessenerBeiträge zur Entwicklungsforschung* 24: 1–17.

Shelton, H. M., S. Franzel, and M. Peters. 2005. "Adoption of Tropical Legume Technology around the World: Analysis of Success." In *Grassland: A Global Resource,* ed. D. A. McGilloway, 149–66. Wageningen, Netherlands: Academic Publishers.

Steinfeld, H., P. Gerber, T. Wassenaar, V. Castel, M. Rosales, and C. de Haan. 2006. *Livestock's Long Shadow: Environmental Issues and Options.* Rome: Food and Agriculture Organization.

't Mannetje, L., ed. 2000. *Silage Making in the Tropics with Particular Emphasis on Smallholders.* Rome: Food and Agriculture Organization.

White, D., F. Holmann, S. Fujisaka, K. Reátegui, and C. Lascano. 2001. "Will Intensifying Pasture Management in Tropical Latin America Protect Forests (or Is It the Other Way Around)?" In *Agricultural Technologies and Tropical Deforestation,* ed. A. Angelsen and D. Kaimowitz, 91–111. Wallingford, U.K., and New York: CAB International.

White, D., R. A. Labarta, and E. J. Leguía. 2005. "Technology Adoption by Resource-Poor Farmers: Considering the Implications of Peak-Season Labor Costs." *Agricultural Systems* 85 (2): 183–201.

SELECTED READINGS

Wollny, C., A. Deininger, N. Bhandari, B. Maass, W. Manig, U. Muuss, F. Brodbeck, and I. Howe. 2003. *Deutscher Tropentag 2003: Technological and Institutional Innovations for Sustainable Rural Development.* Göttingen, Germany: Centre for Tropical and Subtropical Agriculture and Forestry. http://www.tropentag.de/2003/pdf/proceedings.pdf.

WEB RESOURCES

Agricultural Research and Extension Network. The Agricultural Research and Extension Network (AgREN) connects policy makers, practitioners, and researchers in the agriculture sector of developing countries. The network is linked to the broader research of the Rural Policy and Environment Group of the Overseas Development Institute. The program generates research-based policy advice on ways of increasing the effectiveness, efficiency, and accountability of rural resource management and agricultural service delivery. The AgREN Web site contains publications, membership information, research updates, and a link to Overseas Development Institute home page. http://www.odi.org.uk/agren/ publist.html.

International Center for Tropical Agriculture. The International Center for Tropical Agriculture (CIAT) is a non-profit organization that conducts socially and environmentally progressive research targeting the reduction of hunger and poverty and the preservation of natural resources in developing countries. CIAT is one of the 15 centers that make up the Consultative Group on International Agricultural Research. The CIAT Web site has information on its products, regions, research, and services: http://www.ciat.cgiar.org/.

LEAD Virtual Centre. Livestock, Environment And Development (LEAD) is a multi-institutional initiative of FAO formed to promote ecologically sustainable livestock production systems. It focuses on protecting the natural resources that are affected by livestock production and processing and on poverty reduction and public health enhancement through appropriate forms of livestock development. The LEAD web site offers resources through their LEAD Virtual Centre, LEAD language platforms, Decision Support Tools, and Research & Development Projects: http://www.virtualcentre.org/.

Tropical Forages: An Interactive Selection Tool. Tropical Forages: An Interactive Selection Tool is a collaborative effort between CSIRO Sustainable Ecosystems, Department of Primary Industries & Fisheries (Qld), Centro Internacional de Agricultura Tropical (CIAT) and the International Livestock Research Institute (ILRI). A project description can be found in the Overview section and more information about the collaborators and donors can be found in the Acknowledgements section: http://www.tropicalforages.info.

University of Tropical Agriculture Foundation. The University of Tropical Agriculture Foundation (UTA) was established in 1996 in Vietnam, at the University of Agriculture and Forestry (now the Nong Lam University), Ho Chi Minh city. The mission of UTA is to educate people on managing natural resources in a way that will sustain the food and energy needs of present and future generations in tropical regions. The UTA website provides UTA news, publications, studies, resources, and services: http://www.utafoundation.org.

An Approach to Sustainable Land Management by Enhancing the Productive Capacity of African Farms: The Case of the Underused and Versatile Soybean

Soybeans can improve soil fertility, but few African farmers plant them. Crops grown after soybeans can produce larger harvests for household consumption or market sale because of the soybeans' nitrogen-fixing capacity (but note the caveat regarding the important differences between conventional soya, which leaves little for the following crop and sends most of the nitrogen to the grain, and promiscuous soya, which leaves much more nitrogen in the soil). The use of soybeans within an agricultural system also enables farmers to diversify production, thereby spreading their exposure to risk across different crops. Because on-farm investments are minimal, resource-poor farmers can begin production easily. The crop is attractive to women—both as a crop for sale and for home consumption. The Tropical Soil Biology and Fertility Institute (TSBF) of the International Center for Tropical Agriculture (Centro Internacional de Agricultura Tropical, or CIAT) has developed a soybean promotion initiative based on strategic alliances to support market development and provide information about using soybeans. The approach recognizes that successful diversification requires cooperation among farmers and between farmers and service providers to build a viable market chain. Dialogue between the market-chain participants and service providers helps generate better understanding of each other's needs and challenges.

KEY SUSTAINABLE LAND MANAGEMENT ISSUES

Soil nutrient losses in Sub-Saharan Africa are an environmental, social, and political time bomb. Unless these disastrous trends are soon reversed, the future viability of African food systems will be imperiled (Borlaug 2003). Soil degradation is one of the major constraints in achieving food security in developing countries, particularly in Africa.

Degradation may pay in the short term, but not in the long term. Unfortunately, much of Africa is experiencing the long-term effects of degradation (Anderson 2003). Abundant yields do not continue without adequate investments in soil fertility. Many farmers are caught in a poverty trap (Barrett and others 2004), where harvests are insufficient to meet urgent household food needs—let alone generate enough income to invest in fertilizers. Moreover, chemical fertilizers are too expensive (Camara and Heinemann 2006). Organic resources sufficient to replenish nutrient losses through cropping are difficult to produce (African Fertilizer Summit Secretariat 2006). The effects of land degradation are felt beyond the farm. As productivity declines, families often expand production into new areas.

Soybeans can improve soil fertility. In Africa, however, few farmers plant them. Coordinated research and promotion activities are needed to enable soybeans to become a valuable crop within smallholder agricultural systems. This Investment Note shares the experience of TSBF and its partners in advancing soybean use in Kenya. Only by adequately addressing aspects of production, processing, and consumption can soybeans help improve both household earnings and land productivity.

LESSONS LEARNED

Soybeans can add nitrogen to soils (although the conventional varieties channel most nitrogen to the grain and leave little to be returned to the soil). An important development has been the breeding of promiscuous soybeans. Promiscuous varieties nodulate with the natural soil bacteria rather than with the highly variety-specific bacteria that typically have to be pro-

This note was prepared by J. N. Chianu, O. Ohiokpehai, B. Vanlauwe, and N. Sanginga, Tropical Soil Biology and Fertility Institute and the World Agroforestry Centre, Nairobi, and A. Adesina, Rockefeller Foundation, Nairobi.

vided when planting conventional soya. Promiscuous varieties are typically slightly lower in yield but return a significantly higher amount of nitrogen to the soil. For smallholders, where nitrogen is a scarce and expensive input, promiscuous soya are easier to grow and add greater fertility to the overall production system. By cultivating soybeans, farmers can harvest valuable grains while improving the productive capacity of their farms. Such a positive outcome, however, is not always achieved. Only some efforts to promote soybeans have been successful. Perhaps for this reason, soybeans remain a minor crop in African farming systems.

In Nigeria, the International Institute of Tropical Agriculture (IITA) and Canada's International Development Research Center implemented a comprehensive and successful soybean project between 1987 and 1999. During that time, soybean production increased from about 150,000 to 405,000 metric tons, an increase of 166 percent (FAO 2001). Average yields more than doubled from about 340 to 740 kilograms per hectare. Village surveys confirmed dramatic soybean production increases in Benue state. The annual production of 70 soybean farmers (a random sample) was less than 5 metric tons between 1982 and 1984, but it increased to 30 tons by 1989 (Sanginga and others 1999). At present, Nigeria produces about 850,000 metric tons of soybeans annually (figure 3.2).

Increasing demand for soybeans encouraged production and was crucial to project success. An urban market survey in Ibadan (one of Nigeria's largest cities) revealed that whereas only two markets sold soybeans in 1987, there were more than 100 by 2000 (see figure 3.2). Soybean retailers in these markets expanded from 4 to more than 1,500 between 1987 and 1999. A similar success occurred in Zimbabwe following a project intervention led by the University of Zimbabwe (Blackie 2006).

In stark contrast, soybean promotion in Kenya generated few positive results. Despite the contribution of many national and international organizations, soybean production and consumption have not achieved widespread effects. The main reasons for the failure were (a) a lack of awareness about soybean processing and use, (b) low yields, and (c) few markets.

OPPORTUNITIES FOR SUSTAINABLE LAND MANAGEMENT

Because soybean cultivation can fix as much as 100 kilograms of nitrogen per hectare (Sanginga and others 2003) (but note the caveat regarding the important differences between conventional soya, which leaves little for the following crop and sends most of the nitrogen to the grain, and promiscuous soya, which leaves much more nitrogen in the soil), crops grown after soybeans produce larger harvests for household consumption or market sale. Use of soybeans within an agricultural system also enables farmers to diversify production, thereby spreading their exposure to risk across different crops. Such a farm management strategy minimizes the possibility of catastrophic harvest losses at the farm household and landscape levels.

In western Kenya, maize is usually intercropped with common beans. The major cash crops in the area are sugarcane, tobacco, and cotton. Soybeans fit into the maize-base cropping system and are currently either intercropped with maize or rotated with maize. Kenyan scientists have developed the Mbili intercropping system, which greatly increases the efficiency and productivity of maize intercropping. By skillfully altering the spacing both between and within rows of tall-growing maize while maintaining overall plant population, the lower-growing extra intercrop gains additional light and thus provides better yields without compromising the yield of the major food crop—maize. Farmers also intercrop soybeans with sugarcane. In addition, soybeans enable resource-poor farmers to take advantage of the nitrogen-fixing attributes of the promiscuous soybean varieties for their subsequent maize. The effect has been dramatic, especially if two seasons of soybeans are followed by one season of maize.

Figure 3.2   Nigerian Soybean Production (1988–2006) and Markets in Ibadan (1987–2000)

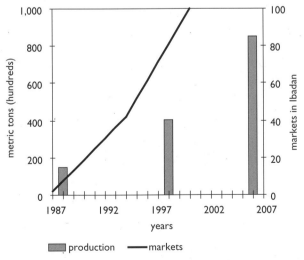

Source: FAO 2001.

RATIONALE FOR INVESTMENT

Good food, nice profit, and better soil fertility are key motivators for cultivating soybeans. Improved and sustainable land management comes as a welcome bonus. With positive incentives, such as households liking the taste of soybeans and a market paying attractive prices, the secondary benefits of soil fertility can easily tag along.

Soybeans are also an important cash crop with many uses. Since the 1960s, the plant has been the dominant oilseed (Smith and Huyser 1987). It is a human food, is used as livestock feed, and has numerous industrial purposes (Myaka, Kirenga, and Malema 2005). The 40 percent protein content of soybeans is approximately twice that of other legumes (Greenberg and Hartung 1998). Despite these apparent uses and benefits, soybean production in Africa remains low. In 2000, Sub-Saharan Africa cultivated only 1 percent of the world's soybean crop.

Soybean cultivation enhances social benefits and gender equity. Because on-farm investments are minimal, resource-poor farmers can begin production easily. Besides preparing meals with soybeans, many women get involved in soybean production (Sanginga and others 1999).

A recent initiative fostered by TSBF aims to broaden the exposure of rural households to soybeans in Kenya. The new initiative aims (a) to capture and hold the interest of farmers in soybeans through an information campaign (to dispel unfounded myths and emphasize benefits) and (b) to create a desire among farmers to process and consume soybeans in different forms through training in processing.

Project partners include the Kenya Agricultural Research Institute, Kenyatta University, the Lake Basin Development Authority, the Kenya Forestry Research Institute, the International Maize and Wheat Improvement Center, and the IITA. Strategic alliances of important stakeholders in the soybean production-to-consumption chain are central to the project. TSBF has developed a three-tier approach for sustainable soybean promotion for Kenya, described as follows:

- *Tier 1—household level.* The approach begins with the creation of widespread awareness on the various benefits of soybean production, consumption, and marketing as well as with practical training. From the beginning, the project confronts unfounded common household myths and stereotypes about soybeans—mistaken information that can undermine an initiative if not adequately addressed with compelling evidence and practical demonstrations. Participatory development of soybean products emphasizes the ease of use within popular local dishes.
- *Tier 2—community level.* Surpluses of soybean production at the household level are absorbed at the community level and processed into soymilk, yogurt, soy bread, cakes, biscuits, and so on. Processing can absorb house-

hold-level production surpluses that could otherwise become a disincentive to further cultivation. Tier 2 action also creates new consumer preferences and potential demand by introducing new products, such as soymilk, soy yogurt, and meat substitutes.
- *Tier 3—industry level.* This tier continues the formalization of the soybean producer in the market. The main emphasis is to link soybean producers with input suppliers (that is, suppliers of seed, fertilizer, value-added knowledge, information, transport, and the like) and output purchasers (especially the industrial market). The project interacts with numerous actors of the supply chain, including (a) industry, to find out what products it wants; (b) farmers, to evaluate their ability to deliver products that meet industrial specifications; and (c) other stakeholders, to determine how they can contribute to the market development process.

RECOMMENDATIONS FOR PRACTITIONERS

Strategic alliances support the three-tier market development for soybeans. Project partners enable smallholder farmers to benefit from soybean production by providing diverse types of necessary and complementary support. The approach recognizes that successful diversification requires cooperation among farmers and between farmers and service providers to build a viable market chain. Dialogue among the market-chain participants and service providers helps generate better understanding of one another's needs and challenges. Different types of knowledge are shared: research, technology, production, equipment, transport, and support services (CIAT 2005). The strategic alliance has seven types of actors, whose participation is crucial for successful soybean promotion:

1. *Soybean farmers and farmer associations.* Farmer representatives are responsible for interacting with other farmers to articulate their views during the alliance meetings. By consolidating relationships with buyers and opening communication channels with all market-chain participants, farmers gain valuable experience and confidence, which in turn enhances their negotiating power.
2. *Input suppliers.* A common feature of the soybean farmers is lack of capital and inputs such as appropriate germplasm. Input service providers include agricultural input and seed suppliers and microcredit agencies.
3. *Nongovernmental organizations.* These organizations provide assistance on postproduction value-added activities: sorting, bulking, grading, packaging, transporta-

tion, haulage, and storage. Such activities enable farmers to increase their prices.

4. *Food processors.* Large-scale industries currently import soybeans. Provided that farmers produce the grains of the quality desired, these industries reaffirm their commitment to purchase grain produced at agreed-on prices.

5. *Communication and information agencies.* Because of the critical role of information, a grassroots information and communication agency, AfriAfya, is in the alliance to backstop extension and to strengthen the provision of information and communication services and soybean technologies. AfriAfya is responsible for creating local content that responds to the needs of rural people.

6. *Government institutions.* The key government institutions represented in the alliance may include the ministries of agriculture, trade and industry, and finance. These institutions assist with both implementing and formulating enabling policies in support of soybeans.

7. *Donor organizations.* Organizations such as the Rockefeller Foundation provide funds for organizing and implementing the alliance.

The alliance (a) creates an opportunity for integrated resource mobilization, (b) involves each stakeholder within a larger problem-solving framework, (c) provides assistance in analyzing distinct perceptions of different actors, (d) strengthens capacity of business services, (e) effectively brokers and addresses industry needs, and (f) develops enduring public-private partnerships for long-term success.

REFERENCES

African Fertilizer Summit Secretariat. 2006. "Frequently Asked Questions: Fertilizers and the Africa Fertilizer Summit." Africa Fertilizer Summit Secretariat, Midrand, South Africa. http://www.africafertilizersummit.org/FAQ.html.

Anderson, J. 2003. *Nature, Wealth, and Power in Africa: Emerging Best Practice for Revitalizing Rural Africa.* Washington, DC: U.S. Agency for International Development. http://www.usaid.gov/our_work/agriculture/land management/pubs/nature_wealth_power_fy2004.pdf.

Barrett, C. P., J. Marenya, B. McPeak, F. Minten, W. Murithi, F. Oluoch-Kosura, J. C. Place, J. Randrianarisoa, J. Rasambainarivo, and J. Wangila. 2004. "Poverty Dynamics in Rural Kenya and Madagascar." BASIS Brief 24, Collaborative Research Support Program, BASIS Research Program on Poverty, Inequality, and Development, University of Wisconsin–Madison, Madison. http://www.basis.wisc.edu/live/basbrief24.pdf.

Blackie, M. 2006. "Indigenous Knowledge and the Transformation of Southern African Agriculture." In *Zimbabwe's Agricultural Revolution Revisited*, ed. M. Rukuni, P. Tawonezvi, and C. Eicher, with M. Munyuki-Hungwe, and P. Matondi. Harare: University of Zimbabwe Press.

Borlaug, N. E. 2003. *Feeding a World of 10 Billion People.* Muscle Shoals, AL: International Center for Soil Fertility and Agricultural Development. http://www.ifdc.org/PDF_Files/LS-3%20Feeding%20a%20World%2010%20Billion.pdf.

Camara, O., and E. Heinemann. 2006. "Overview of the Fertilizer Situation in Africa." African Fertilizer Summit background paper, Abuja, Nigeria, June 9–13.

CIAT (Centro Internacional de Agricultura Tropical). 2005. *CIAT in Focus 2004–2005: Getting a Handle on High-Value Agriculture.* Cali, Colombia: CIAT.

FAO (Food and Agriculture Organization). 2001. FAOSTAT Database. http://faostat.fao.org/.

Greenberg, P., and H. N. Hartung. 1998. *The Whole Soy Cookbook: 175 Delicious, Nutritious, Easy-to-Prepare Recipes Featuring Tofu, Tempeh, and Various Forms of Nature's Healthiest Bean.* New York: Three Rivers Press.

Myaka, F. A., G. Kirenga, and B. Malema, eds. 2005. "Proceedings of the First National Soybean Stakeholders Workshop." Morogoro, Tanzania, November 10–11.

Sanginga, N., K. Dashiell, J. Diels, B. Vanlauwe, O. Lyasse, R. J. Carsky, S. Tarawali, B. Asafo-Adjei, A. Menkir, S. Schulz, B. B. Singh, D. Chikoye, D. Keatinge, and O. Rodomiro. 2003. "Sustainable Resource Management Coupled to Resilient Germplasm to Provide New Intensive Cereal-Grain Legume-Livestock Systems in the Dry Savanna." *Agriculture, Ecosystems, and Environment* 100 (2–3): 305–14.

Sanginga, P. C., A. A. Adesina, V. M. Manyong, O. Otite, and K. E. Dashiell. 1999. *Social Impact of Soybean in Nigeria's Southern Guinea Savanna.* Ibadan, Nigeria: International Institute of Tropical Agriculture.

Smith, K., and W. Huyser. 1987. "World Distribution and Significance of Soybean." In *Soybeans: Improvement, Production, and Uses,* ed. J. R. Wilcox, 1–22. Madison: American Society of Agronomy.

WEB RESOURCES

Africa Fertilizer Summit. The New Partnership for Africa's Development (NEPAD) called for an Africa Fertilizer Summit from June 9–13, 2006 in Abuja, Nigeria, to be implemented by the International Fertilizer Development Center (IFDC). The Summit's objective was to increase the awareness of the role that fertilizer can play in stimulating sustainable pro-poor productivity growth in African agriculture and to discuss approaches for rapidly increasing efficient fertilizer use by African smallholder farmers. For more information on the summit, access the Africa Fertilizer Summit Web site: http://www.africafertilizersummit.org/FAQ.html.

Tropical Soil Biology and Fertility Institute. The Tropical Soil Biology and Fertility Institute (TSBF) of CIAT develops and disseminates strategic principles, concepts, methods, and management options for protecting and improving the health and fertility of soils by manipulating biological processes and efficiently using soil, water, and nutrient resources in tropical agroecosystems. The TSBF of the CIAT Web site has information on its products, networks, research focus, and other information and services: http://www.ciat.cgiar.org/tsbf_institute/index.htm.

Balancing Rainforest Conservation and Poverty Reduction

The Alternatives to Slash-and-Burn (ASB) Programme is a global alliance of more than 80 local, national, and international partners dedicated to action-oriented integrated natural resources management (INRM) research in the tropical forest margins.

ASB research in Cameroon and Indonesia has revealed the feasibility of a middle path of development involving smallholder agroforests and community forest management for timber and other products. The Brazilian Amazon, in contrast, presents much starker trade-offs between global environmental benefits and the returns to smallholders' labor. Here, the most commonly practiced pasture-livestock system, which occupies the vast majority of converted forestland, is profitable for smallholders (at least in the short term) but entails huge carbon emissions and biodiversity loss. The land-use alternatives that are attractive privately are at odds with global environmental interests.

Results from ASB research at all the benchmark sites show that attempting to conserve forests in developing countries is futile without addressing the needs of poor local people. The issues are well illustrated by a study of options facing settlers in Brazil's Acre state. Using a specially developed bioeconomic model, ASB researchers showed that only in the unlikely event that prices quadrupled over their current level might the rate of deforestation slow. Even in that case, the braking effect is slight, and the modest saving in forestland would probably be short-lived.

KEY SUSTAINABLE LAND MANAGEMENT ISSUES

Occasionally, tropical forests can be conserved while poverty is being reduced, but more often these two objectives conflict. Without action to resolve this conflict, tropi-cal forests will continue to disappear. Striking an equitable balance between the legitimate interests of development and the equally legitimate global concerns about the environmental consequences of tropical deforestation is one of the greatest challenges of today's generation.

Everyone in the world wants something from tropical forests. Forest dwellers wish to continue their traditional way of life based on hunting and gathering. They are losing their land to migrant smallholders, who clear small amounts of forest to earn a living by raising crops and livestock. Both groups tend to lose out to larger, more powerful interests—ranchers, plantation owners, large-scale farmers, or logging concerns—whose aim is to convert large areas of forest into big money. Outside the forests is the international community, which wishes to see forests preserved for the carbon they store—that carbon would otherwise contribute to global warming—and for the wealth of biological diversity they harbor.

Deforestation continues because converting forests to other uses is almost always profitable for the individual. However, society as a whole bears the costs of lost biodiversity, global warming, smoke pollution, and degradation of water resources.

Every year the world loses about 10 million hectares of tropical forest—an area more than three times the size of Belgium. None of the land-use systems that replace this natural forest can match it in terms of biodiversity richness and carbon storage. However, these systems do vary greatly in the degree to which they combine at least some environmental benefits with their contributions to economic growth and poor peoples' livelihoods. What will replace forest (and for how long) is, therefore, always worth asking, both under the current mix of policies, insti-

This note was prepared by T. Tomich, J. Lewis, and J. Kasyoki, World Agroforestry Centre; J. Valentim, Empresa Brasileira de Pesquisa Agropecuária; and S. Vosti and J. Witcover, University of California–Davis.

tutions, and technologies and compared with possible alternatives. In other words, what can be done to secure the best balance among the conflicting interests of different groups?

INTEGRATED NATURAL RESOURCES MANAGEMENT APPROACH

The ASB Programme is a well-established global alliance of more than 80 local, national, and international partners dedicated to action-oriented integrated natural resources management research in the tropical forest margins. It is the only global partnership devoted entirely to research on the tropical forest margins. The goal of the ASB Programme is to raise productivity and income of rural households in the humid tropics without increasing deforestation or undermining essential environmental services. The program applies an INRM approach to analysis and action through long-term engagement with local communities and policy makers at various levels.

KEY DRIVERS FOR DEGRADATION DYNAMICS: THE ASB MATRIX—LINING UP THE FACTS

Faced with the diverging goals of conserving forests and addressing the needs of local inhabitants, policy makers need accurate, objective information on which to base their inevitably controversial decisions. To help them weigh up the difficult choices they must make, ASB researchers have developed a new tool known as the ASB matrix (table 3.2).

In the ASB matrix, natural forest and the land-use systems that replace it are scored against various criteria reflecting the objectives of different interest groups. So that results can be compared across locations, systems specific to each are grouped according to broad categories, ranging from agroforests to grasslands and pastures.

The criteria may be fine-tuned for specific locations, but the matrix always includes indicators for the following:

- Two major global environmental concerns: carbon storage and biodiversity
- Agronomic sustainability, assessed according to a range of soil characteristics, including trends in nutrients and organic matter over time
- Policy objectives: economic growth and employment opportunities
- Smallholders' concerns: their workload, returns to their labor, food security for their family, and start-up costs of new systems or techniques
- Policy and institutional barriers to adoption by smallholders, including the availability of credit, markets, and improved technology.

Table 3.2   ASB Summary Matrix: Forest Margins of Sumatra

Land use	Global environment		Agronomic sustainability	National policy-makers' concerns		Adoptability by smallholders
				Potential profitability (at social prices)		Production incentives (at private prices)
	Carbon sequestration	Biodiversity	Plot-level production sustainability		Employment	
Description	Aboveground, time averaged (metric tons per hectare)	Aboveground, plant species per standard plot	Overall rating	Returns to land (US$ per hectare)	Average labor input (days per hectare per year)	Return to labor (US$ per day)
Natural forest	306	120	1	0	0	0
Community-based forest management	136	100	1	11	0.2	4.77
Commercial logging	93	90	0.5	1,080	31	0.78
Rubber agroforest	89	90	0.5	506	111	2.86
Oil palm monoculture	54	25	0.5	1,653	108	4.74
Upland ricebush fallow rotation	7	45	0.5	(117)	25	1.23
Continuous cassava degrading to *imperata*	2	15	0	28	98	1.78

Source: Tomich and others 1998.
Note: Natural forest and the land-use systems that replace it are scored against criteria (global environmental benefits, agronomic sustainability, profitability, labor, and incentives) that are important for the diverse range of stakeholders in the landscape.

Between 1995 and 2005, ASB researchers have filled in this matrix for representative benchmark sites dotted across the humid tropics. Political and economic factors at work at these sites vary greatly, as does their current resource endowment: from the densely populated lowlands of the Indonesian island of Sumatra, through a region of varying population density and access to markets south of Yaoundé in Cameroon, to the remote forests of Acre state in the far west of the Brazilian Amazon, where settlement by small-scale farmers is relatively recent and forest is still plentiful.

At each site, ASB researchers have evaluated land-use systems both as they are currently practiced and in the alternative forms that could be possible through policy, institutional, and technological innovations. A key question addressed was whether the intensification of land use through technological innovation could reduce both poverty and deforestation.

LESSONS LEARNED

The matrix allows researchers, policy makers, environmentalists, and others to identify and discuss trade-offs among the various objectives of different interest groups.

The studies in Cameroon and Indonesia have revealed the feasibility of a middle path of development involving smallholder agroforests and community forest management for timber and other products. Such a path could deliver an attractive balance between environmental benefits and equitable economic growth. Whether this balance is struck in practice, however, will depend on the ability of these countries to deliver the necessary policy and institutional innovations.

Take the examples of Sumatran rubber agroforests and their cocoa and fruit counterparts in Cameroon. These systems offer levels of biodiversity that, although not as high as those found in natural forest, are nevertheless far higher than those in single-species tree plantations or annual cropping systems. Like any tree-based system, they also offer substantial levels of carbon storage. Crucially, technological innovations have the potential to increase the yields of the key commodities in these systems—thereby raising farmers' incomes substantially—to levels that either outperform or at least compete well with virtually all other systems. However, to realize this potential, policy makers, researchers, and others must find ways of delivering improved planting material—the key input needed.

The Brazilian Amazon, in contrast, presents much starker trade-offs between global environmental benefits and the returns to smallholders' labor. Here, the most com-monly practiced pasture-livestock system, which occupies the vast majority of converted forestland, is profitable for smallholders but entails huge carbon emissions and biodiversity loss. Systems that are preferable from an environmental point of view, such as coffee combined with *bandarra* (a fast-growing timber tree), can pay better but have prohibitively high start-up costs and labor requirements and are riskier for farmers. An alternative pasture-livestock system, in which farmers are expressing interest, offers even higher returns to land and labor but only slightly improves biodiversity and carbon storage. In other words, the land-use alternatives that are attractive privately are at odds with global environmental interests. Only a radical overhaul of the incentives available to land users, including smallholders, could change things.

Just how radical would the overhaul have to be? Very radical—even for a small effect—according to ASB research. Consider the gathering of wild Brazil nuts, one of the most environmentally benign uses of the Amazon's forests. At current prices offered to smallholders, Brazil nut harvesting pays well below the going rate for wage labor. To persuade smallholders merely to slow the pace of deforestation, the price of nuts would have to rise more than fourfold.

Research by ASB scientists of the Empresa Brasileira de Pesquisa Agropecuária on the pasture-livestock system in the western Amazon of Brazil shows that, with a combination of legumes to enrich pastures and solar-powered electric fences to control the pattern of grazing by their cattle, smallholders could double milk production per cow and triple the carrying capacity of their land, bringing a marked increase in profitability. In addition, because this pasture system is sustainable without annual burning to control weeds, seasonal smoke pollution would be reduced (see ASB Programme 2002).

So why have these practices not been adopted widely already? First, the vast majority of smallholders cannot get access to the necessary credit, seeds, or hired labor and are too far from markets to be able to sell the increased milk supplies. Second, aiming for these higher profits entails increased risk, in part because of the higher initial investment costs. But even if these barriers were eliminated, widespread adoption of such improvements would likely increase—not decrease—the pressure on neighboring forests. The reason is that the greater profitability of the improved system would make the agricultural frontier more attractive to new settlers. Thus, under the present mix of policies and institutions, plus the incentives they create, the forests in Brazil's western Amazon will continue to fall whether the smallholder succeeds or fails.

OPPORTUNITIES FOR SUSTAINABLE LAND MANAGEMENT: PRODUCTS AND SERVICES

Given these results, what can be done to balance the objectives of forest conservation and poverty reduction in these tricky settings? Some assert that the best opportunities for meeting both objectives lie in the harvest of various products from community-managed forests. In practice, such extensive systems require low population densities plus effective mechanisms for keeping other groups out if they are to prove sustainable.

Where forests are converted, agroforests often represent the next best option for conserving biodiversity and storing carbon, while also providing attractive livelihood opportunities for smallholders. For both economic and ecological reasons, however, no single land-use system should predominate at the expense of all others. Mixes of land uses increase biodiversity at a landscape level, if not within individual systems, and also can enhance economic and ecological resilience. A mixed landscape mosaic represents an especially attractive option in cases such as Brazil, where no single system offers a reasonable compromise between different objectives.

Where productivity of the natural resource base has already sunk to very low levels, concentrating development efforts on the simultaneous environmental and economic restoration of degraded landscapes is an option that is well worth exploring.

The precise mix of interventions needed—hence the benefits and costs of restoration—varies from place to place. In Cameroon, improved cocoa and fruit tree systems could be a win-win proposition in place of unsustainably short fallow rotations. In Indonesia, millions of hectares of *Imperata* grasslands are the obvious starting point.

The direction of change in land-use systems determines the environmental consequences. For example, if farmers replace unsustainable cassava production with an improved rubber agroforest, they help restore habitats and carbon stocks. But if such a system replaces natural forest, the environment loses. Intensification of land use through technological change is a two-edged sword. It has great potential to increase the productivity and sustainability of existing forest-derived systems, thereby raising incomes. By the same token, however, these higher incomes attract more landless people to the agricultural frontier in search of a better living. Therefore, technological innovation to intensify land use will not be enough to stop deforestation. Indeed, it often will accelerate deforestation. If both objectives are to be met, policy measures intended to encourage intensification will need to be accompanied by measures to protect those forest areas that harbor globally significant biodiversity.

RATIONALE FOR INVESTMENT

The main point for policy makers is that without tangible incentives linked to the supply of global environmental benefits, people will continue to cut down tropical rainforests. Results from ASB research at all the benchmark sites show that attempting to conserve forests in developing countries is futile without addressing the needs of poor local people. But how can the necessary incentives to conserve be put in place? Only a limited number of policy instruments have so far been tried, and there is still much to learn about what does and does not work. Part of the answer lies in the developing countries themselves, where such measures as securing land tenure and use rights can be taken. But should these countries have to shoulder the entire financial burden of forest conservation when all face urgent development imperatives, such as educating and vaccinating rural children?

The bottom line is that if the international community wants the global benefits of rainforest preservation, it is going to have to pay for some of the costs.

RECOMMENDATIONS FOR PRACTITIONERS

The issues are well illustrated by a study of options facing settlers in Brazil's Acre state. (Faminow, Oliveira, and Sá 1997). These farmers clear forest gradually over the years, with pasture for cattle becoming the dominant land use. In addition, about 50 percent of farm families harvest nuts from the part of their farms that remains forested.

Using a specially developed bioeconomic model, ASB researchers explored how labor, capital, and land would be allocated to different on-farm activities over a 25-year period under different price and market scenarios. When they applied the model to Brazil nuts, the researchers found that doubling the farm-gate price of nuts would not decrease and might even increase the rate of deforestation. The reason is that farmers probably would reinvest the extra cash they earned in clearing forest faster. From the farmers' perspective, even at the higher price, cattle production remains by far the more profitable activity. Only in the unlikely event that nut prices quadrupled over their current level might the rate of deforestation slow. Even then, the braking effect would be slight and the modest saving in forest would probably be short-lived.

The researchers concluded that subsidizing the price of Brazil nuts would not by itself be an effective policy measure for conserving forests.

REFERENCES

ASB (Alternatives to Slash-and-Burn) Programme. 2002. "Policybrief 04." ASB Programme, Nairobi. http://www.asb.cgiar.org/publications/policybriefs.

Faminow, M., S. Oliveira, and C. Sá. 1997. "Conserving Forest through Improved Cattle Production Technologies." EMBRAPA/IFPRI Policy Brief, Empresa Brasileira de Pesquisa Agropecuária, Rio Branco, Brazil, and International Food Policy Research Institute, Washington, DC.

Tomich, T. P., M. van Noordwijk, S. A. Vosti, and J. Witcover. 1998. "Agricultural Development with Rainforest Conservation: Methods for Seeking Best Bet Alternatives to Slash-and-Burn, with Applications to Brazil and Indonesia." *Agricultural Economics* 19 (1–2): 159–74.

SELECTED READINGS

Cattaneo, A. 2002. "Balancing Agricultural Development and Deforestation in the Brazilian Amazon." IFPRI Research Report 129, International Food Policy Research Institute, Washington, DC.

Gockowski, J., G. Nkamleu, and J. Wendt. 2001. "Implications of Resource-Use Intensification for the Environment and Sustainable Technology Systems in the Central African Rainforest." In *Tradeoffs or Synergies? Agricultural Intensification, Economic Development, and the Environment*, ed. D. R. Lee and C. B. Barrett, 19–219. Wallingford, U.K., and New York: CAB International.

IUCN (World Conservation Union). 2002. *Beyond Rhetoric: Putting Conservation to Work for the Poor.* Gland, Switzerland: IUCN.

Tomich, T. P., M. van Noordwijk, S. Budidarsono, A. Gillison, T. Kusumanto, D. Murdiyarso, F. Stolle, and A. Fagi. 2001. "Agricultural Intensification, Deforestation, and the Environment: Assessing Tradeoffs in Sumatra, Indonesia." In *Tradeoffs or Synergies? Agricultural Intensification, Economic Development and the Environment*, ed. D. R. Lee and C. B. Barrett, 221–44. Wallingford, U.K., and New York: CAB International.

Vosti, S. A, C. Carpentier, J. Witcover, and J. F. Valentim. 2001. "Intensified Small-Scale Livestock Systems in the Western Brazilian Amazon." In *Agricultural Technologies and Tropical Deforestation*, ed. A. Angelsen and D. Kaimowitz, 113–34. Wallingford, U.K., and New York: CAB International.

Vosti, S. A., J. Witcover, and C. Carpentier. 2002. "Agricultural Intensification by Smallholders in the Western Brazilian Amazon: From Deforestation to Sustainable Use." IFPRI Research Report 130, International Food Policy Research Institute, Washington, DC.

Vosti, S. A, J. Witcover, C. Carpentier, S. Oliveira, and J. Santos. 2001. "Intensifying Small-Scale Agriculture in the Western Brazilian Amazon: Issues, Implications, and Implementation." In *Tradeoffs or Synergies? Agricultural Intensification, Economic Development and the Environment*, ed. D. R. Lee and C. B. Barrett, 245–66. Wallingford, U.K., and New York: CAB International.

World Agroforestry Centre. 2003. "Forests as Resources for the Poor: The Rainforest Challenge." World Agroforestry Centre, Gigiri, Kenya. http://www.worldagroforestry.org/AR2003/downloads/SO_Rainforest.pdf.

WEB RESOURCES

ASB Partnership for the Tropical Forest Margins. ASB is a global partnership of research institutes, non-governmental organizations, universities, community organizations, farmers' groups, and other local, national, and international organizations. ASB is the only global partnership that is entirely devoted to researching the tropical forest margins. Since 1994, it has operated as a system-wide program of the Consultative Group for International Research in Agriculture (CGIAR). The ASB Partnership for the Tropical Forest Margins Web site contains information on its impact, regions, themes, publications, and other resources: http://www.asb.cgiar.org/.

ASB Policybriefs series. ASB's Policybriefs series takes the lessons learned from experiences at the local or national levels and distills them for a broader, international audience. ASB aims to deliver relevant, concise reading to key people whose decisions will make a difference to poverty reduction and environmental protection in the humid tropics: http://www.asb.cgiar.org/publications/policybriefs.

ASB reports. ASB has summary reports on Brazil, Cameroon, and Indonesia, as well as working group reports on climate change, biodiversity, and socioeconomic indicators. http://www.asb.cgiar.org/publications/countryreports/.

ASB Voices series. The ASB Voices series aims to provide insights and perspectives from people's real-life experiences and challenges in the humid tropics for a broad audience. The series is able to highlight the implications for the global environment of peoples' choices under severe resource constraints: http://www.asb.cgiar.org/publications/asbvoices/.

Rewarding Upland Poor for Environmental Services. The Rewarding Upland Poor for Environmental Services (RUPES) program aims to enhance the livelihoods and reduce poverty of the upland poor while supporting environmental conservation on biodiversity protection, watershed management, carbon sequestration and landscape beauty at local and global levels. Through partnership with its major donor, the International Fund for Agricultural Development (IFAD), the World Agroforestry Centre (ICRAF) has taken on the role of coordinating a consortium of partners interested in contributing and being a part of RUPES. The RUPES website offers information on RUPES sites, partnerships, and activities: http://www.worldagroforestry.org/sea/Net works/RUPES/index.asp.

World Agroforestry Centre. Using science, the World Agroforestry Centre generates knowledge on the complex role of trees in livelihoods and the environment, and fosters use of this knowledge to improve decisions and practices to impact the poor. The World Agroforestry Centre Web site provides information on their news and events, recent publications, agroforestry information and other information resources: http://www.worldagroforestry .org/es/default.asp.

Groundwater Declines and Land Use: Looking for the Right Solutions

Countries are increasingly relying on finite groundwater reserves (built up over centuries) for household, agricultural, and industrial needs. Although addressing water shortages in the short term, groundwater exploitation brings its own host of problems. Solving these problems means conducting holistic studies of hydrologic systems to find appropriate solutions that will result in real water savings.

The North China Plain is China's most important agricultural center, producing more than half the country's wheat and a third of its maize. The deficit between rainfall and crop requirements has been met by irrigation from aquifers underlying the plain. Pumping water from the aquifers has led to the continued decline of groundwater levels despite improved irrigation efficiency and reduced pumping.

An International Water Management Institute (IWMI) study (Kendy and others 2003) used a water-balance approach—a simple accounting method to quantify hydrologic changes. The model shows clearly that simply changing the amount of water applied for irrigation will not affect the rate of groundwater depletion, which leaves only two other variables: rainfall and evapotranspiration. With rainfall beyond management control, the only way to reduce groundwater depletion and to achieve real water savings is to address evapotranspiration. The water-balance approach allowed IWMI to formulate successful water-saving choices. The sets of options comprise a combination of changing cropping patterns, leaving certain areas of land to lie fallow, and changing land use to urban uses. Each set of options is a different combination of land uses that will deplete no more than 460 millimeters per year—bringing rainfall and evapotranspiration into equilibrium.

KEY SUSTAINABLE LAND MANAGEMENT ISSUES

With growing populations, changing weather patterns, and increasing pollution of bodies of surface water, countries around the world are relying more and more on finite groundwater reserves built up over centuries for household, agricultural, and industrial needs. Although addressing water shortages in the short term, groundwater exploitation brings its own problems. It can cause surface water depletion, saltwater intrusion into freshwater aquifers, and subsidence of the land surface (box 3.2). Governments are quick to turn to improving water efficiency as the best solution to the problem but are too often disappointed. Research increasingly shows that in devising water management strategies to conserve water and halt the decline of groundwater levels, policy makers must conduct holistic studies of hydrologic systems to find appropriate solutions that will result in real water savings. What is needed is not a simple one-size-fits-all policy or solution but varying management approaches to suit specific situations. The concept of hydronomic zones, which categorizes a hydrologic system into different zones—each having its own best set of water-saving measures—could be a useful tool in this exercise.

The paradox of increasing irrigation efficiency and reduced pumping yet declining groundwater levels (see box 3.2) has puzzled water policy experts and resource managers. It provided the impetus for an IWMI study (Kendy and others 2003) in Luancheng county, located in the Hai River basin, one of the three rivers draining the North China Plain. The study examined the nexus between agricultural policies in the area, water management approaches, and actual water use in an effort to explain the steady decline in groundwater levels and to find appropriate solutions to halt this decline.

TRENDS IN RESOURCE USE

As agricultural policies and water management strategies evolved over the years, water-use trends changed accordingly. With increased winter wheat cropping and a shift

This note was prepared by E. Kendy, The Nature Conservancy, Washington, DC.

Box 3.2   Examining Hydrological Contradictions in the North China Plain

The North China Plain is China's most important agricultural center, producing more than half the country's wheat and a third of its maize. It is 320,000 square kilometers in extent and home to more than 200 million people. It is bordered by mountains on the west and the Yellow Sea on the east. Three rivers drain into the plain. The climate is temperate and monsoonal, with cold, dry winters and hot, humid summers. The shortage and seasonal distribution of water are two key factors that inhibit agriculture. Annual rainfall averages between 500 millimeters in the north and 800 millimeters in the south. The typical winter wheat and summer maize cropping pattern currently practiced consumes 660 to 920 millimeters of water annually. The deficit between rainfall and crop requirements has been met by irrigation from aquifers underlying the plain. Pumping water from the aquifers has led to the continued decline of groundwater levels despite improved irrigation efficiency and reduced pumping.

from cotton to more irrigation-intensive maize, an increase in groundwater use that would mirror the cropping patterns could be expected. However, the reality is quite different. Contrary to expectations, groundwater pumping did not grow with the increase and change in cropping. Even more surprisingly, pumping rates actually decreased during the late 1970s and early 1980s before finally stabilizing in the 1980s (figure 3.3). Nevertheless, groundwater levels have declined steadily throughout the period under study. This seeming contradiction has puzzled water policy experts and resource managers and provided the impetus for IWMI's study (Kendy and others 2003).

KEY DRIVERS FOR DEGRADATION DYNAMICS: THE POLICY–WATER USE NEXUS

IWMI's study used a water-balance approach to try to find the answer. It is a simple accounting method used to quantify hydrologic changes. The soil/water balance and the groundwater balance in Luancheng county were both studied. The study concluded that the continued decline in groundwater levels is caused by the long-standing agricultural policy of achieving food self-sufficiency by continually increasing the irrigated area, coupled with the use of groundwater to supplement precipitation. Even more interesting is what the study reveals about the connection between increasing irrigation efficiency and groundwater

Figure 3.3   Irrigation History of Luancheng County: Estimated Pumping for Irrigation, 1949–99

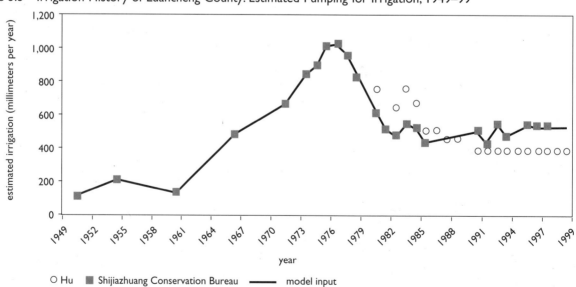

Source: Author's elaboration, based on E. Kendy, personal communication; Chanseng Hu, Chinese Academies of Science, unpublished data.
Note: "Pumping" in the 1950s was primarily hauling, rather than pumping, from shallow, brick-lined wells. "Model input" indicates groundwater pumping and irrigation values used to calculate annual water balances.

levels. In Luancheng county, irrigation efficiency has increased, causing more than a 50 percent decrease in groundwater pumping since the 1970s (figure 3.4). However, groundwater levels continue to drop steadily. Because excess irrigation water seeps through the soil back to the aquifer underlying irrigated areas and replenishes the water supply, the only significant inflows and outflows to the system are through precipitation and crop evapotranspiration. As long as those two factors remain constant, increased irrigation efficiency will save no water. Instead, other options, such as reducing the length of the growing season and reducing the extent of irrigated land, need to be considered to halt the decline of groundwater levels.

The model clearly shows that simply changing the amount of water applied for irrigation will not affect the rate of groundwater depletion, which leaves only two other variables: rainfall and evapotranspiration. With rainfall beyond management control, the only way to reduce groundwater depletion and to achieve real water savings is to address evapotranspiration. This conclusion is further borne out by the relationship among rainfall, evapotranspiration, and resulting depletion in groundwater over the study period (figure 3.4).

In the early years before irrigation development, precipitation exceeded evapotranspiration and the excess water recharged the aquifer, sometimes causing it to overflow. As irrigated areas grew and the number of crops harvested each year rose, evapotranspiration increased until it exceeded rainfall (see figure 3.4). At that point, groundwater mining began, and since that time, the amount of groundwater mined has been the difference between rainfall and evapotranspiration, regardless of the amounts pumped out of the aquifer. As long as this difference remains virtually constant, the rate of groundwater depletion, too, will remain constant.

Taking into consideration the entire hydrologic system, including the soil profile and the underlying aquifer, water policy experts and resource managers have overlooked a simple but nevertheless vital factor over the years: as long as crop evapotranspiration remains constant or increases, no reduction in the rate of groundwater depletion can occur. The answer lies in methods that will either maintain or reduce the rate of evapotranspiration. The holistic study of the hydrologic system points in the right direction in the search for these solutions.

A concept that is useful in studying hydrologic systems is that of hydronomic zoning. A hydrologic system such as a

Figure 3.4   General Relationships between Precipitation and Evapotranspiration for Cropland in Luancheng County, 1947–2000

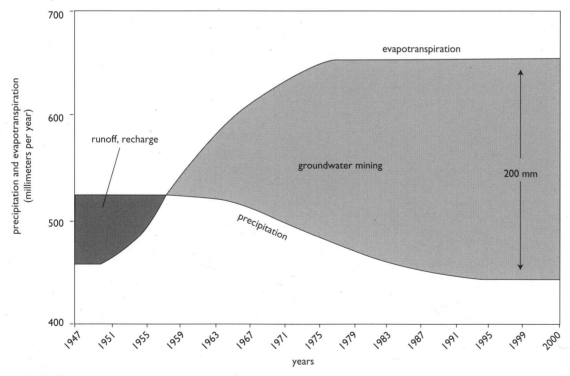

Source: Author's elaboration.

river basin is divided into hydronomic (*hydro* [water] + *nomus* [management]) zones, which are defined primarily according to the destination of the drainage outflow from water uses. Thus, there are zones where water can be reused and where it cannot, because of location and quality. Moreover, each hydrological system can be classified into all or some of the following zones: water source, natural recapture, regulated recapture, stagnation, environmentally sensitive, and final-use zones (figure 3.5).

The classification of the system into the different hydronomic zones (Molden, Sakthivadivel, and Keller 2001) helps identify the best methods of saving water because each zone has its own best set of water-saving measures. In identifying these sets of measures, researchers must account for the extent to which the system has excess water available for depletion, the level of groundwater dependence, and the extent of pollution and salinity loading.

OPPORTUNITIES FOR BOTH WATER AND LAND MANAGEMENT: A SELECTION OF POSSIBLE ANSWERS

The most popular and the most politically acceptable way of attempting to save water is to increase irrigation efficiency. However, IWMI's study has clearly shown that this method will not always be effective. Examining a hydrological system as a system of hydronomic zones has shown that efficiency technologies will not be effective in natural and regulated recapture zones with groundwater storage and low salt buildup. If significant salt buildup or pollution occurs in a regulated recapture zone, efficiency technologies will be useful in controlling pollution. These methods will also be useful where no significant recharge of the aquifer occurs or where the recharge is heavily polluted. Such technologies will also decrease energy use. In a natural recapture zone such as Luancheng county, irrigation efficiency will not be effective in stemming groundwater decline. Thus, a variety of other options has been suggested and considered.

Water price increases to increase irrigation efficiency are often suggested as a water conservation measure. In the case of Luancheng county, this measure might not be appropriate because reducing pumping but irrigating the same area will not stop groundwater decline. Rather, what is required is a change in land use; whether this result will ensue from higher prices is debatable.

Aside from irrigation efficiency, a variety of water-saving technologies are put forward as possible solutions. Some of the technologies may exacerbate the problem if used inappropriately. For example, although sprinkler irrigation will save energy and allow for more precise application of water

Figure 3.5   Hydronomic Zones in a River Basin

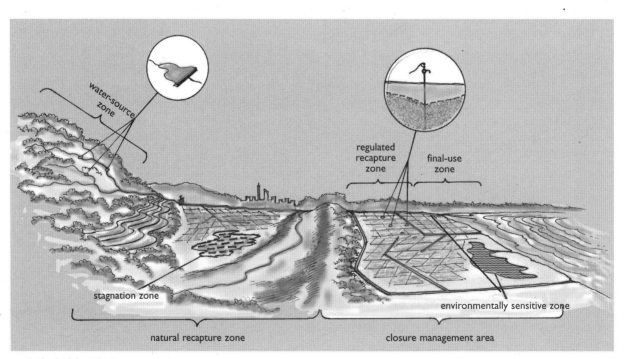

Source: Author's elaboration.

and fertilizers, leading to higher yields, it will not always be effective in reducing groundwater decline. In some situations, it might even aggravate the problem if farmers decide to irrigate more crops with the water they save. Technologies that reduce evaporation, such as the use of mulching and the establishment of greenhouses, would be ideal for Luancheng county.

Changing the cropping pattern is one possibility that needs to be carefully looked at. Adopting less water-intensive cropping patterns than the currently predominant winter wheat and summer maize combination is one suggestion. The amount of water saved will depend on the length of the growing season, the crop's root depth, and its leaf area. Studies have shown, however, that any cropping routine that includes a winter wheat cycle will not show any significant reduction in groundwater depletion. Thus, reintroducing a winter fallow season appears to be the only way of seeing any significant water savings through crop changes. This option, unfortunately, is not likely to be socially and economically palatable.

Another option is the transformation of land use from rural to urban. Although specific data are not available for Luancheng county, urban land use is commonly accepted as depleting much less water than crop evapotranspiration. An urban setting would call for a different range of water conservation measures. In the city of Shijiazhuang, overpumping of groundwater has resulted in the deformation of the water table into a funnel shape, which has affected elevations of water levels at different points and has caused directional changes to the natural flow of groundwater. Thus, water that would naturally have flowed to the aquifers of Luancheng county is flowing instead to the aquifers of Shijiazhuang city. Reducing the net amount of water pumped for the city is imperative if this unsustainable situation is to be reversed.

In an urban setting, precipitation tends to leave the system as runoff, rather than recharging the underlying aquifer, because many of the land surfaces are impermeable. Here, unlike in the study area, efficiency technologies would have a significant effect. A more expensive option is to treat wastewater and then use it to recharge the aquifer. Studies in California have shown that both measures, although they are expensive, show better results in terms of water yield-to-cost ratios than agricultural water conservation, land fallowing, and surface storage construction.

With respect to improving water-use efficiency in urban areas, industrial facilities provide greater potential savings than do households. Water use per industrial product in China is 3 to 10 times greater than in other industrial countries. Discouraging water-intensive industries is a measure that has been adopted in some Chinese cities. Likewise, many different measures can be considered singly or together in the urban context to provide optimal water-use efficiency.

RATIONALE FOR INVESTMENT

None of the measures described earlier will be sufficient on its own to solve the problem of groundwater depletion. Thus, an appropriate mix of measures must be identified to achieve optimal water savings and reduced levels of groundwater depletion. Using the kind of thinking underlying the concept of hydronomic zoning, together with a water-balance approach, the study in Luancheng county set out to identify the right mixture of solutions. It formulated water-saving choices that could be adopted. The sets of options are made up of a combination of changing cropping patterns that leave certain areas of land to lie fallow and changing land use to urban uses. Each set of options is a different combination of land uses that will deplete no more than 460 millimeters per year—bringing rainfall and evapotranspiration into equilibrium.

LESSONS LEARNED

- One must not automatically assume that improving irrigation efficiency will save water. First, consider the fate of excess irrigation water and whether it replenishes the hydrologic system. If excess irrigation water replenishes the hydrologic system, then improved irrigation efficiency will not save water and may, in fact, consume more water by increasing crop production.
- Land and water must be managed in conjunction to achieve sustainable water use. A water-balance approach should be used to associate each land use with its associated net water depletion and to create a sustainable mosaic of land uses.
- For landscape-scale land-use planning, hydronomic zoning should be used to identify areas where improved irrigation efficiency would actually improve water management.
- In places where improved irrigation efficiency does not save water, the only way to reduce the rate of hydrologic depletion (such as water-table declines) is to reduce evapotranspiration. Evapotranspiration reduction can be accomplished by reducing the area devoted to cropland (replacing it with less water-consumptive land use)

and by reducing the growing season on cropland. Reducing the evaporation component of evapotranspiration, for example, by mulching with plastic, can save a smaller amount of water. In the North China Plain, however, the amount of water that could potentially be saved by reducing evaporation is not enough to stabilize declining water tables.

- One should not blindly invest in improvements to irrigation efficiency. They are expensive and often are ineffective in saving water at the basin scale. Moreover, downstream water uses and valuable aquatic ecosystems often rely on the "excess" irrigation water that would be "saved."

INVESTMENT NEEDS AND PRIORITIES

- Establish comprehensive worldwide databases of water use, consumption, and availability by basin.
- Research to understand water consumption (depletion) rates for different land uses—especially urban areas—to facilitate combined land- and water-use planning.
- Design and implement urban wastewater treatment to convert final use of hydronomic zones (contaminated by polluted wastewater) into water-reuse zones
- Improve urban water-use efficiency and stormwater recharge.
- Locate cities upstream from irrigated agricultural areas, which can reuse treated urban wastewater. (The converse—locating irrigation upstream from cities—is less efficient because crops consume most of the water that they use, whereas cities consume only a small fraction of the water they use.)

REFERENCES

Kendy, E., D. J. Molden, T. S. Steenhuis, C. Liu, and J. Wang. 2003. "Policies Drain the North China Plain: Agricultural Policy and Groundwater Depletion in Luancheng County, 1949–2000." IWMI Research Report 71, International Water Management Institute, Colombo, Sri Lanka. http://www.iwmi.cgiar.org/Publications/IWMI_Research _Reports/PDF/pub071/Report71.pdf

Molden, D. J., R. Sakthivadivel, and J. Keller. 2001. "Hydronomic Zones for Developing Basin Water Conservation Strategies." IWMI Research Report 56, International Water Management Institute, Colombo, Sri Lanka.

SELECTED READINGS

Kendy, E. 2003. "The False Promise of Sustainable Pumping Rates." *Ground Water* 41 (1): 2–4.

Kendy, E., and J. D. Bredehoeft. 2006. "Transient Effects of Groundwater Pumping and Surface-Water-Irrigation Returns on Streamflow." *Water Resources Research* 42: W08415.

Kendy E., W. Jinxia, D. J. Molden, C. Zheng, L. Changming, and T. S. Steenhuis. 2007. "Can Urbanization Solve Intersector Water Conflicts? Insight from a Case Study in Hebei Province, North China Plain." *Water Policy* 9 (1): 75–93.

Molden, D. J., and R. Sakthivadivel. 1999. "Water Accounting to Assess Use and Productivity of Water." *International Journal of Water Resources Development* 15 (1): 55–72.

WEB RESOURCES

International Water Management Institute Publications. The publications Web site of the International Water Management Institute contains numerous peer-reviewed reports, papers, and other publications. http://www .iwmi.cgiar.org/Publications/.

Environmental Services Payments and Markets: A Basis for Sustainable Land Resource Management?

The concept of payment for environmental services (PES) arises from the recognition that those who protect resources require compensation for the services they provide to the wider community. One of the most important prerequisites for a functioning PES scheme is an appropriate regulatory framework that establishes property rights and obligations for land use through which environmental services may be negotiated.

A number of PES schemes and pilot programs have been initiated in recent years, particularly in Latin America and the Caribbean. However, experience is inadequate for a thorough comparison of the relative effectiveness of different approaches—and for their replication elsewhere. Transaction costs and the need for government intervention in critical resource areas may prove more expensive than the potential benefits. With skillful analysis of experience, however, PES schemes may be able to overcome some of the limitations of regulatory instruments associated with the creation of incentives for conservation and sustainable use of natural resources. At the same time, these schemes may stimulate the formation of social capital in the regions where they are established.

PES schemes implemented to date have not been beneficial to the poor: they attract as service providers those who hold titles, own larger areas, and obtain incomes from sources outside the production unit (thus making land retirement from production represent little in terms of opportunity cost to the landowner). To improve equity requires that schemes restrict or differentiate payments to low-income households. PES schemes involving market creation should be linked to a regulatory system that establishes specific limitations on productive activities and that creates the need for those who possess environmental liabil-

ities to negotiate trades with those who exceed the stipulated norms. Without this regulatory framework, there is little hope of creating markets for environmental services.

KEY SUSTAINABLE LAND MANAGEMENT ISSUES

New opportunities for adding value to sustainable rural land resources management are being created in many parts of the world under the rubric of payments for environmental services. Such opportunities arise from the growing perception that ensuring nature's services in the long run requires not only that they should be valued by society, but also that these values inspire compensation to those who protect resources.

As described in box 3.3, natural resources protection and good land-use practices generate a gamut of services of both economic and cultural importance, besides ensuring continuation of functions essential to support and maintain living organisms, including humans.

LESSONS LEARNED

Experience in a number of countries to date, particularly in the Americas, suggests that creation of environmental services markets and payment schemes is viable and offers opportunities for equitable and efficient provision of public goods. Environmental services markets function best when they meet the following conditions:

- They provide measurable benefit to the environment from adopting best practices.
- The sources of services are identifiable (for example, improved agricultural practice, new protected areas).

This note was prepared by P. H. May, Department of Agriculture, Development and Society, Federal Rural University, Rio de Janeiro, Brazil.

Box 3.3 Types of Environmental Services Generated by Good Land-Use Practices

Water and Soil-Related Services
- Flow regulation
- Quality maintenance
- Aquatic habitat
- Cultural values (recreation, worship)
- Control of erosion and sedimentation
- Nutrient cycling
- Reduced salinity

Climate Services
- Microclimate regulation
- Reduced emissions from burning
- Carbon sequestration
- Maintenance of terrestrial carbon stocks

Biodiversity Conservation Services
- Connectivity and scale for wildlife conservation
- Sustainable use
- Cultural values (recreation, worship, existence value)

- A regulatory framework establishes limits within which negotiations can occur.
- Services provided are contingent on payment (that is, one should not have to pay for what one would probably receive anyway).
- Beneficiaries and providers agree on compensation amounts and terms.

Scientific research can help identify the origin of services provided and monitor the provision of downstream benefits, relating the latter to the quality of resources protection at the source. However, science has few good tools to arrive at appropriate and equitable values for PES. These values must be negotiated between "buyers" and "sellers." Economic analysis of the willingness of beneficiaries to pay for these services can provide a useful benchmark. In most instances where payment schemes have begun, the opportunity cost of income forgone from alternative land uses has served as a yardstick for the maximum that should be paid to a property owner to retire land from nonconserving uses. Although this measure is a good indicator of cost to the provider, it may fail to take into account future opportunities for productive land use and need to be adjusted over time.

One of the most important prerequisites for a functioning PES scheme is an appropriate regulatory framework that establishes property rights and obligations for land use and sets conditions within which environmental services may be negotiated. For example, in some countries, such as Brazil, land-use codes establish a minimum share of private land that must remain under native vegetation in each biome. Many landowners have not complied with this rule, finding occupation of all or a good part of their properties more lucrative. Others have retained more forest cover than required by law. When the government began to enforce this legislation more rigorously, trading was permitted between deficit and surplus forestland owners. This trade became the germ of a PES scheme that is now being tested in various parts of Brazil. In the same vein, carbon trading could not take place if quantitative limits were not placed on greenhouse gas emissions.

A number of PES schemes and pilot programs have been initiated in recent years, particularly in Latin America and the Caribbean. Descriptions of these experiences are summarized in table 3.3.

The first and largest PES scheme to be implemented was Costa Rica's program for environmental service payments. Created at a national scale in 1997, the program by 2005 had been applied to 500,000 hectares of privately owned forests. The program is administered through the National Forestry

Table 3.3 Incidence of Costs and Benefits for Environmental Services

Services	Opportunity costs	Beneficiaries	Payment mechanisms
Carbon sequestration	Local farmers and landowners (avoiding deforestation)	Global society	Clean development mechanism, biocarbon fund, and non-Kyoto funds
Watershed protection	Farmers in upper watersheds and catchment areas (forgoing production on fragile lands)	Local downstream communities and enterprises	Water-use charges, taxation of water-using enterprises, royalties for electricity generation
Biodiversity conservation	Local ranchers and farmers and wood-producing enterprises (protecting ecosystems)	Global society and traditional peoples	Compensation funds and benefit sharing for traditional knowledge and germplasm

Source: Author's elaboration.

Financing Fund (Fondo Nacional de Financiamiento Forestal, or FONAFIFO) financed from a combination of sources, including a 3.5 percent gasoline levy, electrical utility payments for hydroelectric catchment protection, and grant funds for an ecomarkets project from the Global Environment Facility (GEF) that began in 2001. In Costa Rica, there is now broad public recognition that intact forests and their environmental services have value. GEF support has ensured greater attention to biodiversity conservation and to a more equitable distribution of payments; recipients include women and indigenous communities whose activities promote environmental services (Hartshorn, Ferraro, and Spergel 2005).

More recently, in 2003, the Mexican government created a national program of payments for water services provided by private forest landowners who agree to protect existing forests and to restore forest cover on degraded lands. In its first year alone, the program reached more than 128,000 hectares in rural communities and ejidos (collective properties) in 15 states. In contrast to the program in Costa Rica, the Mexican program is financed from general government revenues rather than from earmarked sources associated with specific environmental service beneficiaries. A GEF-financed project to extend the program and its global benefits, as well as to test market-based mechanisms, is in initial stages of implementation (Guillén 2004).

The GEF has also cofinanced two programs involving research and PES trials in agricultural and forest management systems. The programs primarily focus on Central America. The first is under way in Belize, El Salvador, Honduras, and Nicaragua, under the auspices of the Meso-American Biological Corridor and the Program for Sustainable Hillside Agriculture in Central America. Its objectives are to enable these countries to better adapt to climatic events and water scarcity in prolonged dry seasons and to ensure clean, sufficient, and regular water supplies to communities within this isthmus of globally important biodiversity. PES pilot schemes were initiated in 2002 in six microwatersheds in which municipal governments established funds to finance conservation treatments and modest payments to farmers for improvement in water supplies. The payment scheme led farmers to adopt soil and water conservation technologies that include ceased burning, and use of green manures, terracing, and hedgerows. As a result, water sources are showing signs of recovery. Implementing local pilot actions is perceived to be an effective instrument for developing sound policies at a national level. In Belize and El Salvador, the pilots are intended to provide the basis for structuring national PES programs.

A second pilot program, the Integrated Silvopastoral Approaches to Ecosystem Management, involves pilot valuation studies and PES payment trials with livestock producers in three sites in Colombia, Costa Rica, and Nicaragua. In these locales, land users agreed under contract to receive annual payments averaging US$500 per hectare up to a maximum of US$4,500 per property over four years based on incremental provision of biodiversity-related services in their production systems. The payments were to reach a total of 35,000 hectares over the project's cycle. Payments are defined on the basis of a point system ascribing weights to different land-use attributes insofar as they contribute to biodiversity conservation. As the project evolves, each landowner has the opportunity to increase his or her payment through implementation of agreed practices (Pagiola and others 2004).

Finally, in Brazil, government agencies, small farmers' organizations, and nongovernmental organizations have joined forces to create a program for sustainable development of rural family production in the Amazon (ProAmbiente). The program began in 2004 in 11 pilot areas in the nine Amazon states. In each state, 500 rural households—primarily land reform beneficiaries—were selected to participate in the scheme. Operationally, ProAmbiente combines conventional credit operations with regular monthly payments for farmers, equivalent to up to 40 percent of the credit. These payments are contingent on compliance with land-use criteria based on certified environmental services. Such services include avoiding deforestation, allowing carbon sequestration, reestablishing hydrologic functions, conserving biodiversity, protecting the soil, and reducing risk of fire. The scheme is operating on a pilot basis using general government revenues and seeking funds from international donors and carbon traders for the environmental services payments.

OPPORTUNITIES FOR SUSTAINABLE LAND MANAGEMENT

Devising a workable PES scheme also requires looking at the incidence of costs and benefits. If changes in land use are proposed as a means of benefiting the global environment through climate change mitigation or biodiversity conservation, the costs should be borne by global society and not by farmers in developing nations. If the majority of benefits are received locally, however, such as through clean and reliable water supply, local water users should share the costs. In most cases, however, cross-benefits occur: in integrated watershed management, biodiversity may be protected and water supplies ensured simultaneously. This dual benefit provides opportunities for environmental services to be financed jointly by different beneficiaries through the same resource-protective activities in a geographic area. This facet makes it logical to create an environmental services fund to receive and disburse contributions from different beneficiaries to finance installation and maintenance of a bundle of land-use practices in a given locale. The differential incidence of environmental service benefits and payment mechanisms is described in table 3.3.

Despite the promise of PES, a number of perils and pitfalls can unnecessarily encumber those who seek to set up PES schemes and those who might benefit from them, particularly the rural poor. These difficulties may be summed up in the concept of transaction costs. The contract negotiations, time, and money involved may actually exceed the net benefits of setting up such a scheme, thereby making adoption of land-use codes or other regulations seem easier or more cost-effective than relying on the magic of the marketplace.

RECOMMENDATIONS FOR PRACTITIONERS

Experience with the establishment of PES schemes, even in Latin America where they have a longer history, is as yet quite new. Therefore, it is not possible to thoroughly compare the relative effectiveness of different approaches for replication elsewhere.[1] Expectations for PES schemes generally soar but in all likelihood greatly exceed their probable potential to reduce transaction costs and the need for government intervention in critical resource areas. Nevertheless, PES schemes may be able to overcome some of the limitations of regulatory instruments associated with the creation of incentives for conservation and sustainable use of natural resources. At the same time, they may stimulate the formation of social capital in the regions where they are established. The following principal lessons have been learned from PES experiences to date, focused primarily on watershed services:

■ Calculating the value of benefits arising from specific land-use practices is a gray area subject to great uncertainties. PES schemes will be more effective, for example, if they are directed at water quality than at water supply associated with enhancement of forest cover, because conventional wisdom and scientific proof diverge a number of ways regarding the water-flow regulation functions of forests.

■ At the outset of program design, it is best to begin with services for which a clear established demand exists (for example, improvement in water quality associated with discharge of animal residues) and for which a relationship between the change in practices and the condition of ambient water quality supplied is relatively easy to prove.

■ The best "bang for the buck" is obtained by promoting practices that offer multiple benefits, such as restoration of streambank vegetation, which can simultaneously reduce sedimentation of water courses, sequester carbon, and reestablish biological connectivity between forest fragments.

■ Rather than invest in complicated procedures to calculate environmental benefits, PES should be estimated initially on the basis of opportunity costs associated with adoption in comparison with a baseline scenario (for example, the net income forgone from land retired from production to permit regeneration). It is not always necessary to cover the full opportunity costs of such practices to attract an adequate number of service providers.

In general, PES schemes implemented to date have not been beneficial to the poor. They attract service providers who hold titles, own larger areas, and obtain incomes from sources outside the production unit (thus making land retirement from production represent little in terms of opportunity cost to the landowner). To improve equity requires that schemes restrict or differentiate payments to low-income households.

PES schemes involving market creation should be linked to a regulatory system that establishes specific limitations on productive activities and that creates the need for those who possess environmental liabilities to negotiate trades with those who exceed the stipulated norms. Without this regulatory framework, there is little hope of creating markets for environmental services.

NOTE

1. See Waage and others (2006) for an assessment of capacity-building opportunities for dissemination of PES approaches worldwide.

REFERENCES

Guillén, M. J. G., ed. 2004. "Valuación del Programa de Pago de Servicios Ambientales Hidrológicos (PSAH)." Colegio de Postgraduados, Comisión Nacional Forestal, Zapopan, Mexico.

Hartshorn, G., P. Ferraro, and B. Spergel. 2005. "Evaluation of the World Bank–GEF Ecomarkets Project in Costa Rica." North Carolina State University, Raleigh.

Pagiola, S., P. Agostini, J. Gobbi, C. de Haan, M. Ibrahim, E. Murgueitio, E. Ramírez, M. Rosales, and J. P. Ruíz. 2004. "Paying for Biodiversity Conservation Services in Agricultural Landscapes." Environment Department Paper 96, World Bank, Washington, DC.

Waage, S., S. Scherr, M. Jenkins, and M. Inbar. 2006. A *Scoping Assessment of Current Work on Payments for Ecosystem Services in Asia, Latin America, and East and Southern Africa.* Washington, DC: Forest Trends.

SELECTED READINGS

Faleiro, A., and L. R. de Oliveira. 2005. "ProAmbiente: Conservação ambiental e vida digna no campo." In *Instrumentos Econômicos para o Desenvolvimento Sustentável da Amazônia: Experiências e Visões,* ed. Paulo Haddad and Fernando Rezende, 69–76. Brasília: Ministry of the Environment, Secretariat for Coordination of Amazonia.

Pagiola, S., J. Bishop, and N. Landell-Mills, eds. 2002. *Selling Forest Environmental Services: Market-Based Mechanisms for Conservation and Development.* London: Earthscan.

Pérez, C. J. 2005. "Recovering Positive Mountain Externalities: Reversing Land Degradation through Payment for Environmental Services at the Local Level." Program for Sustainable Agriculture in the Hillsides of Central America.

Wunder, S. 2005. "Payments for Environmental Services: Some Nuts and Bolts." CIFOR Occasional Paper 42, Center for International Forestry Research, Jakarta.

Zbinden, S., and D. R. Lee. 2005. "Paying for Environmental Services: An Analysis of Participation in Costa Rica's PSA Program." *World Development* 33 (2): 255–72.

WEB RESOURCES

Flows. The FLOWS bulletin provides a review of selected topics pertaining to the assessment of the effectiveness of payment arrangements for watershed services and lessons being learned. Each issue provides a space for reader commentary and responses to previous issues, and announcements of pertinent new reports and papers, and upcoming events: http://www.flowsonline.net/.

Species Diversity in Fallow Lands of Southern Cameroon: Implications for Management of Constructed Landscapes

Humid tropical forests provide a range of products and services. Fallow cycles are considered the most common source of deforestation in southern Cameroon and are attributed to smallholder agriculture. As fallow periods become shorter, fallow composition changes, ultimately endangering the succession process of the natural forest.

Lands that have been fallow fewer than 10 years form an important component of the agricultural landscape in the humid forest zone of southern Cameroon. These fallow types of land have been shown to be an essential part of local livelihoods. They are used not only for cropping but also as key reserves of nontimber forest products. There are good reasons to focus on the development of sustainable fallow shifting cultivation systems, which may be more environmentally acceptable than permanent farming systems in terms of deforestation, soil erosion, and carbon storage.

INTRODUCTION

Two major environmental concerns face policy makers and stakeholders regarding the humid forests of Cameroon: deforestation and forest degradation. Humid tropical forests provide a range of products and services that include timber and nontimber forest products, forest biomass used as a fertility input (when converted to ash through slash-and-burn techniques), conservation of important biodiversity, protection of soil resources and watersheds, prevention of desertification, and regulation of local and global climatic patterns through carbon sequestration. Fallow cycles are considered the most common source of deforestation in southern Cameroon and are attributed to smallholder agriculture (Gockowski and Essama-Nssah 2000). As popula-

tion pressures increase and fallow periods become shorter, fallow composition changes, ultimately endangering the succession process of the natural forest.

Most studies on shifting cultivation have assumed that species diversity declines when the length of fallow periods is reduced. A wide range of authors have adopted this theoretical presentation of the essence of ecological dynamics in shifting cultivation (for example, Ruthenberg 1980; Sanchez 1976). This theory has helped fuel the condemnation of fallowing by many governments because it clearly shows that when fallow periods are shortened because of land scarcity and population pressure or other factors, this farming system will in all cases create a downward spiral of low species diversity and declining yield in the subsequent cropping seasons.

Fallow lands fewer than 10 years old form an important component of the agricultural landscape in the humid forest zone of southern Cameroon. These fallow types of land have been shown to be an essential part of local livelihoods. They are used not only for cropping but also as key reserves of nontimber forest products. However, a consequence of increasing resource-use pressure and subsequent shortening of fallow duration is the invasion of these land-use systems by the Asteraceous species *Chromolaena odorata* (L.) (Ngobo, McDonald, and Weise 2004; Weise 1995; Weise and Tchamou 1999).

Chromolaena is widely regarded as a serious threat to agriculture in West Africa and is rapidly spreading throughout Southeast Asia into the South Pacific and into central and eastern Africa from the infestations in western Africa and South Africa. Moreover, shorter fallow periods are believed to cause environmental damage in the form of soil mining and accelerated erosion. In combination with national interests in protecting forest resources for other

This profile was prepared by M. Ngobo and S. Weise, International Institute of Tropical Agriculture, Yaoundé, Cameroon.

purposes, this result has, in many cases, led to an official antipathy toward fallowing practices, making development of sustainable fallow shifting cultivation—which may be more environmentally acceptable than permanent farming systems in terms of deforestation, soil erosion, and carbon storage—more difficult to focus on.

The reported resource-use intensification in the study area and the increasingly acknowledged need for more productive and environmentally friendly agricultural systems for local resource-poor farmers have stimulated renewed interest in the mechanisms by which, among other functions, fallow systems restore ecosystem fertility and biodiversity. Concern for more profitable and ecologically sustainable fallow systems provided impetus for initial research, particularly given the reported increasing abundance of fallows of shortened duration in the humid forest zone of Cameroon. A lack of reliable information regarding the characteristics of these land-use systems in the humid forest zone of southern Cameroon has hindered resource managers' attempts to develop adapted strategies.

DESCRIPTION OF FOREST FALLOW MANAGEMENT INNOVATION

The activity reported here underlines the need to distinguish forest fallows dominated by *Chromolaena* from fallow types that have recently been a forest when designing strategies and policies for sustainable management of short fallows in the humid forest zone of southern Cameroon. The low frequency of forest species recorded in frequently cropped fallows emphasizes the urgent need to develop vegetation management strategies that aim at accelerating plant succession during the fallow phase. The information and knowledge presented are specific to the Mengomo, located in the southern part of the humid forest zone of Cameroon, but they are relevant for similar humid forest sites in Africa.

The major site where the information for this note was derived is situated at 2°20'N and 11°03'E. Mengomo is a small locality (598 inhabitants and 83 households) that lies 52 kilometers south of the city of Ebolowa. It is characterized by a hot and moist equatorial climate, with a minimum mean annual temperature of about 20°C and a maximum of 29°C (National Meteorological Station of Yaoundé, mean of 11 years: 1983–94, as cited in Santoir and Bopda 1995). The mean annual rainfall is about 1,800 millimeters, falling in a bimodal pattern, which determines two rainy seasons (March to July and August to November) and two drier seasons (July to August and November to March) of unequal duration. The main natural vegetation is a mosaic of semi-

deciduous tropical forest, fallow fields of various length, and vegetation (Letouzey 1968). The farming system is one of the least intensified among villages of the area, and production is highly oriented toward subsistence. The site is characterized by yellow ferralitic and highly desaturated soils that fall into the Food and Agriculture Organization class of orthic ferrasols (Koutika, Kameni, and Weise 2000).

EFFECTS ON VEGETATION COMMUNITY AND BIODIVERSITY

Both species and functional diversity were significantly associated with vegetation structure and plant community composition in fallows of five to seven years under different land-use intensity regimes. Recently forested fallow types displayed the highest values of stand structural parameters, except for the site disturbance index. There was no significant effect of fallow type on the mean basal area or crown cover.

Approximately 225 species of vascular plants were recorded in the study sites, belonging to 72 to 74 families. The most richly represented families were Euphorbiaceae, Fabaceae (or Papilionaceae), and Sterculiaceae, respectively; with 23, 21, and 12 genera. Although up to 85 plant species were common to all fallow types, about 67 plants were exclusive to stands that had been forests before the previous cropping cycle (table 3.4). Among the species most frequently found in all study sites were *Chromolaena*, *Haumania danckelmaniana* Milne-Redh., *Milletia* spp., *Dioscorea* spp., *Cissus* spp., *Cnestis ferruginea* DC, and *Nephroplepis biserrata* (Sw.) Schott, which were present in more than 70 percent of the sites.

Frequently cropped fallows were characterized by the abundance of *Chromolaena*, *Albyzia zygia* Macbride, and *Dioscorea* spp, with the understory characterized by a few Poaceae and some Cyperaceae. The vegetation in moderately cropped fallows was consistently least diverse (58 to 132 species). Although *Chromolaena* was still abundant, this fallow type was characterized by the importance of Commelinaceae and Marantaceae species, represented by different species of *Palisota* and *Megaphrynium*. There was more understory than in the previous fallow type, and it comprised some forest herbaceous species like *Aframomum* spp., *Harungana madagascariensis*, and *Haumania danckelmaniana*. A high number of species (150 to 171) was recorded in recently forested fallows. The vegetation in fallow sites of this type was clearly stratified in three distinguishable layers: (a) an upper story dominated by pioneer semiwoody species (of up 8 meters height), (b) an intermediate stratum that

Table 3.4   Total Number of Plant Species Recorded in Three Fallow Types in the Humid Forest Zone of Southern Cameroon

Plant community composition	Frequently cropped	Moderately cropped	Recently forested lands	Total fallows
Total species	111–165	58–132	150–171	224–225
Species with frequency of presence greater than or equal to 70 percent	12	13	17	7
Species with frequency of presence greater than or equal to 50 percent	26	33	47	27
Total families	54	37	64	72–74
Families with 1 species	31	25	33	34
Species exclusive to fallow type	4	33	34	—

Source: Author's elaboration.

comprised small individuals of mostly secondary or primary forest species, and (c) a lower story dominated by secondary forest herbaceous species. Characteristic species of the mature secondary forest were consistently present in this fallow type.

PATTERNS OF VARIATION IN SPECIES COMPOSITION AMONG FALLOW TYPES

Ordination analyses showed a clear pattern of distribution of species along a gradient of resource-use intensity. Except for mean litter depth, a significant positive correlation was found between plant biodiversity (as indicated by the number of species and other diversity indices) and fallow structural features. Conversely, there was a negative significant correlation between plant species diversity and crown cover of woody plants as well as site disturbance index. The influence of vegetation composition and vegetation structure on species assemblages reported in this study, which was highly correlated with litter depth and basal area, suggests that there is a gradient of soil organic matter content and soil moisture from less intensively farmed to more intensively farmed fallow types.

LESSONS LEARNED

The results of this study suggest that increasing land-use intensity (reflected here by increasing the number of fallow cultivation cycles) will initially have little effect on the species diversity of the shortened fallow plant community. However, as the link to the forest is reduced, altering the site vegetation's structural characteristics and decreasing shade (leading to a more homogeneous microclimate), an adverse effect will occur, and the species richness will decline. Nevertheless, other studies have shown that increasing land-use intensity results in the loss of some uncommon useful species of

shortened fallow systems, such as *Megaphrynium* spp. and *Sarcophrynium* spp. (Aweto 2001; van Dijk 1999). As in this study, lack of replacement with uncommon weed species may occur because they are being exposed to competition from ubiquitous species through habitat disturbance.

In Cameroon, smallholder agriculture is held to be the major source of deforestation. Therefore, any proposed multisectoral approach for addressing deforestation must start with agriculture. A summary of the lessons and challenges while designing sustainable vegetation management strategies for the humid forest area of southern Cameroon follows:

- Sustainable pathways for rural development in the humid forest zones can minimize the damage and, in some cases, even improve the environmental services of the cultivation-forest mosaic ecosystem. The productivity of fallow lands needs to be assessed to evaluate their sustainability and economic viability for local resource-poor farmers.

- Measures to achieve these goals are (a) to focus on the collection and dissemination of relevant and reliable information, (b) to work with a larger set of stakeholders, and (c) to use Cameroonian expertise to gain local perspective and build capacity.

- Given the global importance of fallows of 5 to 10 years in the humid forest zone of southern Cameroon, as well as the considerable variation in published estimates of plant species diversity and change, development of a reliable and indisputable monitoring mechanism is imperative. The rapid evolution in remote-sensing technologies offers the best potential for quantifying patterns of change. Reliable and replicable estimates from such techniques would be of great use to policy makers and other stakeholders.

- It is, therefore, necessary to develop improved systematic data gathering to update understanding of the contributions of fallows (and shortened fallows, in particular) to household, community, and national livelihood strategies. Such data will be of great use to policy makers and development organizations in developing improved and sustainable fallow systems that may benefit both small-scale farmers and the environment.

REFERENCES

Aweto, A. O. 2001. "Trees in Shifting and Continuous Cultivation Farms in Ibadan Area, Southwestern Nigeria." *Landscape and Urban Planning* 53 (1–4): 163–71.

Gockowski, J., and B. Essama-Nssah. 2000. *Cameroon Forest Sector Development in a Difficult Political Economy: Evaluation Country Case Study Series.* Washington, DC: World Bank.

Koutika, L. S., R. Kameni, and S. Weise. 2000. "Variability of Nutrient Content in Topsoils under Fallow in Three Villages in the Humid Forest Zone (Southern Cameroon)." In *La jachère en Afrique tropicale,* ed. C. Floret and R. Pontanier, 223–28. Paris: John Libbey Eurotext.

Letouzey, R. 1968. "Étude phytogéographique du Cameroun." In *Encyclopédie Biologique* 69, 511. Paris: Editions Paul LeChevalier.

Ngobo, M., M. McDonald, and S. Weise. 2004. "Impact of Fallow and Invasion by *Chromolaena odorata* on Weed Communities of Crop Fields in Cameroon." *Ecology and Society* 9 (2): 1. http://www.ecologyandsociety.org/vol9/iss2/art1.

Ruthenberg, H. 1980. *Farming Systems in the Tropics.* Oxford, U.K.: Clarendon Press.

Sanchez, P. A. 1976. *Properties and Management of Soils in the Tropics.* New York: John Wiley and Sons.

Santoir, C., and A. Bopda. 1995. *Atlas régional du Sud-Cameroun.* Paris: Office de la Recherche Scientifique et Technique d'Outre-Mer.

van Dijk, J. F. W. 1999. *Non-Timber Forest Products in the Bipindi-Akom II Region, Cameroon: A Socio-economic and Ecological Assessment.* Tropenbos-Cameroon Series 1. Kribi, Cameroon: Tropenbos Cameroon Programme.

Weise, S. F. 1995. "Distribution and Significance of *Chromolaena odorata* (L.) R. M. King and H. Robinson across Ecological Zones in Cameroon." In *Proceedings of the Third International Workshop on Biological Control and Management of* Chromolaena odorata, ed. U. K. Prasad, R. Muniappan, P. Ferrar, J. P. Aeschliman, and H. de Foresta, 29–38. Mangilao: University of Guam.

Weise, S. F., and N. Tchamou. 1999. "*Chromolaena odorata* in the Humid Forests of West and Central Africa: Management or Control?" *Proceedings of the Brighton Crop Protection Conference: Weeds.* Farnham, U.K.: British Crop Protection Council.

SELECTED READINGS

Gockowski, J., D. Baker, J. Tonye, S. Weise, M. Ndoumbè, T. Tiki-Manga, and A. Fouaguégué. 1998. "Characterization and Diagnosis of Farming Systems in the ASB Forest Margins Benchmark of Southern Cameroon." International Institute of Tropical Agriculture, Humid Forest Ecoregional Center, Yaoundé.

Tiki-Manga, T., and S. F. Weise. 1995. "Alternatives to Slash-and-Burn Project." Cameroon Benchmark Site Final Report, Yaoundé.

Domestication and Commercialization of Forest Tree Crops in the Tropics

The harvesting of indigenous fruit trees (IFTs) represents an important food supplement and cash income for rural people in many tropical countries. Most of the fruits from IFTs are still being harvested from the wild, and traditional crops and fruits play a valuable role in supporting household food security. However, this role could be significantly enhanced if improved varieties and production, harvesting, and storage techniques could be made available to the rural poor. Thus a pro-poor strategy involves moving away from depending only on wild harvesting.

Participatory domestication is defined as genetic improvement that includes farmer-researcher collaboration and is farmer led and market driven. It was devised to overcome the shortcomings of earlier top-down approaches of conventional breeding and forestry. It leads to consideration of the wider context in which it is possible to identify which traditional crops and fruits are becoming marginalized; how much diversity occurs within them; and what their productive and genetic potentials, postharvest requirements, and processing and marketing potentials are. These efforts involve plant taxonomists, ethnobotanists, crop breeders, crop scientists, food scientists, agricultural engineers, human nutritionists, and economists and are conducted in conjunction with farmer associations and commercial establishments.

INTRODUCTION

The harvesting of indigenous fruit trees from the wild predated settled agriculture and represents an important food supplement and cash income for rural people in many tropical countries. Evidence is accumulating that IFTs can contribute significantly to household income in every region in the tropics (Akinnifesi and others 2007; Leakey and others 2005) and is a major opportunity for asset building for smallholder farmers. For example, in southern and eastern Africa, most of the food crops grown by small-scale farmers did not originate from Africa. Maize, beans, groundnuts, sweet potatoes, and cassava are all exotics from tropical America and have largely displaced the sorghum, millet, cowpeas, and yams produced by yesteryear's traditional farmers. Marginalizing African crops has resulted in collapsed traditional seed systems, reduced farm biodiversity, poorer diets, decreased food security, and declining cultural tradition. Ironically, today the demand for traditional foods by urban consumers is increasing because indigenous small grains, pulses, fruits, and leafy green vegetables are both tasty and nutritious. However, often these foods are not readily available. In addition, in times of food scarcity, these traditional crops and fruits play a valuable role in supporting household food security. This role could be significantly enhanced if improved varieties and production, harvesting, and storage techniques could be made available to the rural poor.

A large amount of knowledge on the opportunities, challenges, knowledge gaps, and constraints of IFTs has been gathered in recent years. Continued enthusiasm exists among researchers and development practitioners (especially in the past two decades) to explore the opportunities to meet the food needs of humanity through IFTs. As a result, increasing emphasis is placed on tree domestication strategies (promoting IFTs with economic potential as new cash crops), product development, and commercialization and marketing of agroforestry tree products. This profile highlights the opportunities, achievements, and challenges of IFT domestication, use, and marketing in Africa, Asia, and Latin America.

This profile was prepared by F. K. Akinnifesi, O. C. Ajayi, and G. Sileshi, World Agroforestry Centre, Makoka, Malawi.

TREE DOMESTICATION INNOVATION

Participatory domestication is defined as genetic improvement that includes farmer-researcher collaboration. It is farmer led and market driven. It was devised to overcome the shortcomings of earlier top-down approaches of conventional breeding and forestry. Participatory domestication approaches have been applied by the World Agroforestry Centre for *U. kirkiana, Sclerocarya birrea,* and *S. cocculoides* in southern Africa (Akinnifesi and others 2006) and for *Dacryodes edulis* and *Irvingia gabonensis* in West Africa (Tchoundjeu and others 2006). In Latin America, *Bactris gasipaes* Kunth and cupuaçu (*Theobroma grandiflora*) have been subjected to domestication, especially in Brazil and Peru (Clement and others 2008). The objectives of the domestication projects led by the World Agroforestry Centre are (a) to identify technically, economically, and socially viable investment opportunities for indigenous fruit domestication in the context of sustainable land management and (b) to establish pilot projects that meet preestablished investment criteria.

The domestication research started by identifying species preference depending on the extent they are able to meet the subsistence and cash-income needs of the producers and market participants. Franzel, Jaenicke, and Janssen (1996) described the seven principles and application of priority setting that were tested in various regions. Results of the priority setting across regions are presented in table 3.5.

Akinnifesi and others (2007) described detailed principles and strategies for participatory domestication based on clonal selection and vegetative propagation. These strategies have had significant benefits—for example, the long juve-

nile phase (period before first fruiting) has been reduced from 10–15 years to 3–4 years for *D. edulis* in western Africa, for *U. kirkiana* in southern Africa, and for cupuaçu (*Theobroma grandiflora*) in Latin America.

BENEFITS OF ACTIVITY AND ITS IMPLICATIONS FOR SUSTAINABLE LAND MANAGEMENT

The IFT species previously mentioned are important in many ecosystems, and farmers make efforts to conserve and cultivate them on farmlands. Five factors are important in cultivation and sustainable management of IFTs: site requirements, genetic variability and improvement potential, propagation methods, nutritional properties, and commercial potential (Jama and others 2007). Knowledge is important for tree management and sustained land management. Akinnifesi and others (2007) provide insights into the potential of integrating IFT cultivation into smallholder production in ways that contribute to livelihoods, biodiversity conservation, and sustainable land productivity.

Trees can contribute to improved organic matter accumulation, erosion control, and nutrient recycling from deeper soil layers. In a farming system that includes income from tree crops, the farmer can use some of the returns from fruits to invest in fertilizers, seeds, and other inputs in other parts of the system.

LESSONS LEARNED AND ISSUES FOR SCALING UP TREE DOMESTICATION

Most of the fruits from IFTs are still being harvested from the wild, and traditional crops and fruits play a valuable role in

Table 3.5   List of the Four Most Preferred Priority Indigenous Fruit Tree Species in Selected Regions

Region	Rank 1	Rank 2	Rank 3	Rank 4	Method
East Africa (Ethiopia, Kenya, Sudan, and Uganda)	*Adansonia digitata* (baobab)	*Tamarindus indica* (tamarind)	*Ziziphus mauritiana* (ber)	*Sclerocarya birrea* (marula)	Field surveys (n = 167)
Southern Africa (Malawi, Tanzania, Zambia, and Zimbabwe)	*Uapaca kirkiana* (wild loquat)	*Strychnos cocculoides* (wild orange)	*Parinari curatellifolia* (maula)	*Ziziphus mauritiana* (ber)	Field surveys (n = 451)
West Africa (Cameroon, Ghana, and Nigeria)	*Irvingia gabonensis* (wild mango)	*Dacryodes edulis* (African plum)	*Chrysophyllum albidum* (star apple)	*Garcinia cola* (bitter cola)	Workshops + field surveys (n = 94)
Sahelian zone (Burkina Faso, Mali, Niger, and Senegal)	*Adansonia digitata* (baobab)	*Tamarindus indica* (tamarind)	*Vitellaria paradoxa* (shea)	*Ziziphus mauritiana* (ber)	Field surveys (n = 470)
Latin America (Bolivia, Brazil, Colombia, Ecuador, Peru, and R.B. de Venezuela)	*Euterpe oleraceae* (açaí)	*Bactris gasipaes* (pupunha)	*Theobroma grandiflora* (cupuaçu)	*Myrciaria dubia* (camu-camu)	Workshop (Roraima, Brazil, October 2006)

Source: For East Africa, Jama and others 2007; Teklehaimanot 2007. For southern Africa, Akinnifesi and others 2007; Maghembe and others 1998. For West Africa, Franzel and others 2007. For the Sahelian zone, Bounkoungou and others 1998; Franzel and others 2007; Techlehaimanot 2007. For Latin America, regional workshop organized by Iniciativa Amazonica in 2006. Sources are cited in Akinnifesi and others 2007.

supporting household food security. However, this role could be significantly enhanced if improved varieties and production, harvesting, and storage techniques could be made available to the rural poor. Thus, a pro-poor strategy involves moving away from depending only on wild harvesting. Domestication research and development for IFTs have progressed significantly, especially in Africa and Latin America; efforts to prioritize, select, and cultivate superior cultivars of IFTs using participatory approaches are noted across the regions. Such strategies generally involved the following:

- Application of farmer-centered, market-led approaches involving careful participatory selection of the right species and elite cultivars to be promoted; development of low-cost simple propagation techniques; and establishment and management practice in cooperation with farmers
- Postharvest handling, product development, and prospecting of IFT products
- Market research, enterprise development, and commercialization.

The overall objective is to identify, conserve, improve, and promote traditional crops and fruits as a means of improving their seed systems and markets, thereby making the crops more attractive to small-scale farmers. Specific aims are

- To better understand which traditional foods are becoming marginalized and explore avenues for their revitalization
- To explore opportunities for processing traditional foods in ways that make them more attractive and easily prepared by urban consumers, thereby strengthening their demand and markets.

In the wider context, it is possible to identify which traditional crops and fruits are becoming marginalized; how much diversity occurs within them; and what their productive and genetic potentials, postharvest requirements, and processing and marketing potentials are. These efforts involve plant taxonomists, ethnobotanists, crop breeders, crop scientists, food scientists, agricultural engineers, human nutritionists, and economists and are conducted in conjunction with farmer associations and commercial establishments.

Following is a summary of the lessons learned and challenges encountered:

- The investment needs for wider cultivation and scaling up of tree domestication of IFTs include (a) quality planting material in sufficient quantity, (b) adequate skills and resources for village-level nurseries in decentralized systems, and (c) facilities for micropropagation and tissue culture centers for rapid multiplication of specialized propagules (Akinnifesi and others 2006).
- Measures to speed up the multiplication of improved planting materials are necessary. They include the application of biotechnology and tissue culture techniques in germplasm multiplication. Delivery deserves greater attention.
- Research and development on the domestication of IFTs has advanced in only a few species, such as *Uapaca kirkiana*, *Sclerocarya birrea*, *Parinari curatellifolia* in southern Africa; *Dacryodes edules* and *Irvingia gabonensis* in western Africa; and *Theobroma grandiflora* and peach palm (*Bactris gasipaes*) in Latin America. There is a need to expand the range of IFTs currently being researched in different regions of the tropics.
- Droughts and climate affect fruiting potentials, cycles, and seasonal variability and cause major reduction in fruit production and quality. It is important to investigate how tree planting affects climate change, on one hand, and how trees are or can be affected by climate change, on the other. This information will ensure that sufficient resilience is built into tree domestication efforts.
- Farmers and researchers have complementary knowledge and knowledge deficiencies, so integrating both parties' knowledge through participatory processes has been shown to speed up technology adoption and performance.
- Comparatively few studies provide conclusive evidence regarding the profitability and payback periods of IFT cultivation or wild collection. Smallholder farmers may need initial incentives or credit lines for tree establishment, management, and value addition.
- Tree-based practices such as IFTs are more complex than conventional crop practices because of the multiyear cycles required for testing, modification, and eventual adoption by farmers. The key factors that drive adoption of improved IFTs and their effects at multiple scales (that is, household and landscape levels) need to be studied. These studies will provide insights into the level of technology change that would stimulate adoption and effects of IFTs. Such studies are important to guide investment, adoption, and policy decisions regarding IFTs.
- As the technology development processes become complex, the uptake of the technologies by farmers will remain low. The development and dissemination of IFT systems must continue to emphasize practices that

require little capital and simple methods of scaling up improved processes and techniques to wider communities. Such low-cost techniques include small-scale nursery operations, vegetative propagation, use of organic manures, and tree management.

- For market-led IFT initiatives, the market attribute of IFT products must be unique or substantial enough and should be comparable or superior to conventional product sources to make a dent in the market. For instance, camu-camu (*Myrciaria dubia*) is being promoted in Latin America for the extremely high vitamin C content in its pulp (2.8 to 6.0 grams of ascorbic acid per 100 grams), which is 30 times as high as the equivalent weight of orange.

- Second-generation issues, such as the potential occurrence of new pests following the introduction of new trees, must be carefully investigated as IFTs are domesticated and improved germplasm is selected.

- Improved systematic data gathering is needed to update global knowledge on the contributions of IFTs to household, community, and national income and livelihood strategies. This information will enhance the potential opportunities for policy makers and development organizations to use IFTs as an intervention strategy for reducing poverty.

- Innovative research and development efforts on IFTs are needed to help bring about improvements in cultivation, scaling up, markets, and small-scale enterprises in the tropics. The improved performance of the market for agroforestry tree products would stimulate growth in the rural economy.

- Adoption of agroforestry is not a simple direct relationship of only technological characteristics; it is a matrix of several groups of factors that include household- and community-level factors, institutions, and the socioeconomic constraints and incentives that farmers face. As a result, rather than technology change alone, the development of IFTs should place a balanced emphasis on the economics, the people, and the institutional and policy context under which farmers operate.

INVESTMENT NEEDS, PRIORITIES, AND SCALING UP

One of the most effective ways to scale up IFT cultivation is to involve farmers in the entire process of participatory selection, propagation, nursery and tree establishment, and management of superior planting materials. Their involvement will dramatically shorten the time required to produce and disseminate planting materials from centralized nurseries to farmers. It is important to provide farmers with high-quality germplasm and to make it available in a timely manner. Farmers can be organized to produce high-quality seed, seedlings, and vegetative propagule, as evidenced in small-scale nursery enterprises managed by farmer groups, for example, in western and southern Africa and in Peru.

Valuing the contribution of IFTs to the national economy is long overdue, and investment resources should be devoted to their development. Very few cases of active promotion of IFTs have been documented in the tropics. Cross-collaboration and knowledge exchange need to be fostered among regions where species are cultivated, used, or traded; indicators and tools for assessing effects should be developed; and investments in priority IFTs should be increased.

POLICY CONSIDERATIONS

The following key policy priorities emerge from the general literature on the relationship and development of IFTs:

- One way IFTs could be scaled up and mainstreamed into government thinking is to proactively create awareness and raise the profile of the contributions of IFTs during policy debates and in development intervention programs. Such activities will require a long-term investment and an appraisal of policies governing land and tree tenure in many countries in the tropics so that institutional constraints to tree planting can be reduced and policies can be enacted that facilitate cross-border trades and harmonization of exploitation, transportation, and germplasm exchange.

- Regulations must be formulated that will ensure that IFT exploitation, processing, commercialization, and on-farm cultivation does not pose a threat to their conservation. IFTs should be treated as cultivated crops instead of intangible forest products from the wild.

- Policies must be enacted to ensure that intellectual property rights of farmers—such as farmer breeders and community custodians—are well protected. Such policies will ensure that benefits from IFT domestication are not exploited by large-scale commercial growers. Adoption of the International Union for the Protection of New Plant Varieties by governments in the tropics is suggested.

REFERENCES

Akinnifesi, F. K., F. Kwesiga, J. Mhango, T. Chilanga, A. Mkonda, C. A. C. Kadu, I. Kadzere, D. Mithofer, J. D. K.

Saka, G. Sileshi, T. Ramadhani, and P. Dhliwayo. 2006. "Towards the Development of Miombo Fruit Trees as Commercial Tree Crops in Southern Africa." *Forests, Trees, and Livelihoods* 16 (1): 103–21.

Akinnifesi, F. K., R. R. B. Leakey, O. C. Ajayi, G. Sileshi, Z. Tchoundjeu, P. Matakala, and F. R. Kwesiga, eds. 2007. *Indigenous Fruit Trees in the Tropics: Domestication, Utilization, and Commercialization.* Wallingford, U.K.: CAB International.

Bounkoungou, E. G., M. Djimde, E. T. Ayuk, I. Zoungrana, and Z. Tchoundjeu. 1998. *Taking Stock of Agroforestry in the Sahel: Harvesting Results for the Future, End of Phase Report: 1989–96,* ICRAF, PO Box 30677, Nairobi, Kenya.

Clement, C. R., J. P. Cornelius, M. P. Pinedo-Panduro, and K. Yuyama. 2008. "Native Fruit Tree Improvement in Amazonia: An Overview." In *Indigenous Fruit Trees in the Tropics: Domestication, Utilization, and Commercialization,* ed. F. K. Akinnifesi, R. R. B. Leakey, O. C. Ajayi, G. Sileshi, Z. Tchoundjeu, P. Matakala, and F. R. Kwesiga, 100–19. Wallingford, U.K.: CAB International.

Franzel, S., H. Jaenicke, and W. Janssen. 1996. "Choosing the Right Trees: Setting Priorities for Multipurpose Tree Improvement." Research Report 10, International Service for National Agricultural Research, The Hague, Netherlands.

Franzel, S., F. K. Akinnifesi, and C. Ham. 2007. "Setting Priorities among Indigenous Fruit Species: Examples from Three Regions in Africa." In *Indigenous Fruit Trees in the Tropics: Domestication, Utilization and Commercialization,* eds. F. K. Akinnifesi, R. R. B. Leakey, O. C. Ajayi, G. Sileshi, Z. Tchoundjeu, P. Matakala, and F. R. Kwesiga. World Agroforestrt Centre, Nairobi, Wallingford, UK: CAB International Publishing.

Jama, B., A. M. Mohamed, J. Mulatya, and A. N. Njui. 2007. "Comparing the 'Big Five': A Framework for the Sustainable Management of Indigenous Fruit Trees in the Dry Lands of East and Central Africa." *Ecological Indicators* (doi:10.1016/j.ecolind.2006.11.009).

Leakey, R. R. B., Z. Tchoundjeu, K. Schreckenberg, S. E. Shackleton, and C. M. Shackleton. 2005. "Agroforestry Tree Products (AFTPs): Targeting Poverty Reduction and Enhanced Livelihoods." *International Journal for Agricultural Sustainability* 3 (1): 1–23.

Tchoundjeu, Z., E. K. Asaah, P. Anegbeh, A. Degrande, P. Mbile, C. Facheux, A. Tsoberg, A. A. R. Atangana, M. L. Ngo-Mpeck, and A. J. Simons. 2006. "Putting Participatory Domestication into Practice in West and Central Africa." *Forests, Trees, and Livelihoods* 16 (1): 53–70.

Teklehaimanot, Z. 2007. "The Role Of Indigenous Fruit Trees in Sustainable Dryland Agriculture in Eastern Africa." In *Indigenous Fruit Trees in the Tropics: Domestication, Utilization and Commercialization,* eds. Festus K. Akinnifesi, Roger R. B. Leakey, Oluyede C. Ajayi, Gudeta Sileshi, Zac Tchoundjeu, Patrick Matakala, and Freddie R. Kwesiga, 204–23. Wallingford, U.K.: CAB International Publishing.

WEB RESOURCES

World Agroforestry Centre. Using science, the World Agroforestry Centre generates knowledge on the complex role of trees in livelihoods and the environment, and fosters use of this knowledge to improve decisions and practices to impact the poor. The World Agroforestry Centre Web site provides information on their news and events, recent publications, agroforestry information and other information resources: http://www.worldagroforestry.org/es/default.asp.

Avoided Deforestation with Sustainable Benefits: Reducing Carbon Emissions from Deforestation and Land Degradation

Although the clean development mechanism (CDM) of the Kyoto Protocol makes some allowance for afforestation and reforestation, it has so far excluded "avoided deforestation"—for good reasons. However, the global climate change community increasingly recognizes that it must address the challenge of reduction of emissions from deforestation and degradation (REDD). Besides the obvious magnitude of the potential for REDD to reduce climate change, the current situation is creating perverse incentives and disincentives affecting other dimensions of climate change mitigation. The current Intergovernmental Panel on Climate Change (IPCC) good practice guidelines for national greenhouse gas (GHG) inventories provide a coherent framework for dealing with aboveground as well as belowground carbon effects of agriculture, forestry, and other land use (AFOLU).

According to expert opinion in the IPCC community that is responsible for the guidelines, however, the net emission estimates from changes in land use and land cover may carry an unacceptably high uncertainty margin (as much as 60 percent). Data and methods available in national and international research networks can be analyzed to improve the accuracy of estimates, derive better estimates of the uncertainty, and identify ways of reducing it. An effective mechanism for reducing carbon emissions through avoided deforestation would have related but separate mechanisms at the international and national levels. Between countries, political negotiations should be convened to establish commitments to baseline and target emission levels. Countries that attain superior performance in avoided carbon emissions should be eligible for carbon offset payments or credits through multilateral or bilateral arrangements.

The current debate over avoided deforestation offers a chance to correct some of the major inconsistencies in the current system of carbon trading. Some key constraints that need to be overcome relate to scale, scope, political commitment, technical procedures, and data quality. Best practice is emerging on the types of national and local mechanisms that countries can apply with much lower transaction costs than current CDM projects. Avoided deforestation with sustainable benefits can generate both local and global benefits. Research by the Alternatives to Slash-and-Burn (ASB) Programme and others shows that intermediate land uses can store significant quantities of carbon, maintain flows of ecosystem services, generate good economic returns, and reduce pressure on remaining forests.

PROJECT OBJECTIVE AND DESCRIPTION

Climate change and its global effects can no longer be ignored. Although cutting emissions from fossil fuel consumption obviously deserves continued attention by all levels of global society, the approximately 20 percent of emissions that are caused by loss of forests and peatlands cannot remain outside the purview of climate change mechanisms. Recognizing this, the Conference of the Parties to the United Nations Framework Convention on Climate Change invited a discussion "on issues relating to reducing emissions from deforestation in developing countries, focusing on relevant scientific, technical, and methodological issues, and the exchange of relevant information and experiences, including policy approaches and positive incentives" in its 11th session on agenda item 6 (statement FCCC/CP/2005/L.2).

The World Agroforestry Centre (also known as the International Centre for Research in Agroforestry, or ICRAF) prepared a submission for consideration in the discussion. The submission is based on extensive research across the humid tropics by a consortium of international and

---

This profile was prepared by M. van Noordwijk, B. Swallow, L. Verchot, and J. Kasyoki, World Agroforestry Centre.

national organizations operating within the ASB Programme,[1] with key research results generated by Brazil, Cameroon, Indonesia, Peru, the Philippines, and Thailand. This profile summarizes the case for avoided deforestation with sustainable benefits as a simple way to reduce carbon emissions from deforestation and degradation.

PRESENTATION OF INNOVATION: THE ASB OPTION

Several years ago, the international science community established that land-use change and the conversion and degradation of forests generate about 20 percent of global carbon dioxide emissions. Although the CDM of the Kyoto Protocol makes some allowance for afforestation and reforestation, it has so far excluded avoided deforestation. Good reasons exist for this omission:

- The definition of what is and is not a forest is ambiguous.
- The CDM has taken a project approach. Reforestation deals with enhancing tree cover on degraded lands, where monitoring carbon stocks and attributing changes to project activities are easier.
- The CDM pays great attention to *leakage* (making sure that gains in one place do not cause losses in another place) and *additionality* (ensuring that carbon gained or conserved, relative to baselines, would not have occurred without the project). Those issues cannot be reasonably addressed in avoided deforestation projects with limited geographic scope.
- The complexity of rules for applying the CDM to afforestation and reforestation has meant that many of the potential benefits have been offset by the costs of consultants, research organizations, and government agencies. Little carbon value has reached local beneficiaries. In the more difficult case of avoided deforestation, the benefits are even more uncertain.
- The national guidelines for GHG inventories (IPCC 2006) indicate that net emission estimates from changes in land use and land cover may carry an uncertainty margin of as much as 60 percent. This margin makes reaching a valid estimate of the contribution of land-use changes to global carbon dioxide difficult and is the largest uncertainty in quantification of GHG inventories.
- Much deforestation is actually planned by land managers and governments because it leads to land uses with higher economic returns. Completely avoiding deforestation would require offset payments that are not feasible under present circumstances. Negotiating intermediate targets for partial deforestation of a particular landscape would be very complex.

Despite the difficulties, however, the global climate change community increasingly recognizes that it must address the challenge of reducing emissions from deforestation and degradation. Besides the obvious magnitude of the potential for REDD to reduce climate change, the current situation is creating perverse incentives and disincentives affecting other dimensions of climate change mitigation. For example, an annex I country that imports biofuels from non–annex I countries to meet its Kyoto targets is not accountable for forest conversion that biofuel production might cause. Furthermore, public and political willingness to contribute to the control of GHGs through relatively small reductions elsewhere will erode if large and avoidable emissions are not scrutinized. Nonparticipation by Australia and the United States creates similar problems for the Kyoto Protocol.

The current IPCC good practice guidelines for national GHG inventories provide a coherent framework for dealing with aboveground as well as belowground carbon effects of AFOLU. The IPCC framework could become the primary framework for reporting and accountability in non–annex I countries, aligned with the rules that currently apply to annex I countries.

As mentioned previously, expert opinion in the IPCC community that is responsible for the guidelines holds that the net emission estimates from changes in land use and land cover may carry an uncertainty margin of as much as 60 percent. In time, the use of the IPCC guidelines over multiple measurement periods will reduce this margin as annual updates provide better information on which to base future estimates, but the current uncertainty margin is clearly unacceptably high. The opportunity to participate in a market for reduced AFOLU carbon emissions would generate clear incentives to improve the accuracy of the accounts.

Data and methods available in national and international research networks can be analyzed to improve the accuracy of estimates, derive better estimates of the uncertainty, and identify ways to reduce it. The two components of uncertainty are interlinked: the classification of land cover and land-cover change is unsatisfactory, and there is too much uncertainty regarding the mean carbon stocks per unit area in each land-cover class. Clearly, the binary classification (for example, with just "forest" and "nonforest" as classes) is insufficient. Analysis so far suggests that a classification that results in 5 to 10 land-cover classes may lead to the lowest overall uncertainty. Further data compilation and analysis are needed. This work has already started. The IPCC support office is providing support to full-system carbon accounting.

An effective mechanism for reducing carbon emissions through avoided deforestation would have related but separate mechanisms at the international and national levels. Between countries, political negotiations should be convened to establish commitments to baseline and target emission levels. Countries that attain superior performance in avoided carbon emissions should be eligible for carbon offset payments or credits through multilateral or bilateral arrangements.

Each non–annex I country that voluntarily participates in the new REDD rules should have scope for flexible rules to create positive incentives for rural and forest-dependent people to benefit from more sustainable and clean development pathways. Such incentives would ensure the sustainability of the carbon stocks and reserve more of the country's natural capital for the future. A number of countries have gained experience with such mechanisms already, and pilots exist elsewhere. Individual countries involved in the international mechanism should have the flexibility to meet avoided carbon emission targets through national mechanisms appropriate to their own conditions, following principles already established among annex I countries.

BENEFITS AND EFFECT OF ACTIVITY

The current debate over avoided deforestation offers a chance to correct some of the major inconsistencies in the current system of carbon trading. Some key constraints that need to be overcome relate to scale, scope, political commitment, technical procedures, and data quality. Best practice is emerging on the types of national and local mechanisms that countries can apply with much lower transaction costs than current CDM projects. Avoided deforestation with sustainable benefits can generate both local and global benefits. Research by the ASB Programme and others shows that intermediate land uses can store significant quantities of carbon, maintain flows of ecosystem services, generate good economic returns, and reduce pressure on remaining forests.

LESSONS LEARNED AND ISSUES FOR WIDER APPLICATION

Lessons can be learned from the rules of the Kyoto Protocol that already apply between annex I countries, where all land-use and land-cover changes are accounted for, without restriction to any specific concept of forest and without loss of national sovereignty over mechanisms. That accounting framework includes all changes in carbon stock, including peatlands, trees outside forests, agroforestry lands, and flows of other GHGs.

A simple solution to the issue of avoided deforestation at the international level would be to allow developing countries to be voluntarily listed in a new annex X. These countries would follow current rules for emissions related to land use and land cover that exist between annex I countries, while leaving the energy-related emissions for future consideration. The CDM would still apply in the energy sector, but the issuance of carbon credits and associated markets would follow established procedures for annex I countries. No new procedures would be needed, and transaction costs could be much reduced.

Once the playing field is selected and the rules are set (for example, AFOLU accounting at the national level), the real game can begin: determining the baseline of expected emissions that will be used for deciding what will constitute reduction. In some ways, this process is akin to a market where national self-interests need to balance across a range of current issues, including world trade in agricultural and forest-derived commodities.

National and subnational governments would need to know how much avoided emissions they could provide and at what cost. Summary data of this type would require appraisal of scenarios for integrating economic development and land-cover change. Currently, such estimates are not available, although some promising advances have been made in the countries of Meso-America.

In an earlier phase of the discussions on CDMs, an inventory was made of abatement costs, largely in the energy sector. These results indicated that a fraction of hot-air emissions existed that could be avoided at negative total economic costs because they generate net economic costs at the societal level. A range of emissions is also associated with moderate economic gain that could be offset at feasible levels of financial transfer. A range of emissions associated with substantial economic gains that could not be offset under current carbon prices is also likely to exist. Figure 3.6 presents a schematic view of these different types of avoided emissions, plotted in terms of economic benefits from carbon emission against the value of carbon. In addition, displayed across the top of figure 3.6 are some of the policy options that countries might promote to achieve different levels and types of emissions.

For the avoided deforestation debate in tropical countries, to our knowledge no estimates are available for the

Figure 3.6   Schematic Trade-off between Reduced GHG Emissions through Avoided Deforestation
and National Economic Development Opportunities

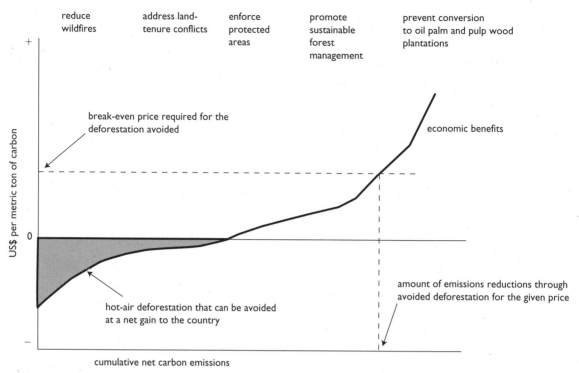

Source: ICRAF.

cumulative abatement costs (see figure 3.6). As an extension of the ideas presented in this profile, the ASB consortium for Indonesia is currently undertaking such an analysis for representative areas of Indonesia for the period since 1990.

Best practice is emerging on the types of national and local mechanisms that countries can apply to reduce carbon emissions from avoided deforestation, potentially with much lower transaction costs than current CDM projects. Incentive and rights-based mechanisms can be put in place to reduce carbon emissions from avoided deforestation while sustaining the asset base, rights, and well-being of people dependent on those resources. Countries such as Costa Rica and Mexico already have substantial experience in implementing such mechanisms at the national and subnational scale. Large-scale afforestation programs, such as those currently implemented in China, India, and Indonesia, could be revised to better address avoided carbon emissions. Forest, landscape, and watershed management projects can be revised to provide greater incentives to avoid carbon emissions through avoided deforestation. Case study evidence from across Asia and a pan-tropical synthesis show that realism, conditionality, voluntarism, and pro-poor are important criteria for evaluating the performance of incentive and rights-based mechanisms.

NOTE

1. The ASB Programme comprises a well-established global alliance of more than 80 local, national, and international partners dedicated to action-oriented integrated natural resource management (INRM) research in the tropical forest margins. It is the only global partnership devoted entirely to research on the tropical forest margins. ASB's goal is to raise the productivity and income of rural households in the humid tropics without increasing deforestation or undermining essential environmental services. The program applies an INRM approach to analysis and action through long-term engagement with local communities and policy makers at various levels.

REFERENCE

IPCC (Intergovernmental Panel on Climate Change (IPCC). 2006. *2006 IPCC Guidelines for National Greenhouse Gas Inventories: Volume 4 Agriculture, Forestry and Other Land Use.* http://www.ipcc-nggip.iges.or.jp/public/2006gl/vol4.htm.

SELECTED READINGS

ADB (Asian Development Bank). 1999. *Asia Least-Cost Greenhouse Gas Abatement Strategy Summary Report.*

Manila: ADB. http://www.adb.org/Documents/Reports/ ALGAS/Summary/default.asp.

Evans, K., S. J. Velarde, R. Prieto, S. N. Rao, S. Sertzen, K. Davila, P. Cronkleton, and W. de Jong. 2006. *Field Guide to the Future: Four Ways for Communities to Think Ahead.* Nairobi: Center for International Forestry Research.

Hairiah K., S. M. Sitompul, M. van Noordwijk, and C. A. Palm. 2001. "Methods for Sampling Carbon Stocks above and below Ground." ASB Lecture Note 4B, International Centre for Research in Agroforestry, Bogor, Indonesia. http://www.worldagroforestry.org/sea/Publications/sear chpub.asp?publishid=1003.

Kandji, S. T, L. V. Verchot, J. Mackensen, A. Boye, M. van Noordwijk, T. P. Tomich, C. K. Ong, A. Albrecht, and C. A. Palm. 2006. "Opportunities for Linking Climate Change Adaptation and Mitigation through Agroforestry Systems." In *World Agroforestry into the Future,* ed. D. P. Garrity, A. Okono, M. Grayson, and S. Parrott, 113–21. Nairobi, Kenya: World Agroforestry Centre. http://www.worldagroforestry.org/sea/Publications/sear chpub.asp?publishid=1481.

Murdiyarso, D., and H. Herawati, eds. 2005. *Carbon Forestry: Who Will Benefit? Proceedings of a Workshop on Carbon Sequestration and Sustainable Livelihoods.* Bogor, Indonesia: Center for International Forestry Research.

Murdiyarso, D., A. Puntodewo, A. Widayati, and M. van Noordwijk. 2006. "Determination of Eligible Lands for A/R CDM Project Activities and of Priority Districts for Project Development Support in Indonesia." Center for International Forestry Research, Bogor, Indonesia.

Murdiyarso, D., and M. Skutsch, eds. 2006. *Community Forest Management as a Carbon Mitigation Option: Case Studies.* Bogor, Indonesia: Center for International Forestry Research.

Palm, C. A, M. van Noordwijk, P. L. Woomer, L. Arevalo, C. Castilla, D. G. Cordeiro, K. Hairiah, J. Kotto-Same, A. Moukam, W. J. Parton, A. Riese, V. Rodrigues, and S. M. Sitompul. 2005. "Carbon Losses and Sequestration Following Land Use Change in the Humid Tropics." In *Slash and Burn: The Search for Alternatives,* ed. C. P. Vosti, S. A. Sanchez, P. J. Ericksen, and A. Juo, 41–63. New York: Columbia University Press. http://www.worldagro-forestry.org/sea/Publications/searchpub.asp?pub-lishid=1306.

WEB RESOURCES

ASB Partnership for the Tropical Forest Margins. ASB is the only global partnership devoted entirely to research on the tropical forest margins. It is a global partnership of research institutes, non-governmental organizations, universities, community organizations, farmers' groups, and other local, national, and international organizations. Since 1994, ASB has operated as a system-wide program of the Consultative Group for International Research in Agriculture (CGIAR). The ASB Program Web site contains information on its impact, regions, themes, publications, and other resources: http://www .asb.cgiar.org/.

CarboFor. The CarboFor website is developed under the main webpage of the Center for International Forestry Research (CIFOR) to serve the communities working on land-use, land-use change and forestry (LULUCF) activities and the associated climate change. The website features Projects carried out by CIFOR and its partners; publications of carbon and climate change-related issues around the LULUCF sector; research activities directed for forest management purpose, as well as highlights of current issues, detailed Events and Links to useful sites: http://www.cifor.cgiar.org/carbofor .

CPWF. The Consultative Group on International Agricultural Research (CGIAR) Challenge Program on Water and Food (CPWF) is an international, multi-institutional research initiative with a strong emphasis on north-south and south-south partnerships. It aims to increase the productivity of water used for agriculture, leaving more water for other users and the environment. The CGIAR Challenge Program on Water and Food features Announcements, Capacity Building Activities, Research, and Publications: http://www.waterandfood.org/.

Food and Agriculture Organization. The Food and Agriculture Organization (FAO) of the United Nations serves as a neutral forum where all nations meet as equals to negotiate agreements and debate policy on efforts to defeat hunger. The FAO webpage on the Quesungual agroforestry farming system describes the Lempira Sur project, where farmers learn new cultivation methods to prevent soil erosion: http://www.fao.org/FOCUS/E/hon duras /agro-e.htm.

IPCC-NGGIP Technical Support Unit. The Technical Support Unit for the Intergovernmental Panel on Climate Change–National Greenhouse Gas Inventories Programme (IPCC-NGGIP) is based at the Institute for Global Environmental Strategies in Japan and is funded by the government of Japan. The IPCC-NGGIP Technical Support Unit's Web site includes information on its internship program, a list of staff members, contact information, and a link to the IPCC home page. http://www.ipcc-nggip.iges.or.jp/tsu/tsustaff.htm.

Rewarding Upland Poor for Environmental Services. Rewarding Upland Poor for Environmental Services (RUPES) is a program that aims to enhance the livelihoods and reduce poverty of the upland poor while supporting environmental conservation on biodiversity protection, watershed management, carbon sequestration, and landscape beauty at local and global levels. With the International Fund for Agricultural Development as a major donor, the World Agroforestry Centre has taken on the role of coordinating a consortium of partners interested in contributing and being a part of RUPES. The RUPES Web site offers information on RUPES sites, partnerships, and activities. http://www.worldagroforestry.org/sea/Networks/RUPES/.

World Agroforestry Centre. Using science, the World Agroforestry Centre generates knowledge on the complex role of trees in livelihoods and the environment, and fosters use of this knowledge to improve decisions and practices to impact the poor. The World Agroforestry Centre Web site provides information on their news and events, recent publications, agroforestry information and other information resources: http://www.worldagroforestry.org/es/default.asp.

On-Farm Integration of Freshwater Agriculture and Aquaculture in the Mekong Delta of Vietnam: The Role of the Pond and Its Effect on Livelihoods of Resource-Poor Farmers

Where there are abundant freshwater resources, valuable opportunities exist to integrate terrestrial and aquatic crops. This fact is illustrated by examples from the Mekong Delta, where high-yielding rice was the priority crop but large areas of rice fields and fruit orchard ponds were underused. The development of integrated agriculture-aquaculture (IAA) systems enhances on-farm nutrient recycling and increases the total farm output. IAA systems are much less capital intensive and risky than conventional aquaculture methods and thus are attractive to both rich and poor farmers.

The adoption of IAA farming was influenced by a combination of biophysical, socioeconomic, and technological settings at community, household, and farm levels. First, at community level, agro-ecology and market accessibility are major driving factors. Better-off farmers, with good access to markets, still tend to favor higher profitability, high-input aquaculture systems. However, IAA farming formed an important innovation, especially in areas with poorer market access and places where farmers faced significant land, capital, or labor constraints.

The main use of the pond is to recycle on-farm nutrients while growing fish for home consumption or income generation. The results from testing the system with a range of farmers in the Mekong Delta show clearly that the conventional, linear approach of technology transfer needs to be replaced by the participatory learning in action approach, which enables the concept to be tailored to the different needs and circumstances of various producers. In addition, systems of IAA farming need to take into account integration with external inputs and diversification toward more commercially valuable crops, which create new off-farm jobs and will particularly benefit poor households.

INTRODUCTION

In areas with abundant freshwater resources, numerous options exist to integrate terrestrial and aquatic crops. Agricultural restructuring and diversification have been considered important for rural economic development and poverty reduction. Before 1999, high-yielding rice culture was the first priority for food security and export. Thus, a vast area of rice fields and fruit orchard ponds remained underused from an aquaculture point of view. In 1999, the Vietnamese government launched the Sustainable Aquaculture for Poverty Alleviation strategy and implementation program as part of a wider poverty-reduction program (Luu 2002). The goal was to culture fish, prawn, or shrimp together with land-based crops and livestock on the same farm, a technique referred to as *integrated agriculture-aquaculture systems* (Nhan and others 2007).

From 1999 to 2005, the freshwater aquaculture farming area increased steadily—on average 12 percent annually. Aquaculture production grew even faster, by 42 percent per year, especially between 2002 and 2005 (figure 3.7). This expansion was in part the result of the development of intensive *Pangasius* culture, characterized by the use of manufactured feeds, by high investments, and by economic risks, making it the domain of rich farmers (Hao 2006; Nhan and others 2007). IAA farming, in contrast, enhances or facilitates on-farm nutrient recycling and increases the total farm output, for rich and poor farmers (Edwards 1998; Prein 2002).

This profile was prepared by D. K. Nhan, D. N. Thanh, and Le T. Duong, Mekong Delta Development Research Institute, Can Tho University, Can Tho Vietnam, and M. J. C. Verdegem and R. H. Bosma, Aquaculture and Fisheries Group, Department of Animal Sciences, Wageningen University, Wageningen, Netherlands.

Figure 3.7 Area and Production Increases in Freshwater Aquaculture in Vietnam, 1999–2005

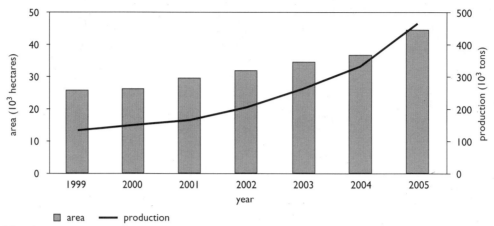

Source: Authors' elaboration.

Two projects, intended to stimulate the development of sustainable agriculture and to improve small-scale farmers' livelihoods in the Mekong Delta, were carried out between 2002 and 2006:

1. Improved resource-use efficiency in Asian integrated pond-dike systems (Pond-Live), funded by the European Commission
2. Impact assessment of policy reforms to agricultural development funded by the Vietnamese Ministry of Agriculture and Rural Development.

Using experience from these two projects, this profile explores the major factors influencing the adoption of various types of aquaculture, describes the resource flows, and reviews roles of ponds in farming systems in the Mekong Delta. Then, it assesses implications for sustainable land management, describes lessons learned for practical application, and makes policy recommendations.

PROJECT DESCRIPTION

The Pond-Live project was implemented at three different sites in the Mekong Delta, with the goal of improving resource-use efficiency of freshwater IAA systems (Nhan and others 2007). A participatory learning-in-action approach was applied, passing through six phases (Little, Verdegem, and Bosma 2007):

1. Expert consultation and literature reviews
2. Formulation of problems and identification of key research and development issues

3. Analysis of interactions among household's conditions and IAA farming performance
4. On-farm monitoring of pond nutrient flows
5. On-farm technology interventions
6. Evaluation, sharing, and dissemination of research results and proposal of further improvements.

Phases 1, 2, and 3 were carried out in the first year of the project. From the second year onward, phases 4, 5, and 6 were implemented, and the process was repeated to create a cycle of continuous development of adaptive technologies of higher productivity and better nutrient use.

A companion study was carried out at eight different sites and was aimed to identify effects of policy reforms on changes in agricultural production and household's livelihoods. The study sites were located in four districts: Cao Lanh and Lai Vung, in Dong Thap province, and Chau Thanh and Cho Gao, in Tien Giang province.

PRESENTATION OF INNOVATION: ADOPTION OF AQUACULTURE PRACTICES

In the Mekong Delta, very few poor farmers adopt aquaculture. Results from the Pond-Live project showed that only 6 percent of poor farmers practiced aquaculture compared with 42 percent and 60 percent for intermediate and rich farmers, respectively (Nhan and others 2007). Richer farmers tended to intensify the fish production, stocking high-value species such as catfish (*Pangasianodon hypophthalmus*) or climbing perch (*Anabas testudineus*) and using commercial feed. Between 2000 and 2004, the percentage of poor households practicing aquaculture increased only 2 percent, while 12 percent and 15 percent more households of intermediate and rich farmers, respectively, took up aquaculture (table 3.6).

The contribution of farming activities to household income was lower for the poor than for the intermediate and the rich. Off-farming or nonfarming jobs are relatively more important for poor people, who generally considered crop production as their most important economic activity and aquaculture as least important. From 2000 to 2004, the contribution of aquaculture to household income increased, but this effect only occurred among the intermediate and the rich groups.

In the Mekong Delta, the adoption of IAA farming was influenced by a combination of biophysical, socioeconomic, and technological settings at community, household, and farm levels. First, at community level, agro-ecology and market accessibility are major driving factors. In rice-dominated areas, more farmers practiced IAA farming than in fruit-dominated areas. Rich farmers with good market accessibility tended to practice commercially oriented aquaculture systems relying heavily on external inputs. Second, the household's wealth status and resource base determine whether the pond culture is adopted or rejected. Nhan and others (2007) identified the major reasons farmers adopt aquaculture: (a) increased use of on-farm resources, given positive contributions of government advocacy, suitability of soil and water, recycling of nutrients, pest control in rice fields, and creation of jobs for family members; (b) income generation through aquaculture; (c) environmental improvements; and (d) improved nutrition of household.

Major factors why farmers did not take up pond farming included (a) insufficient capital to introduce technologies; (b) insufficient landholding; (c) difficult farm management (for example, family labor, distance between homestead and farmland, and poor access to extension service); (d) pesticide use for crop production conflicting with aquaculture activities; and (e) poor soil and water quality.

Table 3.6	Percentage of Farm Households Practicing Freshwater Aquaculture in 2000 and 2004 by Wealth Groups			
Wealth groups	Number of households	2000 (%)	2004 (%)	Difference (%)
Poor	276	4.3	6.2	1.8
Intermediate	303	44.6	56.1	11.6
Rich	292	48.3	63.4	15.1

Source: IPAD project (unpublished data).
Note: Percentages are always given as a fraction of the number of households.

Finally, factors at community and household levels, pond physical properties (such as pond width and depth), and the availability of nutrient sources (on farm or off farm) as pond inputs, together determine to a large extent the type of farming systems adopted. Three major types of IAA systems could be distinguished: (a) low-input fish farming, (b) medium-input fish farming, and (c) high-input fish farming (Nhan and others 2006, 2007). The low-input farming system is commonly practiced in fruit-dominated areas, the medium-input system in rice-dominated areas, and the high-input system in rice-dominated areas with good market accessibility.

ON-FARM RESOURCE FLOWS AND THE ROLE OF THE POND

In the Mekong Delta rural areas, most of households have a pond near the homestead. In the past, the main purpose of digging ponds was to raise the level of low-lying grounds for house construction or for orchards. Fish farming was not considered a high priority because wild fish were abundant in rice fields, floodplains, canals, and rivers. Currently, farm households not practicing IAA farming do not stock hatchery juveniles in their pond, which is used for wild fish capture instead.

The pond within IAA systems plays multiple roles, which differ from one system to another. Currently, the main use of the pond is to recycle on-farm nutrients while growing fish for home consumption or income generation (Nhan and others 2007). In low- and medium-input fish-farming systems, on-farm nutrients are the main input source of the pond (figure 3.8). Livestock and rice-field components that receive nutrients or energy mostly from off-farm sources provide important amounts of nutrient-rich wastes and byproducts (Nhan and others 2006). Byproducts collected from rice fields include not only rice residues but also crabs and golden snails. About 11 percent of the nitrogen in these wastes or byproducts is thrown into ponds and harvested as fish, while 67 percent accumulates in the sediments and 22 percent is lost through water exchange. Annually, farmers typically extract water from the pond to irrigate fruit crops cultivated on dikes during the dry season and remove pond sediments to fill up orchard dikes adjacent to the pond. In this way, the nutrient-rich mud and water can be considered fertilizers for terrestrial crops within the system. Integrating aquaculture into existing land-based farming systems yields various benefits to farmers: (a) higher fish production, (b) low external nutrient inputs, (c) treatment of wastes and byproducts from terrestrial crops, and (d) storage of nutrients in pond sedi-

Figure 3.8   Bioresource Flows of an IAA Pond with Medium-Input Fish Farming in the Mekong Delta

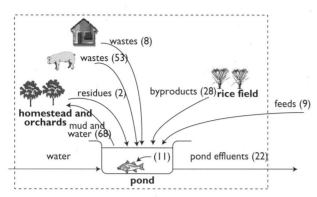

Source: Adapted from Nhan and others 2007.
Note: The numbers in parentheses are the average percentage of total food nitrogen inputs of the pond. Dotted lines refer to farm boundary.

ments for later use as fertilizer. In contrast to intensive fish farming, these benefits are within reach of poor farmers.

BENEFITS OF IAA AND ITS IMPLICATIONS FOR SUSTAINABLE LAND MANAGEMENT

IAA farming can positively affect sustainable land management. These effects include the following:

- Integrating aquaculture into existing land-based farming systems enhances the use of farm resources by creating new nutrient cycles between farming components and by improving overall food productivity and farming profitability.
- A diversified IAA farming system with more synergisms between farm components means a more economically stable farming system. For example, recently in the Mekong Delta, livestock production has not been stable because of disease outbreaks and fluctuations of input and output market prices. Thus, fish produced within an IAA system can compensate for possible losses of livestock production.
- IAA farming rehabilitates farm soil. Intensive fruit and rice production depends highly on heavy use of inorganic fertilizers. Introducing fish into orchard ponds or rice fields enhances farm organic matter recycling and maintains the high fertility of orchard dikes and rice-field soil.
- Improved nutrient recycling between farming components in IAA systems results in a higher fraction of nutrient inputs ending up in farming products while smaller

amounts of nutrients accumulate within the system or flow into the environment.
- IAA farming systems produce low-cost fish not only for the IAA household but also for poor consumers. In the Mekong Delta, fish contribute about 76 percent of the average supply of animal protein (Haylor and Halwart 2001; van Anrooy 2003), but wild fish resources have declined because of rice intensification and overfishing.

LESSONS LEARNED AND ISSUES FOR WIDER APPLICABILITY

The following lessons were learned from applying a participatory learning-in-action approach to develop IAA farming:

- IAA systems are diverse. Identification of biophysical, socioeconomic, and technical factors interacting at different levels (for example, community, household, and pond; phases 1 to 3) is of great importance for finding meaningful interventions at site or household levels.
- A farm bioresource flow diagram is an important tool. At phases 2 and 3, farmers usually have a wide range of options, paying much attention to a particular component rather than the whole system. The diagram helps farmers fully identify their resources and recognize various options to improve their farming system.
- A key factor to success of the participatory learning-in-action approach is the participation of all stakeholders, particularly local farmers and extension workers. Nevertheless, the stakeholders need to understand the whole process of a project, as well as goals and outcomes of each phase within the process. During field visits, researchers and extension workers need to help cooperating farmers gradually upgrade their capacity in technology development by implementing phenomenon observation and explanation, collecting simple data, explaining on-farm trial results, identifying problems, and suggesting possible solutions.
- Improved technologies are context specific. Field visits and discussions among cooperating farmer, local farmers, extension workers, and researchers are necessary so that improved technologies in one place can be taken up adaptively in another.
- Unlike on-station experiments, on-farm trials lack real replications, and data variations between farms are large. Reducing the number of parameters sampled and increasing the number of farms would be advisable. Multivariate data analysis is an important tool in analyzing data and interpreting results (Nhan and others 2006).

INVESTMENT NEEDS AND PRIORITIES

The government advocated developing IAA farming as a way of reducing poverty. Unfortunately, most poor farmers could not respond. The government and extension agencies need to define and implement appropriate solutions. Some of these may include the following:

- The conventional, linear approach that focuses mainly on technology transfer needs to be replaced by the participatory learning-in-action approach, giving attention to integrated resources management rather than a single component.
- A package of immediate and long-term support actions with different choices of appropriate technologies should be provided to pull poor farmers into IAA farming. Time must be taken to categorize local biophysical and socioeconomic contexts to provide tailor-made support actions. Farmers often take up new or improved technologies when they constitute slight improvements to traditional farming practices. After a small improvement has been proven, others will follow more easily.
- Because of the complexity of integrated farming, farm management skills need to be improved.

Extension of IAA farming in the Mekong Delta originally focused on on-farm integration only. Such an approach will hardly produce optimal fish yield considering the large variation in the types, quantity, and quality of on-farm wastes or by-products available. A one-solution-fits-all approach is not feasible.

Integration requires that external contexts be considered. Therefore, propagation of IAA farming should take into account integration with external inputs and diversification toward more commercially valuable crops. Such an approach would create new off-farm jobs and raise the demand for expert advice. The latter concurs with the creation of new jobs directly and will in the long run benefit more poor households than immediate or well-off households (Edwards 1998; Little and others 2007).

REFERENCES

Edwards, P. 1998. "A Systems Approach for the Promotion of Integrated Aquaculture." *Aquaculture Economics and Management* 2 (1): 1–12.

Hao, N. V. 2006. "Status of Catfish Farming in the Delta." *Catch and Culture* 12 (1): 13–14.

Haylor, G., and M. Halwart. 2001. "Aquatic Resources Management for Sustainable Livelihoods of Poor People." In *Using Different Aquatic Resources for Livelihoods in Asia: A Resource Book,* ed. G. Haylor, 11–16. Bangkok: Network of Aquaculture Centres in Asia-Pacific.

Little, D. C., M. Karim, D. Turongruang, E. J. Morales, F. J. Murray, B. K. Barman, M. M. Haque, N. Ben Belton, G. Faruque, E. M. Azim, F. U. Islam, L. Pollock, M. J. Verdegem, W. Leschen, and M. A. Wahab. 2007. "Livelihood Impacts of Ponds in Asia: Opportunities and Constraints." In *Fish Ponds in Farming Systems,* ed. A. J. van der Zijpp, J. A. J. Verreth, L. Q. Tri, M. E. F. van Mensvoort, R. H. Bosma, and M. C. M. Beveridge, 177–202. Wageningen, Netherlands: Academic.

Little, D. C., M. Verdegem, and R. Bosma. 2007. "Approaches to Understanding Pond-Dike Systems in Asia: The POND-LIVE Project Approach." *STREAM* 6 (1): 4–5.

Luu, L. T. 2002. "Sustainable Aquaculture for Poverty Alleviation (SAPA): A New Rural Development Strategy for Viet Nam—Part II: Implementation of the SAPA Strategy." *FAO Aquaculture Newsletter* 28: 1–4.

Nhan, D. K., A. Milstein, M. C. J. Verdegem, and J. A. V. Verreth. 2006. "Food Inputs, Water Quality, and Nutrient Accumulation in Integrated Pond Systems: A Multivariate Approach." *Aquaculture* 261 (1): 160–73.

Nhan, D. K., L. T. Phong, M. J. C. Verdegem, L. T. Duong, R. H. Bosma, and D. C. Little. 2007. "Integrated Freshwater Aquaculture, Crop, and Animal Production in the Mekong Delta, Vietnam: Determinants and the Role of the Pond." *Agricultural Systems* 94 (2): 445–58.

Prein, M. 2002. "Integration of Aquaculture into Crops-Animal Systems in Asia." *Agricultural Systems* 71 (1–2): 127–46.

van Anrooy, R. 2003. "Fish Marketing and Consumption in Vietnam: What about Aquaculture Products?" *FAO Aquaculture Newsletter* 29: 16–19.

SELECTED READING

General Statistics Office. 2006. *Statistical Yearbook.* Hanoi, Vietnam: Statistical Publishing House.

Rainfed Farming Systems in Highlands and Sloping Areas

OVERVIEW

Farming systems in highlands and sloping areas are estimated to provide for an agricultural population of 520 million people, who cultivate 150 million hectares of land, of which 20 percent is irrigated. There is intense population pressure on the resource base, which averages 3.5 people per cultivated hectare.

In most cases, the farms are diversified mixed crop-livestock systems, producing food crops (such as cassava, sweet potatoes, beans, and cereals) and perennial crops (such as bananas, coffee, and fruit trees). Crop productivity is reduced through the high altitudes, lower temperatures, and shorter cropping seasons compared with the lowlands. Steep slopes and thin soil horizons that are prone to erosion characterize these systems. Livestock can be an important system component that depends on the extensive upland grazing areas. Sales of cattle or small ruminants are often the main source of cash income. Many highland areas are home to the last remaining primary forests. Extensive forested areas are sometimes used for grazing and constitute agricultural land reserves that can be put into production through slash-and-burn techniques. In the Andes, Southeast Asia,

and South Asia, uplands are home to large groups of indigenous people. Poverty is usually high.

With intense population pressure on the resource base, farm sizes are usually small. Declining soil fertility is a big problem because of erosion, biomass shortage, and shortage of inputs. Given the lack of road access and other infrastructure, the level of integration with the market is often low. Few off-farm opportunities can be found in the highlands, and seasonal migration is often necessary to find additional income.

POTENTIALS FOR POVERTY REDUCTION AND AGRICULTURAL GROWTH

The driving forces for poverty reduction are emigration (exit from agriculture) and increases in off-farm income. Diversification, especially to high-value products with relatively low transport and marketing costs, can also contribute significantly to poverty reduction. Such products can include crops such as fruit trees, coffee, and tea or, in more temperate areas, olives and grapes, among others. Livestock production also has a potential for further development.

No-Burn Agricultural Zones on Honduran Hillsides: Better Harvests, Air Quality, and Water Availability by Way of Improved Land Management

Hillsides are an important agro-ecosystem in the tropics and subtropics. Traditional slash-and-burn practices, widely used in the hillside areas of Central America, have been a driving force in agricultural expansion and landscape degradation. Farmers in a village called Quesungual, Honduras, developed a slash-and-mulch system and eliminated the burning. This was the origin of the Quesungual Slash-and-Mulch Agroforestry System (QSMAS). With support from the Honduran government and the Food and Agriculture Organization (FAO) of the United Nations, a process to validate the system that involved the active participation of farmers was initiated. Farmers practicing QSMAS can produce sufficient maize and beans to meet their household needs and sell the excess in local markets. In addition, innovative farmers are intensifying and diversifying this system by using vegetables and market-oriented cash crops, as well as raising livestock. QSMAS demonstrated a high degree of resilience to extreme weather events, such as the El Niño drought of 1997 and Hurricane Mitch in 1998. Permanent cover protects the soil from raindrop impact and crust formation, while minimizing surface evaporation. In addition, surface residues favor nutrient recycling, improve soil fertility, and could result in higher carbon storage in soils.

The success of QSMAS is a reflection of a community-based learning process in which local people and extension service providers share ideas and learn together. At the landscape level, QSMAS has contributed to the conservation of more than 40 native species of trees and shrubs. Newer QSMAS farms (two to five years old) serve as sinks for methane with low emission levels of nitrous oxide. These results help mitigate climate change.

KEY SUSTAINABLE LAND MANAGEMENT ISSUES

Hillsides are an important agro-ecosystem in the tropics and subtropics. More than 11 percent of the agricultural lands in these areas are classified as hillsides (4.1 million square kilometers). Tropical hillsides in Africa, Asia, and Latin America are home to about 500 million people, 40 percent of whom live below the poverty line.

In southwest Honduras, most farms are small (80 percent are fewer than 5 hectares) and are located on steep hillsides (a 5 to 50 percent slope). QSMAS is an indigenous land management practice based on planting annual crops with naturally regenerated trees and shrubs. QSMAS enables farmers to achieve food security by simultaneously improving harvests and soil fertility.[1] This Investment Note explains how the International Center for Tropical Agriculture (Centro Internacional de Agricultura Tropical, or CIAT) and its partners combine scientific and local knowledge to further improve the land management practice and foster its use.

Stagnated agricultural productivity coupled with rapid population growth causes uncontrolled expansion of agriculture and ranching into hillside forests. The resulting environmental damage includes not only the loss of trees but also water and soil losses from runoff and erosion. Reversing land degradation while increasing food production is an essential strategy to improve both rural liveli-

This note was prepared by L. A. Welchez, Consortium for Integrated Soil Management, Tegucigalpa, Honduras; M. Ayarza, Tropical Soil Biology and Fertility Institute of Centro Internacional de Agricultura Tropical, Tegucigalpa, Honduras; E. Amezquita, E. Barrious, M. Rondon, A. Castro, M. Rivera, and I. Rao, Centro Internacional de Agricultura Tropical, Cali, Colombia; J. Pavon, Instituto Nacional de Tecnologia Agropecuaria, Managua, Nicaragua; and O. Ferreira, D. Valladares, and N. Sanchez, Escuela Nacional de Ciencias Forestales, Siguatepeque, Honduras.

hoods and natural resource management in hillside regions (Ayarza and Welchez 2004).

Traditional slash-and-burn practices have been a driving force in agricultural expansion and landscape degradation. Such systems are widely used in the hillside areas of Central America. A number of factors have led to this form of land use:

- Lack of opportunities for off-farm employment
- Scarce resources to invest in intensifying production
- The quick economic benefits to farmers from the slash-and-burn system
- A scarcity of technical assistance and little adaptation of appropriate technologies that promote soil cover and eliminate the need for burning
- Increased urbanization (rural areas are rarely a priority for central governments)
- Few national or local policies to encourage the use of environmentally friendly production practices.

BUILDING ON LESSONS LEARNED

Although small farmers practice slash and burn extensively, a small group of farmers in a Honduran village called Quesungual came up with an important change: they planted crops under a slash-and-mulch system and eliminated the burning. This was the origin of QSMAS. In the early 1990s, a development project of the Honduran government with the support of FAO noted this anomaly and concentrated efforts to improve and generalize this practice in the region. The project initiated a process of validation with the active participation of farmers. Local organizations, farmer communities, and small enterprises grew along with the process of supporting the adoption of improved QSMAS practices. Widespread adoption of QSMAS was supported by a local government ban on burning. Before long, several villages of the region had almost completely forgone the use of fire.

Farmers practicing QSMAS could soon produce sufficient maize and beans to meet their household needs and sell the excess in local markets. In addition, innovative farmers are intensifying and diversifying the system by using vegetables and market-oriented cash crops, as well as raising livestock. QSMAS demonstrated a high degree of resilience to extreme weather events, such as the El Niño drought of 1997 and Hurricane Mitch in 1998. Permanent cover protects the soil from raindrop impact and crust formation, while minimizing surface evaporation. In addition, surface residues favor nutrient recycling, improve soil fertility, and could result in higher carbon storage in soils.

QSMAS plots have three layers of vegetation: mulch, crops, and dispersed shrubs and trees. The system starts with the selection of a well-developed fallow (with numerous and diverse trees and shrubs). Farmers selectively slash and prune the fallows, remove firewood and trunks, and uniformly distribute the biomass (leaves and fine shoots) as mulch. Then, pioneer crops such as sorghum (*Sorghum vulgare*) or common beans (*Phaseolus vulgaris*), whose seedlings are capable of emerging through the mulch, are sown by broadcast. Maize (*Zea mays*) is not sown as a pioneer crop because (a) the abundant mulch restricts the emergence of seedlings and (b) late-season planting (August) does not provide adequate soil moisture for grain filling.

For about 10 years after the pioneer crop, the system maintains agricultural production because of the regrowth potential of trees in the system. QSMAS annually produces maize intercropped with beans or sorghum. Management is zero tillage, with continuous slashing and pruning of trees and shrubs for firewood to avoid excessive shading of the crops. Continuous mulching from leaf litter, slashing of trees, and applying crop residues are supplemented with spot fertilization technologies and occasional use of pre-emergence herbicides.

The small farmer was not a major obstacle to larger-scale implementation of QSMAS. Extensionists and their organizations often maintained a monocrop production bias and opposed the comprehensive approach of QSMAS. A lack of training in demand-driven participatory extension dominated rural development projects, which focused efforts on physical, supply-driven indicators. Although much was said about collaboration between local and professional knowledge systems, the approach was rarely implemented (Welchez and Cherrett 2002).

The success of QSMAS is a reflection of a community-based learning process in which local people and extension service providers share ideas and learn together. The strategy to promote adoption and integration consists of three main components: (a) collective action, (b) technological innovations, and (c) policies and negotiations.

The project promoted collective action by strengthening the capacity of households (both men and women), local groups, educational institutions, and development organizations to organize and identify leaders and negotiate their interests with government representatives, service providers, and policy makers. Several local development organizations learned to devise action plans to improve agricultural practices using QSMAS.

Training services strengthened entrepreneurial capacity of men and women to transform and add value to agricultural products and sell them in the market. Technological innovation enhanced the capacity of farmers and household heads to adapt the components of QSMAS to their production systems and to develop appropriate innovations according to their own land and labor constraints.

The bargaining capacity of local communities to negotiate incentives and regulations supporting the adoption of QSMAS was strengthened. Local government officials were informed of the negative effects of burning on crop production and water availability. They enacted laws with severe penalties for people using fire in agricultural practices. Other laws were advanced with respect to common forestlands and water reservoirs. Significant improvements in financial services and infrastructure were negotiated with the Honduran government.

OPPORTUNITIES FOR SUSTAINABLE LAND MANAGEMENT

Letting soils rest as fallow after a cropping cycle has been a traditional management practice throughout the tropics to restore soil fertility. In southwest Honduras, successful restoration of soil fertility after cropping for 2 to 3 years usually requires a 14- to 20-year fallow period. Use of QSMAS can produce 10 years of crops with a fallow period of 5 to 7 years. In QSMAS plots, a key factor that contributes to the restoration of soil fertility is the coexistence of deciduous trees and shrubs. They serve as sources of mulch that protect the soil, retain water, and cycle nutrients during both production and fallow periods. An improved agricultural productive capacity together with provision of several environmental services (including reduced soil losses and improved water quality) can help convince farmers to move away from the traditional slash-and-burn system and toward QSMAS.

Recent research has shown that using QSMAS generates both economic and environmental benefits, which should provide an incentive to national and local authorities to encourage QSMAS. The socioeconomic and biophysical benefits of QSMAS are many:

- *Food security.* Farmers achieve productivity increases of traditional staple crops (such as maize, beans, and sorghum) and can diversify with other food crop options. Other benefits reported by QSMAS farmers are improved incomes, less labor invested in land preparation and weed control, reduced production costs, and higher net profits.
- *Increased market involvement.* Surpluses from improved yields and crop diversification provide householders with the production capacity to link with local markets.

- *Other products.* QSMAS contributes to improved availability and quality of water, not only to local communities but also to users downstream. QSMAS farms are also good sources of firewood for domestic consumption.

QSMAS generated benefits at the farm and landscape levels:

- *Farm level.* QSMAS has proved to be productive and sustainable while providing an improved physical, chemical, and biological resilience to agricultural plots. According to farmers, the following are among the main biophysical benefits of the system: (a) reduced soil erosion, (b) improved soil water-holding capacity when rainfall is erratic (irregular or insufficient), (c) improved soil fertility from efficient recycling of nutrients through mulch, and (d) improved resilience of the system from natural disasters.
- *Landscape level.* The adoption of QSMAS by farmers has contributed to improvements in environmental quality. The widespread use of QSMAS has decreased soil losses and has reduced the sediments in watercourses. QSMAS has contributed to the conservation of more than 40 native species of trees and shrubs. Newer QSMAS farms (two to five years old) serve as sinks for methane, with low emission levels of nitrous oxide. These results help mitigate climate change.

RATIONALE FOR INVESTMENT

QSMAS is a resource-efficient production system that improves livelihoods while conserving the natural resource base. There are four main reasons behind its successful adoption by farmers:

1. *Reduced soil losses from erosion.* A combined effect of permanent soil cover and presence of stones improves crop water productivity and water quality.
2. *Increased availability of soil nutrients.* Trees and organic resources maintain or even increase nitrogen and phosphorus, while enhancing soil biodiversity and biological activity.
3. *Mitigation of climate change.* The no-burn practices reduce the negative effects on greenhouse gas emissions.
4. *Enhanced biodiversity.* Conservation of trees and shrubs favors local biodiversity. Cumulative benefits of widespread QSMAS practices improve biodiversity of the landscape.

In the past decade, more than 6,000 resource-poor farmers have adopted QSMAS on 7,000 hectares in the Lempira department, formerly the poorest region in Honduras. This response has generated a twofold increase in crop yields (for example, maize from 1,200 to 2,500 kilograms per hectare in year 1; beans from 325 to 800 kilograms per hectare in year 1) and cattle stocking rates, along with significant reductions in labor and agrochemical costs (Ayarza and Welchez 2004; Clerck and Deugd 2002). By way of nonformal diffusion processes, the system has also been accepted among farmers in northwest Nicaragua.

Scientists from the CIAT, FAO, and the Consortium for Integrated Soil Management conclude that the Quesungual system—or elements of it—could be adapted for use in hillside areas of Africa, Asia, and South America. The project supported by the Challenge Program for Water and Food expects to identify new areas that could be suitable for QSMAS and to provide the tools for adapting and promoting the entire system or its components in these areas.

RECOMMENDATIONS FOR PRACTITIONERS

- *Reach consensus.* The principle of QSMAS is sustainable land management through the protection of the natural resources that are essential for agricultural productivity. The practices include (a) the use of local natural resources (that is, vegetation, soil, and microorganisms) with introduced crops; (b) field preparation without using burning or tillage; (c) the continuous slash and mulch of naturally regenerated vegetation; and (d) spot application of fertilizers and occasional herbicide use. Successful implementation requires detailed discussion with farmers on all four components.
- *Use local knowledge.* The success of QSMAS depends on local perspectives and knowledge. Close collaboration with local farmers is essential for understanding how to manage system components, particularly the native tree and shrub vegetation.
- *Use local support.* A key factor for the widespread adoption of QSMAS was a decision made in a local referendum to forbid the use of burning to prepare fields for planting. This action would have been impossible without the support of local authorities and a clear understanding by farmers of the negative effects of burning and the multiple biophysical and socioeconomic benefits from the restoration of soil organic matter.
- *Train farmers.* Although maintaining the QSMAS plots is not expensive, the initial investment, especially labor, is higher than the traditional slash-and-burn system. Extensionists need to explain the potential benefits returned

from their labor and costs. QSMAS has some limitations: (a) lower rates of seed germination when the mulch layer is too thick, (b) a higher incidence of pests and diseases during the initial years because of the mulch and the increased humidity from shade, and (c) a similar or even reduced productivity during the first year (FAO 2001).

Although the potential is great for the adoption of QSMAS in other regions of the world, it is important to realize that any project supporting its validation requires substantial commitments of time and resources within the context of a long-term framework. With additional research, development investments would enable more farmers to adapt QSMAS to their local biophysical and socioeconomic conditions. Investments would also permit researchers and development practitioners to analyze the feasibility of establishing payments for environmental services from smallholder QSMAS. Fostering positive incentives for sustainable land management on and off farms could improve the productivity and resilience of tropical hillside agro-ecosystems.

NOTE

1. The system is being used within the upper watersheds of the Lempa River in the department of Lempira, Honduras (around 14 degrees, 4 feet, 60 inches North; 88 degrees, 34 feet, 0 inches West) at 200 to 900 meters above sea level. The region's life zone (Holdridge) is a subhumid tropical forest with semideciduous and pine trees, and its climatic classification is tropic humid-dry (Köppen Aw) with a bimodal rainfall distribution during the year. Mean annual precipitation is about 1,400 millimeters falling mainly from early May to late October, with a distinct dry season of up to six months (November through April). During the dry season, strong winds blow from the north and the enhanced evapotranspiration rates cause severe water deficits (more than 200 millimeters) until the onset of rains. Temperature ranges between 17 and 25 degrees Celsius. Soils are classified as stony Entisols (Lithic Ustorthents) influenced by volcanic ashes associated with igneous and intrusive rocks, usually with low-labile phosphorus (that is, less than 5 mg kg^{-1}) and low soil organic matter content (2.8 to 3.9 percent) with pH values ranging from 4.1 to 6.2.

REFERENCES

Ayarza, M. A., and L. A. Welchez. 2004. "Drivers Affecting the Development and Sustainability of the Quesungual Slash and Mulch Agroforestry System (QSMAS) on Hillsides of Honduras." In *Comprehensive Assessment "Bright*

Spots" Project Final Report, ed. A. Noble, 187–201. Colombo: International Water Management Institute.

Clerck, L., and M. Deugd. 2002. "Pobreza, agricultura sostenible y servicios financieros rurales en América Latina: Reflexiones sobre un estudios de caso en el departamento de Lempira, Honduras." Centro de Estudios para el Desarrollo Rural, Universidad Libre de Amsterdam, San José, Costa Rica.

FAO (Food and Agriculture Organization). 2001. "Conservation Agriculture: Case Studies in Latin America and Africa." FAO Soils Bulletin 78, FAO, Rome.

Welchez, L. A., and I. Cherret. 2002. "The Quesungual System in Honduras: An Alternative to Slash-and-Burn." *Leisa* 18 (3): 10–11.

SELECTED READING

CIAT (Centro Internacional de Agricultura Tropical) and FAO (Food and Agriculture Organization). 2005. "El Sistema Agroforestal Quesungual: Una opción para el manejo de suelos en zonas secas de ladera." FAO, Rome.

Deugd, M. 2000. "No quemar … sostenible y rentable?" Informe Final II: Sistema Quesungual, GCP/HON/021/NET, Food and Agriculture Organization, Honduras.

Hands On. 2008. "Report 1 of 5: Shortage to Surplus—Honduras." Hands On, Rugby, U.K. http://www.handsontv.info/series2/foodworks_reports/shortagetosurplus_honduras.html.

Hellin, J., L. A. Welchez, and I. Cherrett. 1999. "The Quezungual System: An Indigenous Agroforestry System from Western Honduras." *Agroforestry Systems* 46 (3): 229–37.

Penning de Vries, F., H. Acquay, D. J. Molden, S. J. Scherr, C. Valentin, and O. Cofie. 2002. "Integrated Land and Water Management for Food and Environment Security." Comprehensive Assessment Research Paper 1. Comprehensive Assessment Secretariat, Colombo.

TSBF (Tropical Soil Biology and Fertility Institute). 2003. "Quesungual Slash and Mulch Agroforestry System (QSMAS): Improving Crop Water Productivity, Food Security, and Resource Quality in the Sub-humid Tropics." Project Proposal submitted to the Consultative Group on International Agricultural Research Challenge Program on Water and Food, World Bank, Washington, DC.

———. 2006. *Project PE-2: Integrated Soil Fertility Management in the Tropics—Annual Report 2006.* Cali, Colombia: Centro Internacional de Agricultura Tropical.

WEB RESOURCES

International Center for Tropical Agriculture. The International Center for Tropical Agriculture (Centro Internacional de Agricultura Tropical, or CIAT) is a not-for-profit organization that conducts socially and environmentally progressive research aimed at reducing hunger and poverty and preserving natural resources in developing countries. CIAT is one of the 15 centers that make up the Consultative Group on International Agricultural Research. The CIAT Web site has information on its products, regions, research, and services. http://www.ciat.cgiar.org/.

Challenge Program on Water and Food. The Consultative Group on International Agricultural Research (CGIAR) Challenge Program on Water and Food is an international, multi-institutional research initiative with a strong emphasis on North-South and South-South partnerships. Its goal is to increase the productivity of water used for agriculture, leaving more water for other users and the environment. The Web site of the CGIAR Challenge Program on Water and Food features announcements, capacity building activities, research, and publications: http://www.waterandfood.org/.

FAO Web page on the Quesungual agroforestry farming system. The Food and Agriculture Organization (FAO) of the United Nations leads international efforts to defeat hunger by acting as a neutral forum where all nations meet as equals to negotiate agreements and debate policy. The FAO Web page on the Quesungual agroforestry farming system describes the Lempira Sur project, where farmers learn new cultivation methods to prevent soil erosion. http://www.fao.org/FOCUS/E/honduras/agro-e.htm.

Module 5 of the Agriculture Investment Sourcebook. The *Agriculture Investment Sourcebook* addresses how to implement the rural strategy of investing to promote agricultural growth and poverty reduction by sharing information on investment options and identifying innovative approaches that will aid the design of future lending programs for agriculture. Module 5 of the *Agriculture Investment Sourcebook* discusses the investment in sustainable natural resource management for agriculture. http://siteresources.worldbank.org/EXTAGISOU/Resources/Module5_Web.pdf.

World Agroforestry Centre. The World Agroforestry Centre uses science to generate knowledge on the complex role of trees in livelihoods and the environment and fosters the use of this knowledge to improve decisions and practices affecting the poor. Its Web site provides information on news and events, recent publications, agroforestry, and other resources. http://www.worldagroforestry.org/.

Beans: Good Nutrition, Money, and Better Land Management—Appropriate for Scaling Up in Africa?

The common bean is a major staple food crop in Africa. PABRA (the Pan-African Bean Research Alliance) aims to enhance the food security, income, and health of resource-poor farmers in Africa through research on beans. Partners operate in different agro-ecological and socioeconomic environments through a series of collaborations with local agencies and directly with farmers in research groups.

The improved bean varieties have environmental benefits beyond the farm. For example, some require less cooking time than traditional varieties. Fuelwood consumption (as well as the time spent collecting fuel) has fallen sharply, releasing women especially for other livelihood activities. Innovative bean farmers used improved technologies from service providers (such as pest-tolerant high-yielding varieties, fertilizers, commercial pesticides, and improved cultural practices) to blend with local options (the use of wood ash, cow urine, cowshed slurry, and local plant extracts for pest control; the use of animal and green manure for improved soil fertility; and the improvement of agronomy through cultural practices, such as mixed cropping, staggered planting, and use of local crop cultivars). Although the immediate benefit was increased yields from improved bean management, the second benefit, which was broader and even more exciting, was the enhancement of farmer innovation and farmer-to-farmer communication.

PABRA researchers are striving to improve the nutritional content of beans and to improve market access. The PABRA approach also helps in the active exploration of other technologies and improved services (such as quality seeds, markets, credit, improved livestock, fertilizers, tree nurseries, irrigation facilities, and soil and water conservation methods). District authorities in Kenya, Malawi, Tanzania, and Uganda use the PABRA farmers groups to develop and implement community-based project proposals.

CHARACTERISTICS OF KEY SUSTAINABLE LAND MANAGEMENT ISSUE

Beans are popular in Africa—and for good reason. Beans are healthful and profitable, and with good management, they contribute to farm diversification and productivity. Can more farmers benefit from cultivating these fast-growing legumes? Africans confront numerous agricultural, communication, and transportation challenges. This investment note explains how the International Center for Tropical Agriculture (Centro Internacional de Agricultura Tropical, or CIAT) and its partners combine their scientific, organizational, and marketing efforts to address these challenges and reach more farmers.

KEY SUSTAINABLE LAND MANAGEMENT ISSUES

Natural resources are the key to rural development in Africa (Anderson 2003). Despite their importance, a majority of Africans still face both food shortages and degradation of their natural resources. Two-thirds of the population (405 million people) live on small-scale farms (Conway and Toenniessen 2003), where declines in soil fertility severely reduce harvests.

Although overexploitation of natural resources comes in many forms, the results are the same: a loss of both productive capacity and resilience. Soil degradation threatens (a) the sustainability of agricultural yields and (b) the ability of agriculture to deliver crucial services, such as water availability, biodiversity, and carbon storage.

For many generations, traditional farm practices met household food needs. Population growth and accompanying pressure on land, however, have stressed this equilibrium. Farmers typically respond by either intensifying agricultural production or expanding into marginal lands

This note was prepared by D. White, Centro Internacional de Agricultura Tropical and Pan-African Bean Research Alliance.

(Dixon and Gulliver with Gibbon 2001). Nevertheless, harvests from these efforts are typically low because no or few investments in soil fertility maintenance are made. Although chemical fertilizers have produced impressive yield gains in much of the world, fertilizers are rarely available or too expensive in much of Africa (Crawford and others 2003; Gregory and Bumb 2006). There are also serious misunderstandings regarding fertilizer. For example, some farmers believe that to be effective, the fertilizer actually needs to touch the seed—which in fact hinders germination and damages both the crop and the farmers' faith in the technology. Furthermore, the advice farmers are typically given in the use of fertilizer is poor; recommendations ignore crucial differences in soil type and, as importantly, key economic factors about the prices of both inputs and outputs (Conroy and others 2006). Local ways to enhance farm productivity are needed (Giller 2001).

LESSONS LEARNED

The common bean is a major staple food crop in Africa. Farmers plant approximately 4 million hectares of beans, which represent 20 percent of the total crop area planted. In many parts of eastern, central, and southern Africa, beans are referred to as the "poor man's meat." Beans provide nearly 40 percent of dietary protein and are valued as one of the least expensive sources of protein. Many people eat beans twice a day. During hard times in some areas, households survive on just one meal of beans a day.

A major lesson learned is the importance of having an active regional and local institutional partnership to facilitate the dissemination and scaling up of cropping and land management innovations. PABRA's goal is to enhance the food security, income, and health of resource-poor farmers in Africa through research on beans. PABRA works in partnership with farmers and rural communities, nongovernmental organizations, national agricultural research institutes, traders, and other private sector partners. Crucial roles and responsibilities of partners include improving bean varieties, producing and disseminating seed, sharing information, and training extensionists and researchers.

Collaborative PABRA efforts enhance farmer access to improved quality seeds that farmers prefer. This process involves the following:

- Understanding farm household needs, their taste preferences, and their sources of bean seed
- Supporting partners involved in decentralizing bean variety selection, seed production, and distribution

- Strengthening and catalyzing partnerships with strategic actors
- Facilitating access to information and preferred seed varieties by commercial seed producers
- Providing key support services: technical inputs, outreach products, and colearning
- Sharing lessons learned, including successful cases of wider effect at the local, national, and regional levels (for example, Ethiopia and southern Tanzania) that demonstrate how change processes work with PABRA partners
- Adapting lessons to new areas and crops (such as cassava and teff) with new partners.

Since the early 1980s, the bean research network has worked to improve the productivity, resilience, and acceptability of bean varieties. National agricultural research systems and extension partners released about 200 improved beans in 18 countries. Partners operate in different agro-ecological and socioeconomic environments. PABRA partners have overcome production problems, such as bean pests and diseases and poor soil fertility, and have made new bean varieties available to more farmers.

PABRA has fostered strategic partnerships that play complementary roles in reaching end users. By late 2006, PABRA partner organizations had trained more than 300 associations with about 15,000 farmers. Topics included variety testing, seed production, and agronomic practices. Knowledge sharing among farmers has greatly accelerated technology dissemination and adoption. National programs have been encouraged to conduct participatory varietal selection or plant breeding with farmers. Those approaches have ensured that new varieties are quickly made available to farmers before their formal release. To speed up dissemination, PABRA has supported the development of community-based seed production as an agro-enterprise strategy. Technical resource manuals in 11 local languages have been developed and supplied to farmers and extension organizations.

OPPORTUNITIES FOR SUSTAINABLE LAND MANAGEMENT

Beans generate environmental benefits both on and off farms. Farmers often cultivate beans in rotation or in association with other crops. This strategy diversifies farm production against risks and can enable farmers to improve soil fertility. Bean cultivation within a farm management strategy may enhance the yields of other crops, such as maize.

Although PABRA has promoted the use of improved bean varieties that thrive in poor soils, such beans perform better when integrated with good farm management practices. PABRA researchers look for and examine a wide range of locally generated solutions for improving soil fertility, such as green manures and organic soil amendments. In many parts of Africa (Ethiopia, Kenya, and Rwanda), bean crop residues are used as (a) a green manure to increase soil organic matter or (b) a livestock feed, with manure applied to fields. PABRA also serves as a forum for sharing management practices.

Pests and diseases can destroy harvests and cause food shortages. The early 1990s were troubling times for both bean farmers and consumers in eastern Africa. Bean root rot disease decimated harvests in intensely cultivated areas, causing severe food shortages and high prices. To help solve the problem, PABRA scientists from CIAT and the Institut des Sciences Agronomiques du Rwanda identified bush and climbing bean varieties with resistance to the disease. Partners introduced these varieties to Kenya and southwest Uganda.

Improved bean varieties are not the only way to achieve better harvests and possibly improve soil fertility. Climbing beans can generate higher yields than bush beans, enabling farmers to sustainably intensify production on tiny plots. Integrated pest and disease management (IPDM) can be effective in improving system outputs. Farmers typically combine local knowledge and researcher-generated innovations (such as timely planting, weeding, use of botanical pesticides, and sowing or use of *Tephrosia* to restore soil fertility while warding off pests).

Results show that such practices are effective in countering bean root rot and other diseases and pests. According to PABRA, improved practices to counter pests, diseases, and poor soils reached 400,000 farmers by 2005. Although this figure is well behind the numbers of those adopting improved varieties, it represents a very promising start.

Improved bean varieties have environmental benefits beyond the farm. Some of the improved beans require less cooking time than traditional varieties. Women report reduced fuelwood consumption of almost 50 percent. Women can also spend less time collecting firewood during the day and can dedicate that time to other livelihood activities.

RATIONALE FOR INVESTMENT

Beans can play a role in achieving sustainable land management in Africa. Their ability to be profitable while contributing to overall farm production and resilience makes them an attractive crop for many African farmers. Evidence suggests that bean varieties generate substantial benefits for producers, consumers, and other actors in the bean supply chain. Significant effects, however, tend to be found in areas of intense efforts to disseminate seed. As part of the revised PABRA strategy of 2003, the network aims to achieve greater use of improved bean varieties. The goal was to deliver and ensure training in improved bean technologies to 2 million households (10 million end users) in 18 countries by 2008. Expectations have already been exceeded. As a result of the strategic partnerships, about 6.5 million households (30 million end users) had been reached at the end of 2006. Critical to that success was packaging seed in small, affordable quantities. Fifty tons of seed can reach a million farmers with 50-gram seed packets. More work is required to reach the hundreds of millions in need of improved bean technologies.

According to PABRA, farmers who planted improved varieties reported increased yields, had fewer losses to pests and diseases, enhanced family nutrition and health, and realized higher incomes. In some countries, bean research and development activities have brought substantial economic returns. For example, in Tanzania the internal rate of return to research investments was estimated at 60 percent over a 20-year period (1985 to 2005). Economic benefits can be seen from the farmer's perspective. In eastern Democratic Republic of Congo, farmers' incomes from beans increased nearly fivefold. Higher incomes were generated not only from increased bean sales for consumption but also from the sale of seeds. In some countries, seed production and sales have become moneymaking enterprises and generated employment, often with PABRA support.

Cultivating beans appears to be a wealth-neutral agricultural activity. Farmers in several countries, particularly Rwanda, reported that poor or very poor members of the community were as likely to adopt the new varieties as better-off farmers. Many adopters are women, who have seen their incomes rise substantially. To reduce the risk of men trying to appropriate the income gains by taking over what is traditionally a women's crop, PABRA has sought to build the capacity of women's groups and associated service providers in starting and running agro-enterprises. Other social benefits realized by participating bean farmers include exposure to new services providers (that is, credit and input supplies) and to new information on health and nutrition.

Beans are highly vulnerable to climatic stresses, especially drought. In recent years, PABRA partners have developed varieties that combine drought tolerance with other desirable traits. These efforts must continue and intensify so that new varieties are produced, screened, and tested for early dissemination and release.

PABRA's second decade will be even more challenging than its first. PABRA's focus on seed-based technologies has been effective. Plant breeding, as the source of these technologies, will continue to be a key activity. The fight against pests and diseases must intensify and broaden, because new threats constantly arise. Besides bean root rot, other critical diseases that need tackling include angular leaf spot, anthracnose, leaf rust, common bacterial blight, and bean mosaic virus. Priority pests include bean stem maggots, aphids, and cutworms. In addition, focus will continue on low soil fertility and drought. Selection and breeding for resistance or tolerance will, as now, be combined with IPDM approaches that maximize the gains to farmer and ecosystem health. Besides addressing drought, PABRA is extending traditional bean areas to the hot and humid areas of West Africa, where consumer demand and prices are high (Kimani 2006).

RECOMMENDATIONS FOR PRACTITIONERS

To reach marginalized farmers, PABRA must reinforce its efforts to disseminate seed-based and other technologies. Adoption patterns reveal three priorities: (a) disseminating technologies in areas that have been neglected or bypassed, (b) offering a greater number of varieties to allow greater resilience of production and household food security, and (c) continuing to develop and adapt knowledge-based technologies (such as IPDM) that typically lag seed technologies.

PABRA researchers are striving to improve the nutritional content of beans. As part of the HarvestPlus initiative, researchers are working to develop biofortified beans, focusing on iron and zinc in agronomically superior varieties. Efforts to enhance the contribution of beans, particularly for those affected by the continuing spread of HIV/AIDS, require coordination with organizations outside the agricultural sectors. Besides developing and disseminating new varieties that are rich in minerals, PABRA must launch promotional campaigns to involve community-based health and nutrition workers.

As African farmers produce more and better beans, they will need to participate in markets. Ensuring that beans remain profitable requires investments in cost-effective processing options and efforts to open up new regional markets. If prices for beans and other cash crops can be sustained, farmers will likely be more willing to invest in their farms, especially in the fertility of their soils.

The PABRA approach reaches well beyond the innovators. Farmers in Kisii, Kenya, cited benefits from the adoption of improved bean technology: increased amounts of household food, increased household income, availability of food year-round, improvements in family health and relationships with other farmers, and increased income controlled by women. Data from Uganda show increasing involvement in local trade of beans as the farmers move beyond subsistence. Farmers have also started to actively explore other technologies. For example, farmers in northern Tanzania experimented with a locally available phosphate-based fertilizer (Minjingu Mazao) on the bean crop. But they quickly went on to test the fertilizer on other crops, such as maize and vegetables, and also modified their fertilizer use on those crops.

Encouraged by their experiences with beans, farmers started to actively seek improved services, such as quality seed, markets, credit, improved livestock, fertilizers, tree nurseries, irrigation facilities, and soil and water conservation methods (Blackie and Ward 2005). They raised these issues openly with local officials and visitors—something they lacked the confidence to do previously. Through the enhanced participation, local officials, community leaders, nongovernmental organizations, and politicians gain information for local planning. The research groups are an important and dynamic component in the local innovation system. Government ministries (agriculture, livestock, health, education, and marketing) and district authorities in Kenya, Malawi, Tanzania, and Uganda use the farmers groups to develop and implement community-based project proposals.

REFERENCES

Anderson, J. 2003. *Nature, Wealth, and Power in Africa: Emerging Best Practice for Revitalizing Rural Africa.* Washington, DC: U.S. Agency for International Development. http://www.usaid.gov/our_work/agriculture/land management/pubs/nature_wealth_power_fy2004.pdf.

Blackie, M. J., and A. Ward. 2005. "Breaking Out of Poverty: Lessons from Harmonising Research and Policy in Malawi." *Aspects of Applied Biology* 75: 115–26.

Conroy, A. C., M. J. Blackie, A. Whiteside, J. C. Malewezi, and J. D. Sachs. 2006. *Poverty, Aids and Hunger: Breaking the Poverty Trap in Malawi.* Basingstoke, U.K.: Palgrave Macmillan

Conway, G., and G. Toenniessen. 2003. "Science for African Food Security." *Science* 299 (5610): 1187–88.

Crawford, E., V. Kelly, T. Jayne, and J. Howard. 2003. "Input Use and Market Development in Sub-Saharan Africa: An Overview." *Food Policy* 28 (4): 277–92.

Dixon, J., and A. Gulliver, with D. Gibbon. 2001. *Farming Systems and Poverty: Improving Farmers' Livelihoods in a*

Changing World. Rome: Food and Agriculture Organization and World Bank. http://www.fao.org/farmingsystems/.

Giller, K. E. 2001. *Nitrogen Fixation in Tropical Cropping Systems*. 2nd ed. Wallingford, UK: CAB International.

Gregory, D., and B. Bumb. 2006. "Factors Affecting Fertilizer Supply in Africa: Agriculture and Rural Development." Discussion Paper 24. World Bank, Washington, DC. http://www.africafertilizersummit.org/Background_Papers/08%20Gregory—Role%20of%20Input%20Vouchers.pdf.

Kimani, P. 2006. "Bean Varieties for Humid Tropical Regions: Reality or Fiction?" Highlights: CIAT in Africa 34. Centro Internacional de Agricultura Tropical, Kampala. http://www.ciat.cgiar.org/africa/pdf/highlight34.pdf.

SELECTED READING

BBC News. 2006. "'Barren Future' for Africa's Soil." BBC News, London. http://news.bbc.co.uk/2/hi/science/nature/4860694.stm.

HarvestPlus. 2006. "Biofortified Beans." HarvestPlus, Cali, Colombia. http://www.harvestplus.org/pdfs/beans.pdf.

Hyman, G., S. Fujisaka, P. Jones, S. Wood, C. de Vicente, and J. Dixon. 2007. "Strategic Approaches to Targeting Technology Generation: Assessing the Coincidence of Poverty and Drought-Prone Crop Production." Centro Internacional de Agricultura Tropical, Cali, Colombia.

Rubyogo, J. C., L. Sperling, and T. Assefa. 2007. "A New Approach for Facilitating Farmers' Access to Bean Seed." *LEISA* 23 (2): 27–29.

WEB RESOURCES

International Center for Tropical Agriculture. The International Center for Tropical Agriculture (CIAT) is a nonprofit organization that conducts socially and environmentally progressive research targeting the reduction of hunger and poverty and the preservation of natural resources in developing countries. CIAT is one of the 15 centers that make up the Consultative Group on International Agricultural Research. The CIAT Web site has information on its products, regions, research, and services: http://www.ciat.cgiar.org/.

Fodder Shrubs for Improving Livestock Productivity and Sustainable Land Management in East Africa

In East Africa, zero-grazing systems constitute the most common smallholder dairy system; farmers cut and carry feed to their confined dairy cows. Fodder legumes have been tested for more than 50 years as protein supplements, but with little adoption. Fodder shrubs are a low-cost, easy-to-produce protein source that could also contribute to sustainable land management (SLM). They are highly attractive to farmers because they require little or no cash. Moreover, they do not require farmers to take land out of use for food or other crops. But the technology is knowledge intensive and requires the farmer to learn new skills.

The spread of fodder shrubs has been substantial, and by 2006 (about 10 years after dissemination began in earnest), they were contributing about US$3.8 million per year to farmer incomes across East Africa. Critical to the expansion were extension approaches involving (a) dissemination facilitators (specialists who promote the use of fodder shrubs among extension providers and support them with training, information, and access to seeds); (b) farmer-to-farmer dissemination; (c) large nongovernmental organization (NGO) promoters, which facilitated seed flows (seed availability was a key constraint in many areas); and (d) civil society campaigns involving a broader set of partners than just farmers and extension providers.

PROJECT OBJECTIVE

Low quality and quantity of feed resources are the greatest constraint to improving the productivity of livestock in Sub-Saharan Africa (Winrock International Institute for Agricultural Development 1992). Dairy production is increasing rapidly in the highlands of East Africa, which hosts roughly 3 million dairy farmers, including some 21 million in Kenya alone (SDP 2006). Milk demand is concentrated in towns and cities, and dairy production has grown rapidly around those urban areas, to take advantage of low marketing costs. But farm sizes are also generally small in such peri-urban areas, exacerbating feed constraints. Land degradation is also a pervasive problem; most of the land is sloping, and soil erosion reduces crop productivity.

Zero-grazing systems are the most common smallholder dairy system; farmers cut and carry feed to their confined dairy cows. Napier grass is the basal feed of choice, but its protein content is too low to sustain adequate milk yields. Manufactured dairy meal is available in most areas, but few small farmers use it because of its high price. Fodder legumes have been tested in East Africa for more than 50 years as protein supplements, but there are few cases of widespread adoption, especially in the smallholder sector. The objective of introducing fodder shrubs in East Africa was to provide a low-cost, easy-to-produce protein source that could also contribute to SLM.

STUDY AREA DESCRIPTION

The highlands of East Africa extend across central and western Kenya, westward to Uganda and Rwanda, and to the south in parts of northern Tanzania. Altitudes range from 1,000 to 2,200 meters. Rainfall occurs in two seasons, March through June and October through December, and averages 1,200 to 1,500 millimeters annually. Soils, primarily nitosols, are deep and of moderate to high fertility. Population density is high, ranging from 300 to more than 1,000 people per square kilometer. In central Kenya, which has the region's highest population density and the most dairy cows, farm size averages 1 to 2 hectares. Most farmers have title to their land; thus, their tenure is relatively secure. The main crops are coffee, which is produced for cash, and

This profile was prepared by S. Franzel, C. Wambugu, H. Arimi, and J. Stewart, International Centre for Research in Agroforestry. Nairobi, Kenya.

maize and beans, which is produced for food. Most farmers also grow Napier grass (*Pennisetum purpureum*) to feed their dairy cows, and farmers crop their fields continuously because of the shortage of land. About 80 percent have improved dairy cows. The typical family has 1.7 cows, kept in zero- or minimum-grazing systems. Milk yields average about 8 kilograms per cow per day, and production is for both home consumption and sale. Dairy goats, which are particularly suited to poorer households, are a rapidly growing enterprise (Murithi 1998; Staal and others 2002).

The main feed source for dairy cows in Kenya is Napier grass, supplemented during the dry season with crop residues (such as maize and bean stover, as well as banana leaves and pseudostems) and indigenous fodder shrubs. Few farmers purchase commercial dairy meal (16 percent crude protein). Dairy meal use has declined in recent years because farmers feel that the price ratio of dairy meal to milk is unfavorable and because they lack cash to buy the meal. Many also suspect the nutritive value of dairy meal, in part because of scandals concerning fraudulent maize seed and agrochemicals sold to farmers (Franzel, Wambugu, and Tuwei 2003; Murithi 1998; Staal and others 2002).

Smallholder dairy systems in Rwanda, northern Tanzania, and Uganda are similar to those in Kenya, but the density of dairy farmers and cows is generally lower, as is government extension support and private sector marketing infrastructure.

PRESENTATION OF INNOVATION

Fodder shrubs are highly attractive to farmers because they require little or no cash. Moreover, they do not require farmers to take land out of use for food or other crops. The only inputs required are the initial seed and minimal amounts of labor, which farmers are usually willing to provide. But like many agroforestry and natural resource management practices, fodder shrubs are knowledge intensive and require considerable skills that most farmers lack. These skills include raising seedlings in a nursery, pruning trees, and knowing the best ways to feed the fodder to livestock. Such skills are difficult to acquire as is, at times, the necessary seed. Thus, the technology does not spread easily.

Farmers prefer planting fodder shrubs in the following locations and arrangements:

- In hedges around the farm compound
- In hedges along contour bunds and terrace edges on sloping land. The shrubs thus help conserve soil and, when kept well pruned, have little effect on adjacent crops

- In lines with Napier grass. Results from intercropping experiments show that introducing the leguminous shrub *Calliandra calothyrsus* into Napier grass does not depress the grass yields (Nyaata, O'Neill, and Roothaert 1998)
- In lines between upper-story trees. Many farmers plant *Grevillea robusta*, a tree useful for timber and firewood, along their boundaries. Fodder shrubs may be planted between the trees in the same line (NARP 1993).

Seeds are planted in nurseries and then transplanted on the farm at the onset of the rains, after about three months in the nursery. Experiments on seedling production have confirmed that the seedlings may be grown "bare root"; that is, they may be raised in seedbeds rather than by the more expensive, laborious method of raising them in polythene pots (NARP 1993).

The shrubs are first pruned for fodder 9 to 12 months after transplant, and pruning is carried out four or five times a year (Roothaert and others 1998). Leafy biomass yields per year rise if the shrubs are pruned less frequently and allowed to grow taller, but as this happens, competition from the shrubs means that adjacent crop yields are negatively affected (Franzel and Wambugu 2007). The most productive compromise is probably in the range of four to six prunings annually at 0.6- to 1-meter cutting height. This approach yields, under farmers' conditions, roughly 1.5 kilograms of dry matter (4.5 kilograms of fresh biomass) per tree per year planted at a spacing of two to three trees per meter in hedges. Thus, a farmer needs about 500 shrubs to feed a cow throughout the year at a rate of 2 kilograms of dry (6 kilograms of fresh) matter per day, providing about 0.6 kilogram of crude protein. This amount provides an effective protein supplement to the basal feed of Napier grass and crop residues for increased milk production. A typical farm of 1.5 hectares could easily accommodate 500 shrubs without replacing any existing crops (Paterson and others 1998).[1]

On-farm feeding trials have confirmed the effectiveness of *C. calothyrsus* as a supplement to the basal diet. Two kilograms of dry *C. calothyrsus* (24 percent crude protein and digestibility of 60 percent when fed fresh) have about the same amount of digestible protein as 2 kilograms of dairy meal (16 percent crude protein and 80 percent digestibility); each increases milk production by about 1.5 kilograms under farm conditions. But the response varies, depending on such factors as the health of the cow and the quantity and quality of the basal feed (Paterson and others 1998).

Since *C. calothyrsus* was introduced in the mid-1990s, several other shrub species have also been tested and disseminated (Wambugu and others 2006). In Kenya, *Leucaena trichandra* (an exotic species), *Morus alba* (mulberry, a naturalized species), and *Sesbania sesban* (an indigenous species) are grown widely but not as commonly as *C. calothyrsus*. In Rwanda, *C. calothyrsus* and *Leucaena diversifolia*, also an exotic, are the most common fodder shrubs. In Uganda, these same two shrubs, along with *Sesbania*, are widely grown. In northern Tanzania, *C. calothyrsus* and *Leucaena leucocephala* are the most widely used species.

BENEFITS AND EFFECT OF THE ACTIVITY

The main benefit to using fodder shrubs is increased milk production. In an economic analysis from Kenya in 2006, the authors compared the value of increased milk production with the costs of establishing a nursery, raising 500 *C. calothyrsus* seedlings, transplanting them on the farm, and harvesting them for feed (Hess and others 2006). In the first year, the farmer spends about US$13 establishing the nursery, raising the seedlings, and transplanting them. About US$1.70 of this amount is for seed and the rest is spent on labor. Beginning in the second year, when the farmer starts harvesting the shrubs, the 500 *C. calothyrsus* shrubs increase net household income by about US$95 to US$122 a year, depending on the location. The main causes of variation in income increases across location were differences in milk prices. The analysis does not take into account several other benefits of fodder shrubs. First, they increase the butterfat content of milk (in the farmers' terms, its "creaminess" and "thickness"). Second, the extra nutrients that the shrubs provide may improve the cow's health and shorten the calving interval. Finally, farmers can also benefit from harvesting and selling seeds.

Fodder shrubs also make important contributions to SLM, which are not taken into account in the previous analysis:

- *Nitrogen fixation.* Five of the six species fix nitrogen from the atmosphere and thus contribute to improving soil fertility. As long as these species are grown in hedges that are 1 meter high, they do not compete with crops grown next to them.
- *Increased quantity and quality of manure.* Most fodder species are high in tannins, which bind protein and increase the levels of nitrogen in manure. The increase in quantity and quality of manure helps improve soil fertility.
- *Soil erosion control.* Fodder shrubs are planted along the contour, thereby reducing soil erosion. The shrubs are particularly effective when combined with grasses.

- *Substitutes for products obtained from forests.* Most of the shrub species provide firewood, fencing, and stakes, thus reducing the need to source them off the farm and deplete woodlands.

In the Kabale area of western Uganda, more than 70 percent of farmers mentioned fencing, firewood, soil fertility improvement, and stakes as important benefits of fodder shrubs (Mawanda 2004). In central Kenya, more than 30 percent mentioned firewood, soil fertility improvement, and improvement in animal health (Koech 2005).

The spread of fodder shrubs has been substantial. By 2006, about 10 years after dissemination began in earnest, 224 organizations across Kenya, Rwanda, northern Tanzania, and Uganda were promoting fodder shrubs, and more than 200,000 farmers had planted them (table 4.1). The number of shrubs averages 71 to 236 per farmer, depending on the country. Note, however, that this number is still well below the 500 shrubs needed to feed a single dairy cow. The explanation is that many farmers adopt incrementally (they plant some shrubs to see how they perform before adding more), and others partially adopt (they apply several different strategies for providing protein supplements—herbaceous legumes, dairy meal, and so forth—to better manage the risks of relying on a single strategy). The number of shrubs per farmer is higher in countries such as Uganda, where NGOs promote fodder shrubs; it is lower in countries such as Kenya, where farmer-to-farmer dissemination is the main cause of the spread.

Fodder shrubs currently contribute about US$3.8 million annually to farmer incomes across East Africa. If all farmers were to adopt them, the potential is more than US$200 million per year.

LESSONS LEARNED

Representatives of 70 organizations promoting fodder shrubs were interviewed and asked to name the most important factor explaining their achievements in disseminating fodder shrubs. With a mean score of 4.1 on a scale of 0 to 5.0, the most important factor was that fodder shrubs met the needs of farmers (Franzel and Wambugu 2007). Other key factors were that the fodder shrubs were profitable, that effective extension approaches were used, and that partnerships with other organizations facilitated success. Less important factors included long-term commitment by key players, farmers' commercial orientation, farmers' skill levels, availability of training materials, and backstopping from research. Many of the reasons for the

Table 4.1 Farmers Planting Fodder Shrubs in Kenya, Northern Tanzania, Rwanda, and Uganda

Country	Number of organizations promoting fodder shrubs	Number of farmers planting according to records	Rough estimate of additional farmers planting	Total	Number of trees per farmer	Notes and sources
Kenya	60	51,645	30,000	81,645	75	Data in "records" column are from 4 random sample surveys and reports from 23 organizations, mostly from 2004 to 2005. Data in "rough estimates" column include numbers in areas with fodder shrubs for which there are no data (for example, Coast, Kisii, and Machakos) and increases in central and eastern provinces since 2003 surveys.
Northern Tanzania	15	17,519	10,000	27,519	99	Data in "records" column are from 14 organizations in Arusha and Kilimanjaro and estimates of numbers of collectors, planters, processors, and users in Tanga. Data in "rough estimates" column are for farmers in Mwanza, Lushoto, and other parts of northern Tanzania where fodder shrubs are promoted.
Rwanda	69	9,590	4,400	13,990	266	Data in "records" column are from 11 of the organizations that promoted fodder shrubs from 2000 to 2005. "Rough estimate" column assumes that each of the other 44 organizations that bought seed helped 100 farmers plant. Many of the organizations were promoting fodder shrubs primarily for soil conservation.
Uganda	80	77,369	5,000	82,369	306	Data in "records" column are from surveys in 2003 and 2005 in which 44 organizations reported on number of farmers planting fodder shrubs. Data in "rough estimates" column include numbers in areas not included in the survey and 16 organizations that were unable to report on number of farmers. Many of the organizations were promoting fodder shrubs primarily for soil conservation.
Total	224	156,123	49,400	205,523	184	

Source: Franzel and Wambugu 2007.

spread are related to the technology itself, its attractiveness to farmers, and the socioeconomic environment (in particular, the rapid growth of the smallholder dairy industry in the region). Franzel and Wambugu (2007) found that five extension approaches were critical for the spread of the practice:

1. *Dissemination facilitators.* Dissemination facilitators are extension specialists who promote the use of fodder shrubs among extension providers and support them by providing training, information, and access to seed. Dissemination facilitators were employed by international organizations such as the World Agroforestry Centre or national agricultural research institutes such as the National Agricultural Research Organization of Uganda. The dissemination facilitators proved to be highly effective. In central Kenya, for example, over a two-year period, a dissemination facilitator assisted 22 organizations and 150 farmer groups comprising 2,600 farmers to establish 250 nurseries and plant more than 1 million fodder shrubs (Wambugu and others 2001).

2. *Farmer-to-farmer dissemination.* Survey results showed that farmers played a critical role in disseminating seeds and information to other farmers. A survey of 94 farmers in central Kenya, randomly selected from farmers who had planted fodder shrubs three years before, revealed that 57 percent had distributed planting material (seeds or seedlings) and information to other farmers. On average, those providing planting material gave to 6.3 other farmers. But most astounding was that 5 percent of the farmers accounted for 66 percent of all dissemination. These master disseminators differed from other farmers in no appreciable way—they included both men and women and had different ages, levels of

education, and farm sizes. Farmers receiving planting material from other farmers had high rates of success in planting; about 75 percent had received fodder shrubs.

3. *Large NGO promoters.* In Rwanda and Uganda, a few large, international NGOs facilitated the dissemination of fodder shrubs to thousands of farmers, accounting for over half the farmers planting in the two countries. Large NGOs were also important in facilitating the spread of the practice in Kenya and Tanzania. Some of the NGOs employed hundreds of extension staff members and thus had significant reach. Many promoted dairy production and wanted to ensure that farmers had sufficient feed for their cows. Others promoted SLM and helped farmers plant shrubs for a range of purposes: soil erosion control, firewood, and fodder.

4. *Facilitation of seed* flows. Seed availability was a key constraint in many areas. *Calliandra calothyrsus,* the main species used, produces relatively little seed, and farmers need to be trained to collect, maintain, and treat it before planting. An assessment of the seed market chain found that private seed vendors in western Kenya were effective in providing seed to big institutional suppliers, such as NGOs, but were ineffective in reaching farmers, particularly in central Kenya where the greatest number of potential adopters were. Following the study, the World Agroforestry Centre and its partners assisted seed vendors in central Kenya in forming an association that forged links with seed providers in western Kenya and in packaging seeds in small packets for sale to farmers in central Kenya (Franzel and Wambugu 2007). Over an eight-month period in 2006, 43 seed vendors sold more than 2.3 tons of seed, sufficient for more than 40,000 farmers. A thriving private seed market is a key to sustainable growth in the adoption of fodder shrubs.

5. *Civil society campaigns.* A much broader set of partners than just farmers and extension providers can add significant value in promoting a new technology such as fodder shrubs. The SCALE (Systemwide Collaborative Action for Livelihoods and the Environment) methodology brings civil society stakeholders together to plan and implement campaigns to promote new practices (AED 2006). By engaging a wide range of stakeholders who represent all aspects of a given system (in this case, dairy production), the SCALE method generates change across many levels and sectors of society, using a combination of different social change methodologies, including advocacy, mass communication, and social mobilization. Experience with the SCALE approach in central Kenya highlights the effectiveness of civil society campaigns as

complements to more conventional extension programs. Religious leaders; media (radio, television, and the press); private input suppliers; local government administrators; and dairy companies each have a critical role to play in sensitizing and training farmers about new practices such as fodder shrubs.

ISSUES FOR WIDER APPLICATION

This paper documents the substantial progress that has been made in promoting fodder shrubs in East Africa. But the 200,000 farmers planting them represent less than 10 percent of dairy farmers in the region. Because of the knowledge-intensive nature of the technology, it will not spread easily on its own and thus requires outside facilitation. Considerable investments are still required to reach the other dairy farmers and to sustain the uptake process. With formal extension systems in decline throughout Africa, more efforts are needed to develop other approaches for spreading the use of fodder shrubs. This profile documents four dissemination approaches that are particularly effective and that indicate where greater investment in research and development is needed:

- Dissemination facilitators to support organizations promoting fodder shrubs offer a high return on investment. These facilitators do not train farmers; rather, they train trainers and therefore have a high multiplicative effect in promoting new practices.

- Mechanisms are needed to promote farmer-to-farmer dissemination and, in particular, master disseminators, who spread new practices in their communities. Research is needed to determine how best to select master disseminators and how to support them. Is it worthwhile to assist them with transportation (such as bicycles) or train them in the use of fodder shrub technologies or extension methods? Can they be assisted by offering cash for providing extension services, either in exchange for the information they provide or through selling inputs, such as fodder shrub seeds and seedlings?

- Seed vendors face an array of constraints: NGOs giving out free seed and undercutting their business, government seed centers selling seed to institutional buyers at subsidized prices, and government services demanding licensing fees. Efforts in Kenya have been successful in helping seed vendors organize and increase their sales and reach. More efforts are needed to support them, by linking them with institutional buyers and lobbying governments for policy reforms to provide them with a level playing field. Efforts are also needed to help seed vendors in other countries emerge and organize themselves.

- Civil society campaigns offer great promise for both sensitizing communities about new practices and training farmers in their use. Key questions that research could address concern the scope of the campaign (for example, fodder shrubs, enriched feeds, or dairy production); the balance between sensitization and training; and the relative importance and effectiveness of involving different types of stakeholders, such as media, religious leaders, and dairy companies.

Finally, investments are needed in two other key areas to sustain progress in fodder shrub adoption and outcomes, especially with regard to SLM:

- *Improved species diversification.* The range of species currently available to farmers should be expanded to include more indigenous shrubs. A broader range will reduce the risk of pests and diseases and promote local biodiversity. The most widely planted shrub, *C. calothyrsus*, has numerous qualities that make it attractive: it is easily propagated, it grows fast and withstands frequent pruning, and it competes little with adjacent crops. But it is not among the most nutritious of feeds (Hess and others 2006); greater efforts are needed to find shrubs that have *C. calothyrsus*'s favorable features and are higher in nutritive quality. Moreover, improved species are needed for marginal environments. Fodder shrub species are currently available for the highlands (1,200 to 2,000 meters), but few are available for higher altitudes or for semiarid areas.

- *Soil erosion prevention.* More research is needed on the role that fodder shrubs can play in curbing soil erosion. In Rwanda, fodder shrub hedges are used for making progressive terraces, which form because soil builds up behind a hedge that stops soil from moving down the hillside. Fodder shrubs are also used to stabilize existing terraces. Policy makers want to know the costs and benefits of using biological means to prevent soil erosion, such as fodder shrubs, as compared with radical terracing, in which manual labor is used to build terraces.

NOTE

1. For example, such a farm would typically have available about 500 meters of perimeter and several hundred meters in each of three other niches: along terrace edges or bunds, along internal field and homestead boundaries, and in Napier grass plots. With the recommended spacing, the needed 500 trees would occupy only 250 meters of this available space.

REFERENCES

AED (Academy for Educational Development). 2006. "SCALE: A Tool for Transformational Development." AED, Washington, DC.

Franzel, S., and C. Wambugu. 2007. "The Uptake of Fodder Shrubs among Smallholders in East Africa: Key Elements That Facilitate Widespread Adoption." In *Forages: A Pathway to Prosperity for Smallholder Farmers 2007*, ed. M. D. Hare and K. Wongpichet, 203–22. Ubon Ratchathani, Thailand: Ubon Ratchathani University.

Franzel, S., C. Wambugu, and P. Tuwei. 2003. "The Adoption and Dissemination of Fodder Shrubs in Central Kenya." AGREN Series Paper 131, Agricultural Research and Network, Overseas Development Institute, London.

Hess, H. D., T. T. Tiemann, F. Noto, S. Franzel, C. Lascano, and M. Kreuze. 2006. "The Effects of Cultivation Site on Forage Quality of *Calliandra calothyrsus* var. Patulul." *Agroforestry Systems* 68 (3): 209–20.

Koech, S. 2005. "Socioeconomic Analysis of Fodder Legumes: The Case of *Calliandra* and *Desmodium* in Smallholder Dairy Farms of Embu District, Kenya." Master's thesis, Egerton University, Njoro, Kenya.

Mawanda, F. 2004. "Socioeconomic and Farmers' Perceived Environmental Impacts of *Calliandra calothyrsus* in Uganda: A Case Study of Mukono and Kabale Districts." Master's thesis, Makerere University, Kampala.

Murithi, F. M. 1998. "Economic Evaluation of the Role of Livestock in Mixed Smallholder Farms of the Central Highlands of Kenya." Ph.D. dissertation, University of Reading, U.K.

NARP (National Agroforestry Research Project). 1993. "Kenya Agricultural Research Institute Regional Research Centre–Embu Annual Report: March 1992–April 1993." AFRENA Report 69, International Centre for Research in Agroforestry, Nairobi.

Nyaata, O. Z., M. K. O'Neill, and R. L. Roothaert. 1998. "Comparison of *Leucaena leucocephala* with *Calliandra calothyrsus* in Napier (*Pennisetum purpureum*) Fodder Banks." In *Leucaena: Adaptation Quality and Farming Systems*, ACIAR Proceedings 86, ed. H. M. Shelton, R. C. Gutteridge, B. F. Mullen, and R. A. Bray, 257–60. Canberra: Australian Centre for International Agricultural Research.

Paterson, R. T., G. M. Karanja, R. Roothaert, Z. Nyaata, and I. W. Kariuki. 1998. "A Review of Tree Fodder Production and Utilization within Smallholder Agroforestry Systems in Kenya." *Agroforestry Systems* 41 (2): 181–99.

Roothaert, R, G., M. Karanja, I. W. Kariuki, R. Paterson, P. Tuwei, E. Kiruiro, J. Mugwe, and S. Franzel. 1998. "*Calliandra* for Livestock." Technical Bulletin 1, Regional Research Centre, Embu, Kenya.

SDP (Smallholder Dairy Project). 2006. "The Uncertainty of Cattle Numbers in Kenya." SDP Policy Brief 10, SDP, International Livestock Research Institute, Nairobi, Kenya.

Staal, S. J., I. Baltenweek, M. M. Waithaka, T. de Wolf, and L. Njoroge. 2002. "Location and Uptake: Integrated Household and GIS Analysis of Technology Adoption and Land Use with Application to Smallholder Dairy Farms in Kenya." *Agricultural Economics* 27 (3): 295–315.

Wambugu, C., S. Franzel, J. Cordero, and J. Stewart. 2006. *Fodder Shrubs for Dairy Farmers in East Africa: Making Extension Decisions and Putting Them into Practice.* Nairobi: World Agroforestry Centre and Oxford Forestry Institute.

Wambugu, C., S. Franzel, P. Tuwei, and G. Karanja. 2001. "Scaling Up the Use of Fodder Trees in Central Kenya." *Development in Practice* 11: 487–94.

Winrock International Institute for Agricultural Development. 1992. *Assessment of Animal Agriculture in Sub-Saharan Africa.* Little Rock, AR: Winrock International Institute for Agricultural Development.

SUGGESTED READING

Angima, S. D., D. E. Stott, M. K. O Neill, C. K. Ong, and G. A. Weesies. 2002. "Use of *Calliandra*–Napier Grass Contour Hedges to Control Erosion in Central Kenya." *Agriculture Ecosystems and Environment* 91 (1): 15–23.

CHAPTER 5

Rainfed Dry and Cold Farming Systems

OVERVIEW

Rainfed dry or cold farming systems cover about 3.5 billion hectares, but they support a relatively modest agricultural population of 500 million. Approximately 231 million hectares of land are cultivated, of which 18 percent is irrigated. Population density is low, with 2.1 people per hectare of cultivated land.

These lower-potential systems are generally based on mixed crop-livestock or pastoral activities, merging eventually into sparse and often dispersed systems with very low productivity or potential because of environmental constraints on production. In Africa, the main crops are millet and sorghum. In the Middle East and North Africa, the system is based on wheat, barley, and a wide variety of pulses and oil crops, among others. Crop-livestock integration is important, especially when cattle are fertilizing fields while browsing on cereal straw after the harvest. In some of the systems, small-scale irrigation opportunities exist, allowing pastoralists to supplement their livelihoods in diet and income. New irrigated areas are developed in the Middle East and North Africa through new drilling and pumping technologies. Market development is limited.

The main source of vulnerability is great climatic variability and drought, leading to crop failure, weak animals, and the distress sale of assets. Population density is modest; however, pressure on the limited amount of cultivated land is very high. Overgrazing is common, resulting in low livestock productivity, environmental damage, and desertification. Poverty is extensive, often severe, and accentuated by drought.

POTENTIALS FOR POVERTY REDUCTION AND AGRICULTURAL GROWTH

The potentials for poverty reduction and for agricultural growth are modest. Rainfed dry or cold farming systems have some characteristics similar to highland rainfed systems because of the low agricultural potential and the poor marketing infrastructure. Exit from agriculture has been judged to be the most important strategy for poverty reduction, followed by increase in off-farm income and diversification.

Diversification is based on livestock, on irrigation where possible, and on improved land management that allows better resistance to climate variability. Animal productivity can be improved by better using crop residues and byproducts, by promoting locally adapted breeds, by controlling epizootic diseases, and by improving village poultry production. Support to small-scale private livestock trading has some potential. Hides and skins, for instance, are often undervalued products. There is limited potential for agricultural development, except where irrigation can be developed and where water resources are not overexploited. The development of higher-value crops, such as fruits and vegetables, is restrained because of rainfall uncertainties and relatively poor market links. Thus, a key priority is reducing the likelihood of crop failure in drought years through improved land and water management and multiplication of palatable, drought-resistant, and early-maturing crop varieties. The regeneration of forests and natural vegetation is necessary for sustainable fuelwood supply and for soil fertility management.

Integrating Land and Water Management in Smallholder Livestock Systems in Sub-Saharan Africa

Livestock perform many functions in the global economy and at the household level, such as providing food, improving economic security, enhancing crop production, generating cash income, and producing value-added goods that can have multiplier effects and create a need for services. With increasing population pressure, farmers and governments are striving to produce more food using the existing land-based resources. The result is a reduction in the land available for pasture and restrictions on the movement of animals for grazing. Increases in livestock production and productivity can be coupled with environmental sustainability if timely interventions are adopted. Without a clear strategy for the closer integration of crops and livestock, the outcome is inevitably widespread environmental degradation.

The International Institute for Land Reclamation and Improvement (ILRI) has identified resource management policy research as a key strategy. Such research includes establishing trends on how current livestock management affects resource use and conservation in the future and on how changes in government policies affecting the institutions that deal with risk, credit, commodity pricing, and macroeconomic policies influence resource use and the environment.

KEY SUSTAINABLE LAND MANAGEMENT ISSUES

Livestock perform many functions in the global economy and at the household level, such as providing food, improving economic security, enhancing crop production, generating cash income, and producing value-added goods that can

have multiplier effects and create a need for services (Sere and Steinfeld 1996).

With increasing population pressure, farmers and governments are striving to produce more food using existing land-based resources. In some regions, such as Africa and Latin America, increased food production is being achieved by expanding croplands into more marginal areas. In South and Southeast Asia, the trend is for rapid expansion of urban areas into former agricultural lands. In both cases, however, the net result is a reduction in the land available for pasture and grazing, thereby restricting the movement of animals. There are two major ways of increasing livestock productivity in the various production systems, either through intensification of systems using high-input production and management principles, including improved breeds, improved animal health, and cut-and-carry industrial systems, or through more intensively managed ranching systems. Increased livestock production and productivity could be coupled with environmental sustainability if timely interventions are adopted.

Land management invariably implies nutrient, water, and vegetation management, and sustainable land management (SLM) demands integrated technological, policy, and institutional interventions. Increases in crop yield or pasture through improved agronomic practices (for example, optimum nutrient inputs) could enhance water-use efficiency while the nutrient outflow through harvested products (for example, livestock feeding on residues) could be high.

This note does not review the available literature on livestock-environment issues but rather uses selected case studies involving livestock-water and livestock-land interactions in Sub-Saharan Africa. These cases are used to indicate potential

This note was prepared by T. Amede, International Livestock Research Institute, Addis Ababa, Ethiopia, and International Water Management Institute, Addis Ababa, Ethiopia; A. Haileslasie and D. Peden, International Livestock Research Institute, Addis Ababa, Ethiopia; S. Bekele, International Water Management Institute, Addis Ababa, Ethiopia; and M. Blümmel, International Livestock Research Institute, Addis Ababa, Ethiopia, and Hyderabad, India.

interventions that could help reduce the degradation of land and water resources in smallholder livestock systems.

Globally, livestock systems cover about 3.4 billion hectares of grazing land (Sere and Steinfeld 1996) and use feed from about 25 percent of the cropland. In 1996, about 442,884,000 metric tons of dry matter (DM) was consumed to provide the meat and milk demanded by world markets (de Haan, Steinfeld, and Blackburn 1997). In the future, even more dry matter will be needed as the demand for meat and milk increases with growing urbanization, human population growth, and increased incomes. For example, in Africa, from 2000 to 2020, ruminant populations are predicted to increase from 279 million to 409 million tropical livestock units (TLUs).[1] About half of the rangelands and a third of the mixed rainfed production systems are in Sub-Saharan Africa (Peden, Tadesse, and Misra 2007).

Livestock production systems vary greatly around the world, as do their management and the relative importance of livestock products and services. Accordingly, various combinations of production systems have evolved in different parts of the world as the result of spatial and temporal diversity in climate, population density, economic opportunities, and cultural practices (Stangel 1993). The typical sequence, however, is that as populations rise, cropping activities expand, fallow periods formerly used to restore soil fertility are no longer possible, and concurrently, cropping takes over marginal or fallow lands previously used for livestock grazing. Without a clear strategy for the closer integration of crops and livestock, the outcome is inevitably widespread environmental degradation (Tarawali and others 2001).

Although they are not entirely distinct from each other, four stages of livestock intensification processes have been observed (Ehui and others 2003; McIntire, Bourzat, and Pingali 1992). These stages dictate the positive or negative relationships between livestock- and land-based resources.

In the first stage, at low population density and abundance of land, crop and livestock activities are extensive and specialized. Limited interaction occurs between crop-livestock producers and pastoralists. In this case, the environmental effect of livestock on land management could be positive, even in areas where the resource base is marginal. Well-managed livestock will do better than crops in these marginal areas.

In the second stage, agriculture intensifies because of population growth and changes in market structures. This stage is typical in mixed-crop livestock systems of Sub-Saharan Africa, where the two components are complementary (in some cases, however, competition for land-based resources between livestock and crop enterprises can be found). This type of intense integrated crop-livestock interactions occurs in systems like the dry savanna of West Africa (Tarawali and others 2001).

In the third stage, both agriculture production and livestock production intensify. Livestock producers use more crops to produce meat and milk; crop farmers need draft power and manure to maintain their intensified cropping systems. Unless market conditions attract external inputs to restore resource balances and minimize depletion of land-based resources by farmers and livestock producers, the long-term consequence is nutrient mining and degradation of water resources.

In the fourth stage, where markets and improved technologies accompany population growth and increased labor prices, the system increasingly depends on external inputs, thereby developing more profitable specialized livestock enterprises. Where markets are weak (as in much of Sub-Saharan Africa), with increasing population pressure and declining farm size, however, even the traditional grazing areas—including steep slopes and communal lands—become converted to crop fields (although the return for investment is relatively low), thereby forcing livestock systems to use even more marginal areas. In contrast, in areas where market access for livestock products is appealing, farmers integrate multipurpose forages with both feed and soil fertility restoration value.

In general, the different livestock production systems developed in various parts of Sub-Saharan Africa are greatly influenced by the way livestock interacts with water and nutrient resources. Attempts to sustain the land resource base also vary greatly across regions, production systems, and economic incentives.

LIVESTOCK WATER AND NUTRIENT INTERACTIONS: IMPLICATIONS FOR SUSTAINABLE LAND MANAGEMENT

Livestock transform poor-quality, bulky vegetation into high-value products of economic importance and nutritional use (Delgado and others 1999). They enhance system productivity by recycling nutrients and providing manure, by supplying draft power for the crop enterprises, and by providing livelihood options. Draft animals provide about 80 percent of the power used for farming in developing countries. The byproduct of crop production (crop residue) is a principal input for livestock production, and the byproduct of livestock (manure and draft power) is a key input for the crop sector. In addition to recycling nutrients, livestock redistribute nutrients between cropland and pastureland or within the cropland between different plots (feeding livestock on agricultural residues). The complementarities between the livestock and crop subcomponents could be much higher than the potential competition between them, particularly when well-managed livestock can contribute positively to sustainable vegetation cover, improved land management, and biodiversity. Moreover, use of livestock may offset the need for petroleum for mechanized agriculture. Although a huge potential exists for a more balanced view of livestock, livelihoods, and environment, the potential role of improved livestock management in promoting SLM is neglected in the scientific and development arena.

In contrast, livestock are most frequently cited as one of the major drivers of changing land use and soil degradation (Steinfeld and others 2006), although that may not always be true in well-managed mixed crop-livestock systems of Sub-Saharan Africa. Livestock could be one of the factors contributing to off-site problems of sedimentation, carbon emissions and climate change, reduced ecosystem function, and changes in natural habitats that ultimately lead to loss of genetic stock and biodiversity, particularly in regions where the livestock density is high, the carrying capacity is low, and the livelihood options are limited.

Although erosion from croplands is commonly considered the major cause of land degradation in the African highlands, Dunstan, Matlon, and Löffler (2004) indicated that overgrazing is one of the primary causes of land degradation (49 percent) in the developing world, followed by agricultural activities (24 percent), deforestation (14 percent), and overexploitation of vegetative cover (13 percent). Land fragmentation and limited farm size also contribute to inappropriate livestock management, resulting in land degradation. High livestock density may lead to trampling, depletion and pollution of water, emission of greenhouse gases, and loss of plant and animal genetic resources (de Haan, Steinfeld, and Blackburn 1997). Livestock production also will have an off-site effect, such as the expansion and intensification of cropland to satisfy the increasing demand for feed, which in turn may lead to erosion and pollution. In crop-livestock systems, where crop production is favored in resource allocation over livestock, arable lands and fertile corners are commonly allocated for production of food crops while less fertile farm corners, hillsides, and degraded outfields are allocated for grazing and pasture. In these systems, livestock can cause huge pressure on the land by greatly reducing chances for rotation and vegetative recovery.

In response to these environmental concerns, various initiatives are being developed or proposed to adopt holistic approaches. However, the effects of livestock on dryland systems are sometimes overstated because changes in rangeland vegetation are often more affected by rainfall, soil type, and topography than by grazing (Tarawali and others 2001). Similarly, grazing could have a positive effect on soil porosity and infiltration rates in the presence of good vegetative cover, whereas the effect could be negative in overgrazed areas (Tarawali and others 2001).

Livestock provide nutrients to global agriculture equivalent to US$800 million per year (Jansen and de Wit 1996). Like that of water, nutrient flow between different ecosystem compartments is highly affected by the livestock production system. In the Sahel, Fernandez-Rivera and others (1995) indicated that if all animals in the sorghum-millet production systems were used for producing manure, manure input would range from 300 to 1,600 kilograms per hectare. The potential of manure to contribute to sustainable farming in these systems could be influenced by livestock population, spatial location of animals at manuring time, manure excretion per animal, efficiency of manure collection, and availability of feed and land resources (Tarawali and others 2001). In contrast, in semiurban small-scale livestock systems of Sub-Saharan Africa, where land is intensively cultivated and animals are stall fed, manure must be handled, stored, transported, and spread on fields. Most nutrients excreted as urine from stall-fed animals may be lost, through either volatilization or leaching. Thus, a move to more stall-feeding of animals could greatly reduce the amount of nutrients recycled to the rural agricultural systems. In extensive land-use systems, animals graze to satisfy feed requirements and are herded close to watering points. In these situations, animal manure and urine is highest in nonproductive areas, such as near watering holes, in resting areas, and along paths of animal movement. This situation results in high accumulation of nutrients in these areas and increases the risk not only of nutrient losses but also of contamination of water resources.

Global livestock population requires considerable amounts of water; however, the estimation of these requirements is crude (Peden, Tadesse, and Misra 2007). Water constitutes about 60 to 70 percent of animal liveweight. Livestock maintain this level by drinking, consuming moisture-laden feed, and capturing metabolic water (from intercellular respiration). The major nutrients required for metabolic function of livestock come from feed, voluntary water intake, and the atmosphere (for example, oxygen). Livestock lose water and nutrients to the subsystem in the form of evaporation, urine, feces, lactation, and respiration. Depending on the scale, these losses could be inputs for other nonlivestock system components as organic fertilizers.

When thinking about livestock and water, most people visualize the direct consumption of drinking water. Evidence suggests that voluntary water intake ranges between 25 and 50 liters per TLU per day (Peden, Tadesse, and Misra 2007). This volume varies greatly by species and breed, ambient temperature, water quality, level and water content of feed, and animal activity. In terms of volume, the most important interaction of water and livestock is through evapotranspiration processes in producing animal feed. In the tropics, animals usually consume (in kilograms of DM per day) between 1.5 and 3.5 percent of their body weight, depending on the quality of the diet, feed availability, environmental conditions, and other factors. If one assumes about 0.5 kilogram cubic meters of rangeland water productivity, water required to produce maintenance feed for one TLU is 100 times more than the water required for drinking. Less than half of the plant material is eaten by animals and about half of what is eaten is returned to the soil as manure (if the animals are in pastureland). Thus, only about 25 percent of pasture could go to animals, and the rest could support ecosystem services.

In general, the farming sector is under huge pressure to produce more crop and animal products per units of water and nutrient investment. Livestock subsystems, which strongly interact with crop and other system components across fields, farms, and landscapes, should be efficient users of resources if the food demand by the growing population is to be satisfied and the environmental services are to be sustained. Therefore, an integrated systems approach that minimizes competition for land-based resources between different system subcomponents needs to be adopted, and interventions must be introduced that would create win-win situations for enhancing livestock water and nutrient productivity at various scales.

LESSONS LEARNED

Water productivity describes the production of more economic agricultural products per unit of water, expressed in terms of product per units of evapotranspiration (Rockström, Barron, and Fox 2003). Peden, Tadesse, and Misra (2007) suggested the following four major strategies to enhance livestock-water productivity:

1. Improving feed strategies by promoting nongrain feed sources with high water productivity, using crop residues and byproducts as feed, and adopting practices that encourage more uniform grazing
2. Conserving water by managing animals in a way that reduces land and water degradation (such as overgraz-

ing, erosion, and nutrient depletion), including adopting nutrient recycling principles
3. Enhancing animal productivity through better livestock health, nutrition, and animal husbandry practices
4. Providing adequate quality of drinking water synchronized with available feed.

Additional interventions that would enhance livestock-water productivity include increasing the availability of mineral blocks in pastures and water, improving the digestibility of low-quality crop residue, and mixing livestock feed strategically.

Furthermore, livestock interventions to reverse degraded lands in small-scale livestock systems include the following:

■ Gaining the confidence of community experimenters
■ Minimizing soil erosion of grazing and pasturelands through physical and biological measures
■ Increasing soil organic matter through improved forages, improved management of pasturelands, and improved manure and crop residues
■ Improving the water budget of the system through water conservation measures
■ Increasing the nutrient status of the soil through improved nutrient recycling and application of key nutrients
■ Adopting integrated approaches enhancing the productivity of the crop-livestock systems, particularly through improved livestock management.

OPPORTUNITIES FOR SCALING UP LIVESTOCK SYSTEMS USING INTEGRATED LAND AND NATURAL RESOURCE APPROACHES

The following interventions, which emerged from the research work of national, regional, and international research institutions in East Africa, could address the growing concerns of livestock-environment interaction at farm and higher scales and are envisaged from the perspective of harmonizing livestock to the existing crop-livestock systems of Sub-Saharan Africa. Feed and fodder requirements for livestock present the crucial interface at which positive and negative of effects of livestock are decided. Feed and fodder obviously drive livestock productivity, and they are commonly the major input factor deciding the economic return from animal husbandry. Ingested feed and fodder carbon and nitrogen inefficiently converted into meat and milk contribute substantially to greenhouse gases (Blümmel, Krishna, and Ørskov 2001).

The following approaches to promoting efficient feeding strategies have shown promise for scaling up:

- *Legume forage banks.* From the early 1980s, the International Institute of Tropical Agriculture and the International Livestock Research Centre for Africa (the current ILRI) promoted alley cropping and forage banks—with multipurpose legume shrubs as key strategies—to boost livestock production and improve soil fertility through nitrogen fixation and addition of nutrients supplied as green manures or mulch.

- *Integrating food-feed crops.* Generally, where land and water are allocated and used exclusively for fodder production, the efficiency of conversion of natural resources into livestock product is low (even though absolute livestock production might be high). A range of management options exist for increasing biomass production in mixed crop-livestock systems. They include intercropping, thinning out of densely planted crops, and of course, fertilizer application (Blümmel, Krishna, and Ørskov 2001). For instance, in the dry savanna of West Africa, Tarawali and others (2001) reported that 1 hectare of improved cowpeas could benefit a farmer by an extra 50 kilograms of meat per year from better-nourished animals and also produce an additional 300 kilograms of cereal grains as a result of improved soil fertility.

- *Increasing livestock feed by growing crop mixtures.* Crop mixtures reduce risk in drought-prone areas (such as much of Sub-Saharan Africa). For example, where forage legumes are relay cropped with another crop, the legumes may still yield a useful harvest after the drought-affected crop or the early-maturing component is harvested. Preliminary empirical findings show that the relay-cropped forage can produce up to 4 metric tons of DM per hectare of high-quality fodder using the residual moisture and nutrients, without competing with the main food or cash crop and thus not interfering with the production objectives of farmers. This finding suggests increased water productivity at farm and higher scales.

- *Forage legumes in degraded farms and systems (decision guides).* Producers using crop-livestock systems need reliable and accurate information on where to grow forages, on the costs and benefits (both long- and short-term) of introducing forage legumes into their systems, and on how to identify the spatial and temporal niches for integration of forages with win-win benefits of soil fertility restoration, erosion control, increased vegetative cover, and minimized land degradation. Decision guides that could help farmers and development actors to target

legume interventions have been tested across communities and systems and are currently available.

- *Soil and water conservation as niches for integration of forages.* Protecting upper watersheds is important not only for preserving sustainable flow of water to downstream users but also for minimizing land degradation and erosion of soils and biodiversity. Besides minimizing erosion and runoff, these interventions became important niches for integration of livestock feed in various systems. The multiple use of forages as biological stabilizers and sources of high-quality feed, particularly for calves and milking cows during the dry season, is a very important incentive for integration and promotion of forages.

- *Zai systems as forage niches.* Livestock water and nutrient productivity could be enhanced through adoption of water- and nutrient-saving technologies, particularly in degraded farms and landscape niches. *Zai* is a water and nutrient harvesting intervention that was developed by farmers in Burkina Faso in response to the recurrent drought of the 1970s and 1980s. When farmers planted forages (for example, vetch, Napier grass) treated by zai pits, forage yield was increased as much as 10–fold. Tuber yields of potatoes increased about fivefold compared to untreated plots. The benefits were highest in degraded farms and systems.

- *Increasing livestock feed through spot application of fertilizers.* In the dryland, mixed crop-livestock systems of Sub-Saharan Africa, crop and livestock productivity is constrained not only by shortage of water but also by nutrient deficiency. At Sadore, Niger, where the annual average rainfall is 560 millimeters, not using fertilizers resulted in a harvest of 1.24 kilograms of pearl millet grain per millimeter of water, whereas using fertilizers resulted in the harvest of 4.14 kilograms of millet grain per millimeter of water (ICRISAT 1985).

- *Improved manure management.* Manure is a key resource for reversing land degradation and improving soil water-holding capacity, thereby enhancing water productivity. Producers can adopt several practical interventions to improve the quality of the manure generated by livestock. Runoff can be prevented from passing across the feedlot surface by installing up-gradient ditches to reduce significantly the volume of wastewater; storage lagoons and holding ponds can be used to contain excess wastewater; manure can be stockpiled at a safe distance away from any water supply; and grass filter strips, filter fencing, or straw bales can filter solids and nutrients in runoff. Composting manure will help reduce volume and enhance the value and acceptance of manure as a source of plant nutrients. The efficiency of manure is also improved when manure use is combined with water conservation technologies, such as zai pits.

- *Outfield grazing management on water and nutrient resources.* Free grazing systems, which are common in pastoral and mixed crop-livestock systems of Sub-Saharan Africa and South Asia, are considered a major cause of land degradation and depletion of water resources. Experience of the African highlands initiative indicates that the following approaches can significantly improve sustainability of outfield grazing: (a) introducing fast-growing forages as forage banks, particularly in homestead areas, improving crop residue management, and introducing rotational pasture management; (b) assisting communities in identifying spatial and temporal niches for forages and in accessing technologies to increase feed production and livestock productivity; and (c) assisting communities in developing local rules and bylaws to guide the management of free grazing.

RECOMMENDATIONS FOR PRACTITIONERS AND POLICY MAKERS

In general, policy makers have not considered the effect of livestock on land productivity as a policy objective in itself but merely as an input for achieving other policy objectives. Land degradation is not seen as posing a serious policy concern unless it threatens livelihood and immediate regional and national objectives (Scherr 1999). The ongoing challenge is therefore to identify policies, institutions, and technologies that will enhance the positive and mitigate the negative effects of livestock on the environment. ILRI has identified resource management policy research as a key strategy (Ehui and others 2003). This strategy includes establishing trends on how current livestock management affects resource use and conservation in the future and on how changes in government policies affect those institutions in terms of risk sharing, credit, commodity pricing, and selected macroeconomic policies on resource use and the environment. The most relevant policy area related to SLM is the policy framework. It should promote the mitigation of negative effects of livestock production on environmental health, including the following:

- Integrate livestock in designing irrigation and other water-related development projects. The current policy of Sub-Saharan African countries is biased toward crop production, but livestock drinking and feeding are not part of the design of irrigation projects. Integrating livestock in the wider water development agenda will boost livestock-water productivity and promote SLM.
- Promote integrated crop-livestock systems, whereby crop and livestock enterprises are complementary, resource recycling is practiced, water depletion and nutrient mining are minimized, and key critical external inputs are introduced.
- Encourage participatory policy formulation to regulate stocking rates in pastoral systems, and allocate land to groups that will enhance resource-use efficiency.
- Promote well-managed corralling, based on keeping livestock on selected areas over a given time period to provide fertilizer for crops while reducing nutrient losses from manures through volatilization and runoff.
- Employ full cost recovery for developing water points and animal health services to encourage livestock keepers to adjust stocking rates to the carrying capacity of the system.
- Promote access to water points and feed resources across scales, particularly for the poor, as an incentive to promote gender equity and improve land and water management practices. Poor farmers may be willing to invest labor and other resources to guarantee the sustainable productivity of their limited number of livestock.

INVESTMENT NEEDS

- Promoting small-scale irrigation through diversions, water harvesting, and groundwater use, with due consideration to environmental consequences and upstream-downstream relationships, could be an important policy strategy to improve livestock-environment interaction. Increased access to irrigation will increase feed availability from crop fields, forages, grasslands, and other niches that will reduce the grazing pressure on marginal lands.
- Incentives for strategically located markets and value-added processing to facilitate livestock sales and thus match livestock resource (that is, feed and water) demands pressure on carrying capacity of the natural resources base.

NOTE

1. A TLU is equivalent to 250 kilograms liveweight.

REFERENCES

Blümmel, M., N. Krishna, and E. R. Ørskov. 2001. "Supplementation Strategies for Optimizing Ruminal Carbon and Nitrogen Utilization: Concepts and Approaches." In *Review Papers: Proceedings of the 10th Animal Nutrition Conference, Karnal, India,* November 9–11, 2001, 10–23. Karnal, India: Animal Nutrition Society of India.

de Haan, C., H. Steinfeld, and H. Blackburn. 1997. *Livestock and the Environment: Finding a Balance.* Report of a study sponsored by the Commission of the European Communities; the World Bank; and the governments of Denmark, France, Germany, the Netherlands, United Kingdom, and United States. Suffolk, U.K.: WRENmedia.

Delgado, C., M. Rosegrant, H. Steinfeld, S. Ehui, and C. Courbois. 1999. "Livestock 2020: The Next Food Revolution." FAO Discussion Paper 28, Food and Agriculture Organization, Rome.

Dunstan, S. C. S., P. J. Matlon, and H. Löffler. 2004. "Realizing the Promise of African Agriculture." Background Paper 1, InterAcademy Council, Amsterdam, Netherlands.

Ehui, S. K., M. M. Ahmed, B. Gebremedhin, S. E. Benin, N. A. Nin-Pratt, and M. L. Lapar. 2003. *Ten Years of Livestock Policy Analysis: Policies for Improving Productivity, Competitiveness, and Sustainable Livelihoods of Smallholder Livestock Producers.* Nairobi: International Livestock Research Institute.

Fernandez-Rivera, S., T. O. Williams, P. Hiernaux, and J. M. Powell. 1995. "Livestock, Feed, and Manure Availability in Semi-Arid West Africa." In *Livestock and Sustainable Nutrient Cycling in Mixed Farming Systems of Sub-Saharan Africa, Volume 2, Technical Papers, Proceedings of an International Conference, November 22–26, 1993,* ed. J. M. Powell, S. Fernandez-Rivera, T. O. Williams, and C. Renard, 149–70. Addis Ababa: International Livestock Research Centre for Africa.

ICRISAT (International Crops Research Institute for the Semi-Arid Tropics). 1985. *Annual Report, 1984.* Niamey, Niger: ICRISAT.

Jansen, J. C. M., and J. de Wit. 1996. *Livestock and the Environment: Finding a Balance—Environmental Impact Assessment of Livestock Production in Mixed Irrigated Systems in the Sub-humid Zones.* Wageningen, Netherlands: International Agriculture Centre.

McIntire, J., D. Bourzat, and P. Pingali. 1992. *Crop-Livestock Interaction in Sub-Saharan Africa.* Washington, DC: World Bank.

Peden, D., G. Tadesse, and A. K. Misra. 2007. "Water and Livestock for Human Development." In *Water for Food, Water for Life: A Comprehensive Assessment of Water Management in Agriculture,* ed. D. Molden, 485–514. London: Earthscan.

Rockström, J., J. Barron, and P. Fox. 2003. "Water Productivity in Rainfed Agriculture: Challenges and Opportunities for Smallholder Farmers in Drought-Prone Tropical Agro-Ecosystems." In *Water Productivity in Agriculture: Limits and Opportunities for Improvement,* ed. J. W. Kijne, R. Barker, and D. Molden, 145–63. Wallingford, U.K.: CAB International.

Scherr, S. J. 1999. "Past and Present Effects of Soil Degradation." IFPRI 2020 Discussion Paper 27. International Food Policy Research Institute, Washington, DC.

Sere, C., and H. Steinfeld. 1996. "World Livestock Production Systems: Current Status, Issues and Trends." Animal Production and Health Paper 127, Food and Agriculture Organization, Rome.

Stangel, P. J. 1993. "Nutrient Cycling and Its Importance in Sustaining Crop/Livestock Systems in Sub-Saharan Africa: An Overview." In *Livestock and Sustainable Nutrient Cycling in Mixed Farming Systems of Sub-Saharan Africa, Volume 1: Conference Summary, Proceedings of an International Conference, November 22–26, 1993,* ed. J. M. Powell, S. Fernandez-Rivera, and T. O. Williams, 37–57. Addis Ababa: International Livestock Research Centre for Africa.

Steinfeld, H., P. Gerber, T. Wassenaar, V. Castel, M. Roslaes, and C. de Haan. 2006. *Livestock's Long Shadow: Environmental Issues and Options.* Rome: Food and Agriculture Organization.

Tarawali, S. A., A. Larbi, S. Fernandez-Rivera, and A. Bationo. 2001. "The Contribution of Livestock to Soil Fertility." In *Sustaining Soil Fertility in West Africa,* ed. G. Tian, J. L. Hatfield, and F. Ishida, 281–304. Madison, WI: Soil Science Society of America and American Society of Agronomy.

SUGGESTED READING

Molden, D. J. 2007. *Water for Food, Water for Life: A Comprehensive Assessment of Water Management in Agriculture.* London: Earthscan. http://www.iwmi.cgiar.org/assessment/.

Integrated Nutrient Management in the Semiarid Tropics

Increasing needs of food, feed, and fiber for the ever-increasing population in the semiarid tropical regions of the developing world are putting pressure on the rainfed areas to make a greater contribution from the vast area under dryland agriculture. The smallholder farmers rely on dryland subsistence productivity for their livelihood, but the productivity of dryland systems remains low because of low and erratic distribution of rainfall coupled with low to negligible inputs of nutrients. Moreover, maintenance of soil organic matter is a challenge because of competing uses for organic and crop residues. Organic matter is not just the source of nutrients; it is essential for preserving the physical, chemical, and biological integrity of the soil so that the soil can perform productivity and environment-related functions on a continuing basis. With little investment in the management of soils, large areas under dryland agriculture are in various stages of physical, chemical, and biological degradation. Strategies that can achieve sustainable improvement in dryland productivity by facilitating an integrated land and water management and conservation approach are highlighted, along with a special focus on integrated nutrient management (INM) of soil.

KEY SUSTAINABLE LAND MANAGEMENT ISSUES

Farm holdings in the subarid tropics not only are distinct in terms of size, shape, and location on a toposequence but also vary widely in the cropping patterns and the quality and quantity of nutrients used for crop production. A major constraint is the timely availability of knowledge and the right information about soil health for the farmers (Singh and others 2004). Farmers do not know what is ailing their farm in general. Establishing high-quality soil analytical laboratories in each district of a state is of utmost importance so that timely and correct information can be provided to the farmers relating to the diagnosis of soil fertility constraints (Wani and others 2003, 2005).

Apart from water shortage, the productivity in rainfed systems is constrained by low soil fertility. The soils in the subarid tropical regions generally have low organic matter and nutrient reserves. Soil erosion removes the top soil layer, which results not only in loss of soil but also in loss of organic matter and plant nutrients, which largely are stored in the top soil layer (Wani and others 2003). Among the major nutrients, nitrogen is universally deficient; phosphorus deficiency ranks second only to nitrogen in most subarid tropical soils. The work of the International Crops Research Institute for the Semi-Arid Tropics (ICRISAT) has shown that potassium reserves in subarid tropical soils are generally adequate (Rego and others 2007). Most subarid tropical soils have low to moderate phosphorus sorption capacity, and most of the rainfed systems require low to moderate rates of phosphorus applications to meet their phosphorus requirements when residual benefits are also considered (Sahrawat 1999, 2000; Sahrawat and others 1995). Many farmers' fields in the subarid tropical regions of India are deficient in secondary nutrients and micronutrients. ICRISAT's extensive survey of farmers' fields in the subarid tropical regions of India revealed that deficiencies of sulfur, boron, and zinc are very widespread, and in most cases 80 to 100 percent of farmers' fields were critically deficient in these nutrients (table 5.1) (Rego and others 2007).

LESSONS LEARNED

Several microorganisms in the soil decompose plant and animal residues, and several groups of microorganisms are involved in important biological processes. Microorganisms

This note was prepared by S. P. Wani, K. L. Sahrawat, and C. Srinivasa Rao, International Crops Research Institute for the Semi-Arid Tropics.

District	Number of fields	Type of measurement	pH	Organic carbon (g kg⁻¹)	Total nitrogen (g kg⁻¹)	Olsen-P test (mg kg⁻¹)	Exchange potassium (mg kg⁻¹)	Extractable nutrient elements (mg kg⁻¹)		
								Sulfur	Boron	Zinc
Nalgonda	256	Range	5.7–9.2	1.2–13.6	144–947	0.7–37.6	34–784	1.4–93.0	0.02–1.48	0.08–16.00
		Mean	7.7	4.0	410	8.5	135	7.00	0.26	0.73
		Percentage deficient[a]						86	93	73
Mahabubnagar	359	Range	5.5–9.1	0.8–12.0	123–783	0.7–61.0	25–487	1.1–44.0	0.02–1.62	0.12–35.60
		Mean	7.1	3.6	342	9.1	117	11.5	0.22	1.34
		Percentage deficient[a]						73	94	62
Kurnool	309	Range	5.6–9.7	0.9–10.6	26–966	0.4–36.4	33–508	1.3–68.2	0.04–1.64	0.08–4.92
		Mean	7.8	3.4	295	7.9	142	5.6	0.34	0.42
		Percentage deficient[a]						88	83	94

Table 5.1 Chemical Characteristics of 924 Soil Samples Collected from Farmers' Fields in Three Districts of Andhra Pradesh, India, 2002–04

Source: Authors' elaboration.

Note: g kg⁻¹ = grams per kilogram of the sample; mg kg⁻¹= milligrams per kilogram of the sample.

a. Represents the critical limits in the soil used: 8–10 mg kg⁻¹ for calcium chloride extractable sulfur; 0.58 mg kg⁻¹ for hot water extractable boron; 0.75 mg kg⁻¹ for DTPA (diethylene triamine pentaacetic acid) extractable zinc.

regulate nutrient flow in the soil by assimilating nutrients and producing soil biomass (immobilization) and by converting carbon, nitrogen, phosphorus, and sulfur to mineral forms (mineralization). Among the important findings were the following:

- *Symbiotic nitrogen fixers.* A symbiotic partnership between bacteria (*Rhizobium* and *Bradyrhizobium*) and legumes contributes substantially (up to 450 kilograms of nitrogen per hectare per year) to total biological nitrogen fixation (BNF).
- *Nonsymbiotic and associative nitrogen fixers.* Inoculation with bacteria (*Aztobacter* and *Azospirillum*) reduces the nitrogen requirement of cereals or nonlegume crops up to 20 kilograms per hectare.
- *Plant growth–promoting rhizobacteria.* These bacteria improve plant growth through hormonal effects and reduce disease severity.
- *Phosphate-solubilizing microorganisms.* These bacteria and fungi solubilize inorganic phosphates and make them available to plants in usable form.
- *Vesicular-arbuscular mycorrhizae.* These fungi help increase uptake of nutrients such as phosphorus, sulfur, and copper and improve plant growth.

BIOLOGICAL NITROGEN FIXATION

BNF is an economically attractive and ecologically sound process and is an integral part of nitrogen cycling in nature. *Rhizobium* inoculation is practiced to ensure adequate nodulation and BNF. Efficient strains of *Rhizobium* and

Bradyrhizobium supplied as inoculants are used as biofertilizers by seed or soil inoculation.

Recent results from a long-term study conducted under rainfed conditions on a vertisol for 12 years demonstrated that the inclusion of grain legumes such as pigeonpeas and chickpeas in the production systems not only provided extra income but also increased the productivity of succeeding or intercropped cereal such as sorghum and maize. Such systems also maintained the soil nitrogen status (Rego and Nagewara 2000). Nitrogen mineralization potential of soil under legume-based systems was twofold higher than under a cereal-cereal system (Wani and others 1995). Another long-term study showed that in cropping systems involving legumes, land and water management factors, such as the broad-bed and furrow landform and use of inorganic fertilizers, increased the organic matter, increased available nitrogen and phosphorus status of soils, and improved soil physical and biological properties (table 5.2). Results also showed that in the improved system higher carbon was sequestered and the biological properties of the soil were improved, which led to higher productivity of systems and higher carrying capacity of land (both of people and of animals). The application of phosphorus to the improved system increased the amount of carbon sequestered by 7.4 tons of carbon per hectare in 24 years (Wani and others 2003).

OPPORTUNITIES FOR SUSTAINABLE LAND MANAGEMENT: PRODUCTS AND SERVICES

Enhancing and sustaining agricultural productivity and food security in the subarid tropics requires adopting INM

Table 5.2 Biological and Chemical Properties of Semiarid Tropical Vertisols

Properties	System	Soil depth (cm)		SE±
		0–60	60–120	
Soil respiration (kg C/hectare)	Improved	723	342	7.8
	Traditional	260	98	
Microbial biomass carbon (kg C/hectare)	Improved	2,676	2,137	48.0
	Traditional	1,462	1,088	
Organic carbon (tons C/hectare)	Improved	27.4	19.4	0.89
	Traditional	21.4	18.1	
Mineral nitrogen (kg N/hectare)	Improved	28.2	10.3	2.88
	Traditional	15.4	26.0	
Net nitrogen mineralization (kg N/hectare)	Improved	−3.3	−6.3	4.22
	Traditional	32.6	15.4	
Microbial biomass nitrogen (kg N/hectare)	Improved	86.4	39.2	2.3
	Traditional	42.1	25.8	
Nonmicrobial organic nitrogen (kg N/hectare)	Improved	2,569	1,879	156.9
	Traditional	2,218	1,832	
Total nitrogen (kg N/hectare)	Improved	2,684	1,928	156.6
	Traditional	2,276	1,884	
Olsen P test (kg P/hectare)	Improved	6.1	1.6	0.36
	Traditional	1.5	1.0	

Source: ICRISAT.

Note: SE = standard error of mean; C = carbon; N = nitrogen; P = phosphorus; kg = kilogram. The data are for 1998, after 24 years of cropping under improved and traditional systems in catchments at the ICRISAT Center in Patancheru, India.

strategy. INM strategy includes maintenance or adjustment of soil fertility and plant nutrient supply to sustain the desired level of crop productivity, using all available sources of nutrients (for example, soil organic matter, soil reserves, BNF, organic manures, mineral fertilizers, and nutrients) supplied through precipitation and irrigation water. INM is a holistic approach focusing on the cropping system rather than on individual crops. INM focuses on the farming system rather than on individual fields. It does not preclude the use of renewable nutrient sources such as BNF and organic manures and minimal use of mineral fertilizers.

Organic matter is not just the reservoir of plant nutrients. Organic matter favorably influences physical and biological properties and productivity of soils. High prevailing temperatures in the tropics, coupled with low net primary productivity in the dry regions, results in low organic matter reserves in the SAT soils.

Organic manures are of two types:

- *Bulky.* These manures include farmyard manure, composts (rural and town), and crop residues
- *Concentrated.* These manures include oilcakes, poultry manure, and slaughterhouse waste.

Farmyard manure is the most commonly used organic manure, particularly for high-value crops. It is prepared from animal-shed wastes and crop residues, including stover, and contains 0.5 to 1.0 percent nitrogen, 0.05 to 0.07 percent phosphorus, and 0.03 to 0.35 percent potassium. Crop residues can be recycled by composting, vermicomposting, mulching, and direct incorporation. Because of their low nitrogen content, organic manures are less efficient than mineral fertilizers; however, combined use of these nutrient sources is superior to using mineral fertilizer or organic manure alone. A combination of crop residue restitution (based on availability), fallowing, and green manuring can be used to maintain organic matter levels in the soil.

On farms as well as in homes, large quantities of organic wastes are generated regularly. Besides agricultural wastes, large quantities of domestic wastes are generated in cities and rural areas that are burned or put in landfills. These valuable nutrients in residues could instead be effectively used for increasing agricultural productivity by using earthworms to convert the residues into a valuable source of plant nutrients (table 5.3). The process of preparing valuable manure from all kinds of organic residues with the help of earthworms is called *vermicomposting* and this manure is called *vermicompost.*

Vermicompost can be prepared from all types of organic residues, such as agricultural residues, sericultural residues, animal manures, dairy and poultry wastes, food industry wastes, municipal solid wastes, biogas sludge, and bagasse from sugarcane factories. Vermicompost can be prepared by

Table 5.3	Nutrient Composition of Vermicompost	
Nutrient element	**Vermicompost (%)**	
Organic carbon	9.8–13.4	
Nitrogen	0.51–1.61	
Phosphorus	0.19–1.02	
Potassium	0.15–0.73	
Calcium	1.18–7.61	
Magnesium	0.093–0.568	
Sodium	0.058–0.158	
Zinc	0.0042–0.110	
Copper	0.0026–0.0048	
Iron	0.2050–1.3313	
Manganese	0.0105–0.2038	

Source: ICRISAT.

different methods in shaded areas, such as (a) on the floor in a heap, (b) in pits up to 1 meter deep, (c) in an enclosure with a wall 1 meter high constructed with soil and rocks or brick material or cement, and (d) in cement rings. The procedure for preparation of vermicompost is similar for all methods.

Vermicompost can be used on agricultural, horticultural, ornamental, and vegetable crops at any stage of the crop. Vermicompost is a rich source of major and micro plant nutrients (see table 5.3) and can be applied in varying doses in the field.

RATIONALE FOR INVESTMENT

On-farm studies made on smallholder farms for three seasons in the subarid tropical region of Zimbabwe showed that applications of fertilizer nitrogen (8.5 kilograms nitrogen per hectare) in combination with manure application at 3 or 6 tons per hectare have the potential to improve the livelihoods of farmers. The maize yields of the crop were dramatically increased by the applications of manure and nitrogen in small doses (Ncube and others 2007).

ICRISAT's recent on-farm research in the subarid tropical regions of India showed that balanced nutrition of rainfed crops is crucial for sustainable increase in productivity and maintenance of fertility. For example, in the subarid tropical regions of India where most farmers' fields were found deficient not only in nitrogen and phosphorus but also in sulfur, boron, and zinc, the application of sulfur, boron, and zinc with nitrogen and phosphorus significantly increased the yield (by 30 to 120 percent) of field crops, including sorghum, maize, castor, sunflower, and groundnut (Rego and others 2007).

RECOMMENDATIONS FOR PRACTITIONERS

Rainfed production systems have two major constraints: water shortages and general low soil fertility. To make these systems sustainable at reasonable productivity levels, farmers need to integrate soil and water-conserving practices with balanced nutrition of crops by adopting INM. The knowledge available about different sources of nutrients, such as BNF, organic manures, and mineral fertilizers, can be used to develop a suitable strategy for INM to sustain crop productivity. INM strategy is realistic, attractive, and friendly to the environment. INM will enhance the efficiency of biological, organic, and mineral inputs for sustaining productivity of subarid tropical soils. Judicious and balanced use of nutrients from biological sources, mineral fertilizers, and organic matter is a prerequisite for making rainfed agriculture efficient through increased efficiency of rainfall use. Specific recommendations include the following:

- Recognize that different crops require different rhizobia.
- Select the right type of biofertilizer (inoculant).
- Use fresh inoculant that is within the limit of its expiration date.
- Use well-tested inoculants produced by reputable manufacturers.
- In India, insist on high-quality inoculants with the Indian Standards Institution (ISI) mark.
- Prepare inoculum slurry by using a sticking agent such as jaggery, rice porridge, or gum arabic.
- Mix seeds with inoculum slurry by hand.
- Dry seeds on a plastic sheet kept under a shade.
- Sow seeds within 48 hours after inoculation.
- Use high nitrogen-fixing crops or varieties.
- Practice mixed and intercropping agriculture (that is, row and strip) with legumes.
- Use appropriate tillage practices, landform treatments, and nutrient amendments.
- Use appropriate mineral fertilizers in amounts to meet the nutrients requirements.
- Ensure that efficiency of applied fertilizers is optimized through adoption of suitable practices:
  - Form or type—as recommended for the crop
  - Method—furrow placement and covering with soil instead of broadcasting
  - Time—splitting of nitrogen doses instead using one application
  - Quantity—just sufficient to meet plant demand without adversely affecting BNF
- Undertake detailed soil analysis to identify soil fertility constraints limiting crop production.

- Develop suitable nutrient management recommendations from soil analysis results and share that knowledge with the farmers, stressing the need for adoption of INM to maintain fertility and productivity.
- Optimize and harness full potential of available biological and organic sources and use chemical fertilizers to supplement the gap in the nutrient requirements of the production system.
- Adopt an integrated strategy rather than a piecemeal approach for sustainable development (for example, for most land management issues, addressing water management, fertility management, pest management, and improved cultivars is also necessary because all these components are synergistically interlinked with sustainable land management).

INVESTMENT NEEDS BY LOCAL AND NATIONAL GOVERNMENTS OR OTHER DONORS

- Investments are urgently needed to help establish high-quality, reliable, and functional soil-plant analytical laboratories in developing countries. The cost to provide analytical support for analysis of soil and plant samples could range from US$20,000 to US$100,000, depending on the extent of automation and the number of samples to be analyzed in a year.
- Enhancing awareness among the farmers, development agents, and policy makers to discuss soil quality and to adopt sustainable INM practices is necessary. If land degradation is to be minimized, continued investments in capacity building and training of personnel involved are needed.
- Investments to enhance the use of biological and organic resources through incentives for increased adoption are needed for sustainable land management.

POLICY RECOMMENDATIONS

- Enable policies and incentive mechanisms for greater adoption of INM practices.
- Establish appropriate institutions that can ensure timely availability to farmers of high-quality products and knowledge about those products and sustainable INM practices.
- Enable policies and mechanisms to produce, distribute, and use various sources of different plant nutrients.

REFERENCES

Ncube, B., J. P. Dimes, S. J. Twomlow, W. Mupangwa, and K. E. Giller. 2007. "Raising the Productivity of Smallholder Farms under Semi-arid Conditions by Use of Small Doses of Manure and Nitrogen: A Case of Participatory Research." *Agroecosystems* 77 (1): 53–67.

Rego, T. J., and V. Nageswara. 2000. "Long-Term Effects of Grain Legumes on Rainy Season Sorghum Productivity in a Semi-arid Tropical Vertisol." *Experimental Agriculture* 36 (2): 205–21.

Rego, T. J., K. L. Sahrawat, S. P. Wani, and G. Pardhasaradhi. 2007. "Widespread Deficiencies of Sulfur, Boron, and Zinc in Indian Semi-arid Tropical Soils: On-Farm Crop Responses." *Journal of Plant Nutrition* 30 (10): 1569–83.

Sahrawat, K. L. 1999. "Assessing the Fertilizer Phosphorus Requirement of Grain Sorghum." *Communications in Soil Science and Plant Analysis* 30 (11–12): 1593–601.

———. 2000. "Residual Phosphorus and Management Strategy for Grain Sorghum on a Vertisol." *Communications in Soil Science and Plant Analysis* 31 (19–20): 3103–12.

Sahrawat, K. L., T. J. Rego, J. R. Burford, M. H., Rahman, J. K. Rao, and A. Adam. 1995. "Response of Sorghum to Fertilizer Phosphorus and Its Residual Value in a Vertisol." *Fertilizer Research* 41 (1): 41–47.

Singh, H. P., K. D. Sharma, R. G. Subba, and K. L. Sharma. 2004. "Dryland Agriculture in India." In *Challenges and Strategies for Dryland Agriculture,* ed. S. Rao and J. Ryan, 67–92. Madison, WI: Crop Science of America and American Society of Agronomy.

Wani, S. P., P. Pathak, L. S. Jangawad, H. Eswaran, and P. Singh. 2003. "Improved Management of Vertisols in the Semiarid Tropics for Increased Productivity and Soil Carbon Sequestration." *Soil Use and Management* 19 (3): 217–22.

Wani, S. P., T. J. Rego, S. Rajeswari, and K. K. Lee. 1995. "Effect of Legume-Based Cropping Systems on Nitrogen Mineralization Potential of Vertisol." *Plant and Soil* 175 (2): 265–74.

Wani, S. P., P. Singh, R. S. Dwivedi, R. R. Navalgund, and A. Ramakrishna. 2005. "Biophysical Indicators of Agroecosystem Services and Methods for Monitoring the Impacts of NRM Technologies at Different Scale." In *Methods for Assessing Economic and Environmental Impacts,* ed. B. Shiferaw, H. A. Freeman, and S. M. Swinton, 23–54. Wallingford, U.K.: CAB International.

INVESTMENT NOTE 5.3

Integrated Natural Resource Management for Enhanced Watershed Function and Improved Livelihoods in the Semiarid Tropics

The community watershed model has become popular because it brings together, as a package for rural development, the best expertise available locally and from all the consortium partners. The model uses the microwatershed as a geographic unit for soil and water conservation and management, and the effect is strengthened with improved agronomical practices and diversified income-generating activities. Water management is used as an entry point for enhancing agricultural productivity and rural incomes. The consortium's approach aims to showcase increased incomes for villagers. When the villagers are convinced that the innovations improve their livelihood security, they become ambassadors of the cause, convincing neighboring villages to practice community watershed development technologies.

The success of the Kothapally example has led to the acceptance of the watershed approach in large areas of India, as well as in China, Thailand, and Vietnam. Countries and agencies in Sub-Saharan Africa are also becoming involved.

The data show that with the community watershed approach, productivity and incomes can be doubled through collective action and knowledge-based management of natural resources. Water management is just an entry point and not an end in itself. Community watershed development needs to go further and adopt the livelihood approach with technical backstopping from multidisciplinary teams from different institutions working together in a consortium to harness the benefits of a holistic integrated genetic and natural resource management (IGNRM) approach through empowerment of stakeholders.

INTRODUCTION

In rainfed tropical areas of Asia and Africa, natural resources are severely degraded because of soil erosion, nutrient mining, depleted groundwater levels, waterlogging, and removal of vegetative cover. Although drylands have sustained large populations, many dryland areas are increasingly showing up as hotspots of poverty and malnutrition. In addition, many such areas are predicted to face more frequent and severe droughts because of increasing climate variability and eventual change (Wani and others 2002). Monsoon rains are erratic, and a few torrential downpours[1] cause severe runoff, which removes nutrient- and carbon-rich topsoil, thereby contributing to land degradation (table 5.4).

The community watershed approach is being used to overcome the livelihood constraints posed by natural resource degradation by way of the IGNRM approach. In this approach, research and development activities are implemented at landscape scales with benchmark sites representing the different semiarid tropical agro-ecoregions. The entire process revolves around the principles of empowerment, equity, efficiency, and environment, which are addressed by adopting specific strategies prescribed by consortium institutions from the scientific, nongovernment, government, and farmer groups. This approach

This note was prepared by S. P. Wani, T. K. Sreedevi, P. Pathak, Piara Singh, and T. J. Rego, International Crops Research Institute for the Semi-Arid Tropics, Patancheru, Andhra Pradesh, India; Y. S. Ramakrishna, Central Research Institute for Dryland Agriculture, Santoshnagar, Hyderabad, Andhra Pradesh, India; Thawilkal Wangkahart, Agricultural Research and Development, Region 3, Muang, Khon Kaen, Thailand; Yin Dixin, Guizhou Academy of Agricultural Sciences, Integrated Rural Development Center, Guiyang, Guizhou, China; and Zhong Li, Yunnan Academy of Agricultural Sciences, Kunming, Yunnan, China.

addressed the issues of participation, equity, sustainability, and technical support, which were found to be important constraints for enhancing the effect of watershed programs in India in a meta-analysis of 311 case studies (Joshi and others 2005).

PRESENTATION OF INNOVATION

The community watershed model has become popular because it brings together as a package for rural development the best expertise available locally and from all the consortium partners. Although the model uses the microwatershed as a geographic unit for soil and water conservation and management, its effect is strengthened with improved agronomical practices and diversified income-generating activities. Water management is used as an entry point for enhancing agricultural productivity and rural incomes. The knowledge-based entry point to build rapport with the community in place of a money- and capital-based entry point enhanced community participation by providing tangible economic benefits to individuals through enhanced productivity. Farmers' participatory research and development approach is fully operationalized, and no free inputs are provided to farmers. The consortium's approach aims to showcase increased incomes for villagers. After they are convinced that the innovations improve their livelihood security, they become ambassadors for the cause, convincing neighboring villages to practice community watershed development technologies (Wani and others 2006).

Although the activities initiated by the International Crops Research Institute for the Semi-Arid Tropics (ICRISAT) and its partners started with soil and water conservation, the watersheds became the site for implementing IGNRM. In Adarsha watershed, Kothapally, in Andhra Pradesh, India, the package of interventions included introducing broad-bed and furrow cultivation, planting *Gliricidia* on the bunds (an embankment used especially in India to control the flow of water) for green manure, introducing new crops, using high-yielding and stress-tolerant improved cultivars and cropping systems, innovating with pest management techniques, and developing microenterprises for additional income generation along with low-cost rainwater harvesting and groundwater recharging structures throughout the toposequence.

Choosing an appropriate cropping sequence and matching crop rotation with the soil profile and changing rainfall patterns helped minimize the effect of drought in Kothapally. A combination of maize-pigeonpea and maize followed by chickpea proved to be most beneficial because these crops could use the soil moisture more efficiently, thus encouraging farmers to shift from a cotton-based system. Moreover, studies showed that soils in Andhra Pradesh, Gujarat, Karnataka, Madhya Pradesh, Tamil Nadu, and Rajasthan were not only thirsty but hungry too, and they suffered from critical deficiency of micronutrients such as zinc, boron, and sulfur along with nitrogen and phosphorus. Adding those micronutrients to the soil resulted in a 28 to 70 percent increase in the yields of crops, and a balanced fertilizer application with nitrogen and phosphorus along with micronutrients increased yields up to 120 percent (Rego and others 2007).

In Tad Fa and Wang Chai watersheds in Thailand and in Thanh Ha and Huong Dao watersheds in Vietnam, the package of practices included introducing improved crop varieties; constructing and rehabilitating farm ponds; introducing legumes to the cropping systems; using vegetative contour bounds, using staggered trenches, and planting *Gliricidia sepium* trees and vetiver grass on bunds; growing fruit trees on steep slopes; using contour cultivation on mild slopes; introducing innovative integrated pest management (IPM) techniques, such as using molasses to trap moths; and diversifying cultivation with horticultural crops.

In China, farmers from Lucheba and Xioaoxincum watersheds have harvested rainwater in underground cisterns and surface tanks; diversified the systems by growing high-value vegetables and fruits; introduced innovative IPM options, such as use of light traps and tobacco waste; and earned additional income from allied activities, such as rearing of pigs and rabbits as well as biogas production. Leujiagh village in Lucheba watershed has become a model biogas village for the country. The village uses plant and animal wastes (pig manure) for biogas production, thereby allowing sanitation and energy self-sufficiency.

BENEFITS AND RESULTS OF THE ACTIVITY

Many innovations are being implemented with success in watersheds. In Thailand, an innovative IPM technique of mixing molasses with water and storing it in open bottles to trap adult moths before they lay their eggs has practically eliminated the use of chemical pesticides in vegetable crops.

The innovations also provide income-generating activities to women's self-help groups (SHGs) and landless farmers. In Kothapally and hundreds of watersheds in Andhra Pradesh, Gujarat, Karnatka, Madhya Pradesh, and Rajasthan, the members of the SHGs feed parthenium weed to earthworms, generate valuable vermicompost, and earn about Rs 500 per person per month from its sale. The SHGs also produce and sell biopesticide made from neem and *Gliricidia* plant leaves using earthworms. Catering to the needs of generating biodiesel plantations, the SHG members started a nursery to raise seedlings of *Jatropha* and *Pongamia*.

Likewise, the women's SHG in Goverdhanpura in Bundi district of Rajasthan has started manufacturing washing powder as an income-generating activity. The small profit helps run the SHG and provides additional income to women members.

Increasing Crop Productivity

Increasing crop productivity is common in all the watersheds and is evident soon after the inception of watershed interventions. For example, in benchmark watersheds of Andhra Pradesh, improved crop management technologies increased maize yield by two and one-half times and sorghum by three times. Overall, in 65 community watersheds (each measuring approximately 500 hectares), implementing best practices resulted in significant yield advantages in sorghum (35 to 270 percent), maize (30 to 174 percent), pearl millet (72 to 242 percent), groundnuts (28 to 179 percent), and pigeonpeas as a sole crop (97 to 204 percent) and as an intercrop (40 to 110 percent). In Thanh Ha watershed of Vietnam, yields of soybeans, groundnuts, and mung beans increased by three- to fourfold (2.8 to 3.5 tons per hectare) as compared with baseline yields (0.5 to 1.0 tons per hectare), thereby reducing the yield gaps between potential and farmers' yields. A reduction in nitrogen fertilizer (90 to 120 kilograms of urea per hectare) by 38 percent increased maize yield by 18 percent. In Tad Fa watershed of northeastern Thailand, maize yield increased by 27 to 34 percent with improved crop management.

Improving Water Availability

Improved water availability in the watersheds was attributed to efficient management of rainwater and in situ con-servation. Establishing low-cost water-harvesting structures (WHSs) throughout the toposequence improved groundwater levels, benefiting many small farmers. Even after the rainy season, the water level in wells nearer to WHSs sustained good groundwater yield. In the various watersheds of India, such as Lalatora in Madhya Pradesh, the treated area registered a groundwater level rise of 7.3 meters. At Bundi, Rajasthan, the average rise was 5.7 meters, and the irrigated area increased from 207 hectares to 343 hectares (figure 5.1). In Kothapally watershed, the groundwater level rise was 4.2 meters in open wells. The various WHSs resulted in an additional groundwater recharge per year of approximately 428,000 cubic meters on average. This improvement in groundwater availability guaranteed the supply of clean drinking water. In Lucheba watershed in southern China, a drinking-water project, comprising a water storage tank and pipelines to farm households, was a joint effort of the community and the watershed project. It solved the drinking-water problem for 62 households and more than 300 head of livestock and provided major impetus for the excellent farmer participation in the project. Similarly, in Thanh Ha watershed in Vietnam, collective pumping of well water and establishment of efficient water distribution systems enabled the farmers' group to earn more income by growing watermelon, which provided maximum income for households.

Through improved yields and income-generating opportunities, the families in the watershed projects have more money in their hands. For instance, in Kothapally, the average income (including livestock and nonfarming sources) was Rs 42,500 (US$1,036.60) in 2001. In comparison, the average income in the neighboring villages without watershed management approaches was Rs 27,600 (US$673.10). Even in the drought year of 2002, Kothapally farmers earned more from crop cultivation than farmers in the neighboring villages, resulting in reduced migration from Kothapally. In the Tad Fa and Wang Chai watersheds in Thailand, farm income increased 45 percent. On the whole, the farmers

Table 5.4	Seasonal Rainfall, Runoff, and Soil Loss from Different Benchmark Watersheds in India and Thailand					
Watershed	Seasonal rainfall (mm)	Runoff (mm)		Soil loss (tons per hectare)	
		Treated	Untreated	Treated	Untreated
Kothapally, Andhra Pradesh, India	743	44	67	0.82	1.90
Lalatora, Madhya Pradesh, India	1,046	70	273	0.63	3.2
Ringnodia, Madhya Pradesh, India	764	21	66	0.75	2.2
Tad Fa, Khon Kaen, northeast Thailand	1,284	169	364	4.21	31.2

Source: Authors' elaboration.

Figure 5.1   Effect of Watershed Interventions on Groundwater Levels at Two Benchmark Sites in India

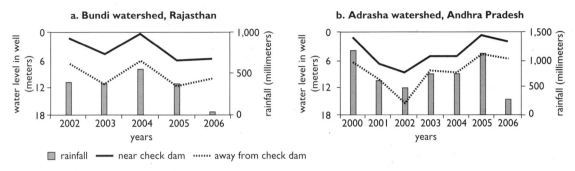

Source: Authors' elaboration.

earned an average net income of B 45,530 (US$1,230) per cropping season (Shiferaw and Rao 2006).

Improved land and water management practices along with integrated nutrient management—consisting of applications of inorganic fertilizers and organic amendments such as crop residues, vermicompost, farm manures, and *Gliricidia* loppings, as well as crop diversification with legumes—not only enhanced productivity but also improved soil quality. Increased carbon sequestration of 7.4 tons per hectare in 24 years was observed with improved management options in a long-term watershed experiment at ICRISAT. Normalized difference vegetation index estimation from satellite images showed that within four years, vegetation cover increased by 35 percent in Kothapally. The IGNRM options in the watersheds reduced loss of nitrate-nitrogen in runoff water (8 kilograms compared with 14 kilograms of nitrogen per hectare). Introduction of IPM in cotton and pigoenpeas substantially reduced the number of chemical insecticidal sprays during the season, and reduced use of pesticides resulted in less pollution of water bodies with harmful chemicals.

Conserving Biodiversity

Conservation of biodiversity in the watersheds was engendered through participatory natural resource management (NRM). The index of surface percentage of crops, crop agrobiodiversity factor (CAF), and surface variability of main crops changed as a result of integrated watershed management interventions. Pronounced agrobiodiversity effects were observed in Kothapally watershed, where farmers now grow 22 crops in a season with a remarkable shift in cropping pattern from cotton (200 hectares in 1998 to 100 hectares in 2002) to a maize-pigeonpea intercrop system (40 hectares to 180 hectares), thereby changing the CAF

from 0.41 in 1998 to 0.73 in 2002. In Thanh Ha, Vietnam, the CAF changed from 0.25 in 1998 to 0.60 in 2002 with the introduction of legumes. Similarly, rehabilitation of the common property resource land in Bundi watershed through the collective action of the community ensured the availability of fodder for all the households and income of US$1,670 per year for the SHG through sale of grass to the surrounding villages. Aboveground diversity of plants (54 plant species belonging to 35 families) as well as belowground diversity of microorganisms (21 bacterial isolates, 31 fungal species, and 1.6 times higher biomass carbon) were evident in rehabilitated common property when compared with the degraded common property (9 plant species, 18 bacterial isolates, and 20 fungal isolates, of which 75 percent belonged to *Aspergillus* genus) (Wani and others 2005).

Promoting Natural Resource Management at the Landscape Level

Data obtained by using new science tools, such as remote sensing, promote a comprehensive understanding of the effects of the changes (that is, vegetation cover on degraded lands) in the watersheds. This knowledge, in turn, has provided the indicators to assess agricultural productivity. Promoting NRM at the landscape level by using tools that provide the needed database is anticipated to have better effect because of the possible integration of all the factors (natural resources with the ancillary information).

Although some interventions took place at plot to farm levels, the effects of NRM—such as sustainability of production, improved soil and water quality, and other environment resources—have been looked at from a landscape perspective. Equal attention was focused on both on-site and off-site effects. The effect of water conservation at the upper ridge on downstream communities was also considered. This effect accounts for some successes in addressing concerns about equity issues, such as benefits for the poorest people—like the landless, who were previously unable to take advantage of improved soil and water conditions in activities implemented only at field scales. Clearly, off-site effects of watershed management—upstream-downstream equity—need to be strengthened for enhanced outcomes.

Enhancing Partnerships and Institutional Innovations

Enhancing partnerships and institutional innovations through the consortium approach was the major impetus for harnessing the watershed's potential to reduce household poverty. The underlying element of the consortium approach adapted in ICRISAT-led watersheds is engaging a range of actors with the locales as the primary implementing unit. Joint efforts of ICRISAT and key partners—the national agricultural research systems (NARSs), nongovernmental organizations, government organizations, agricultural universities, and other private interest groups—with farm households as the key decision makers effectively addressed complex issues. SHGs, such as village seed banks, were established to provide timely and high-quality seeds. These SHGs also created the venue for receiving technical support and building the capacity of members, such as women, in managing conservation and livelihood development activities. Incorporating a knowledge-based entry point in the approach led to the facilitation of rapport and at the same time enabled the community to make rational decisions for its development. As demonstrated by ICRISAT, the strongest merit of the consortium approach is in capacity building, where farm households are not the sole beneficiaries, but researchers, development agents, and students of various disciplines are also trained, and policy makers from the NARSs are sensitized on the entire gamut of watershed activities. Private-public partnership has provided the means for increased investments not only for enhancing productivity but also for building institutions as engines for people-led NRM.

LESSONS LEARNED AND SCALING UP

The success of the Kothapally example led to the acceptance of the watershed approach by the government of Andhra Pradesh for scaling up in 150 watersheds through the Andhra Pradesh Rural Livelihoods Project, which is supported by the U.K. Department for International Development. Observing this success, the government of Karnataka has also adopted productivity enhancement initiatives in pilot watershed sites and scaled out through the World

Bank–funded Sujala Watershed Project. With financial support from the Sir Dorabji Tata Trust, the ICRISAT-led consortium of partners has implemented watershed projects in Madhya Pradesh and Rajasthan in India. Watershed projects are also being implemented in Rajasthan and Tamil Nadu in partnership with the Confederation of Indian Industry and the Coca-Cola Foundation. With funding from the Asian Development Bank, ICRISAT's model of watershed development was implemented in selected villages in China, India, Thailand, and Vietnam.

The outcomes of the ICRISAT's watershed research and development activities are also being used for South-South cooperation among countries in Asia and Africa. Considering the usual long time lag between NRM research and subsequent results, ICRISAT and the Soil and Water Research Management Network are focusing on adapting existing knowledge for local conditions rather than on initiating new research. For example, following visits to India by African officials, the Association for Strengthening Agricultural Research in Eastern and Central Africa and the Indian Council for Agricultural Research (ICAR) entered into a memorandum of understanding to facilitate long-term collaboration. The government of Rwanda, through its agricultural research institute, is working with ICAR to implement pilot sites for the adaptation and demonstration of Indian experiences in integrated management of watersheds.

RECOMMENDATIONS FOR PRACTITIONERS

- Manage natural resources on a smaller catchment scale (500 to 3,000 hectares) by adopting a sustainable livelihoods approach.
- Adopt a holistic community watershed approach using water management as an entry point for improving livelihoods.
- Remember that soil and water conservation measures are just the beginning for watershed development and not an end, as generally adopted.
- Recognize that knowledge-based entry-point activity promotes better community participation than subsidy-based entry-point activity.
- Adopt productivity enhancement and income-generating activities to ensure tangible economic benefits to individuals for increased collective action in the watersheds.

INVESTMENT NEEDS

- Soil and water conservation measures address long-term sustainability issues, and benefits are both on site and off site. This approach calls for investments by governments, development donors, and others.

- Depending on topography, socioeconomic parameters, and infrastructure availability, development costs would vary between US$500 and US$1,500 per hectare.

POLICY AND FINANCIAL INCENTIVES

- Community watershed projects' success depends on participation and collective action by the members. Policies enabling collective action for management of natural resources are needed.

- More investment in upland and upstream areas is needed to minimize land degradation and to address equity and gender parity issues.

- The artificial divide between rainfed and irrigated agriculture needs to be discarded. Work needs to be in a continuum, from rainfed to supplemental to fully irrigated systems, if investments are to improve livelihoods.

- Financial incentives for poor upstream people who provide environmental services to downstream people need to be provided to encourage them to be better managers of natural resources.

NOTE

1. For example, Adarsha Watershed, Kothapally, in Andhra Pradesh, India, received 345 millimeters of rainfall in 24 hours on August 24, 2000. This downpour constituted about 40 percent of mean annual rainfall.

REFERENCES

Joshi, P. K, A. K. Jha, S. P. Wani, L. Joshi, and R. L. Shiyani. 2005. "Meta-Analysis to Assess Impact of Watershed Program and People's Participation: Comprehensive Assess-

ment." Research Report 8, International Water Management Institute, Colombo.

Rego, T. J., K. L. Sahrawat, S. P. Wani, and G. Pardhasaradhi. 2007. "Widespread Deficiencies of Sulfur, Boron, and Zinc in Indian Semi-arid Tropical Soils: On-Farm Crop Responses." *Journal of Plant Nutrition* 30 (10): 1569–83.

Shiferaw, B., and K. P. C. Rao, eds. 2006. *Integrated Management of Watersheds for Agricultural Diversification and Sustainable Livelihoods in Eastern and Central Africa: Lessons and Experiences from Semi-arid South Asia.* Patancheru, Andhra Pradesh, India: International Crop Research Institute for the Semi-Arid Tropics.

Wani, S. P., P. Pathak, H. M. Tam, A. Ramakrishna, P. Singh, and T. K. Sreedevi. 2002. "Integrated Watershed Management for Minimizing Land Degradation and Sustaining Productivity in Asia." In *Integrated Land Management in Dry Areas,* ed. Z. Adee, 207–30. Beijing.

Wani, S. P., Y. S. Ramakrishna, T. K. Sreedevi, T. D. Long, T. Wangkahart, B. Shiferaw, P. Pathak, and A. V. R. Kesava Rao. 2005. "Issues, Concepts, Approaches, and Practices in the Integrated Watershed Management: Experience and Lessons from Asia." Paper submitted for the Indian Council for Agricultural Research, International Water Management Institute, International Crop Research Institute for the Semi-Arid Tropics, and Association for Strengthening Agricultural Research in Eastern and Central Africa joint mission to Nairobi, Kenya, November 30–December 2, 2004.

Wani, S. P., Y. S. Ramakrishna, T. K. Sreedevi, T. Wangkahart, N. V. Thang, S. Roy, Z. Li, Y. Dixin, Z. H. Ye, A. K. Chourasia, B. Shiferaw, P. Pathak, P. Singh, G. V. Ranga Rao, R. P. Mula, S. Sitaraman, and Communication Office at ICRISAT. 2006. "Greening Drylands and Improving Livelihoods." International Crop Research Institute for the Semi-Arid Tropics, Patancheru, Andhra Pradesh, India.

Enhancing Mobility of Pastoral Systems in Arid and Semiarid Regions of Sub-Saharan Africa to Combat Desertification

Pastoral systems in arid and semiarid regions of Sub-Saharan Africa are well suited to cope effectively—and in an environmentally sustainable manner—with the prevailing harsh and erratic ecological conditions of those regions. The ability of pastoralists to move their herds over large distances and to take refuge in more favorable sites during droughts was critical to their livestock and livelihoods. Moreover, by maintaining the supply of animal food products during regional droughts, they also mitigated the impact of simultaneous crop failures on food security in adjacent, more humid areas. Today, however, unfortunately, mobility of pastoralists is increasingly being constrained, which is causing the effectiveness of the pastoral system to deteriorate fast. Furthermore, development policies have undermined the basic foundations of pastoralism.

For many years, the multiple values and needs of traditional mobile pastoralism have been neglected or misunderstood. Only from the mid-1970s have field studies on pastoral systems emerged to help explain seasonal livestock movements, herd-sex structures and productivity, rangeland ecology, and the multiple functions of pastoralism. The advantages of opportune and flexible use of natural resources, rather than control of stocking rates, have only recently been accepted as the recommended scientific basis of livestock development.

Mobile pastoralism can be an efficient and sustainable system. Improving natural rangelands in arid and semiarid regions would also improve the world's carbon storage capacity, biodiversity, and water quality. Arid and semiarid lands represent about two-thirds of Africa's total land area of nearly 30 million square kilometers and host about 189 million people. Enhancing the condition and availability of natural rangelands and water resources for pastoral production would simultaneously improve wild food availability, provide critical micronutrients, and diversify regional rural economies. Moreover, increasing the area and condition of rangelands adjacent to cropping areas would favor the sustainability and productivity of the cropping systems through (a) reduced soil erosion resulting from the increased water retention capacity of the rangelands and (b) increased availability of animal manure per cropping area unit. Finally, mixed crop-rangeland systems would reduce the impact of food-crop failure induced by drought and crop-specific pests or diseases, thus contributing to the livelihood of the 180 million people in Sub-Saharan Africa who are food insecure.

INTRODUCTION

Pastoral systems in arid and semiarid regions of Sub-Saharan Africa used to cope effectively and in an environmentally sustainable manner with the prevailing harsh and erratic ecological conditions of those regions. The ability to move their herds over large distances and take refuge in more favorable sites during droughts was critical to the livestock and livelihoods of pasturalists. Moreover, by maintaining the supply of animal food products during regional droughts, they mitigated the impact of simultaneous crop failures on food security in adjacent, more humid areas. Unfortunately, mobility is increasingly being constrained by various developments, and the effectiveness of the pastoral system is deteriorating fast. As a result, pastoralists are now burdening rather than supporting larger societies. This note provides the rationale for investment in the recovery of mobility of these pastoral systems.

This note was prepared by S. Leloup, consultant.

KEY SUSTAINABLE LAND MANAGEMENT ISSUES

Mobile pastoral systems in arid and semiarid regions make sustainable use of natural resources by tracking climatic and landscape variability (Niamir-Fuller 2000). However, land degradation will occur when livestock is forced to stay year round in restricted areas. In semiarid and adjacent subhumid regions, land degradation is clearly linked to settlement and to the combined effect of growing human populations and uncoordinated different land uses. For example, in West Africa, uncontrolled expansion of low-input cropping systems, accompanied by uncontrolled bush fires, fuelwood collection, and increasing numbers of sedentary livestock, induces severe degradation of both croplands and rangelands (Leloup 1994). Hence, the notion that overgrazing or livestock holding in general is the primary cause of desertification in Africa is no longer justified.

TRENDS OF RESOURCE USE

During the past century, frequency and distances of herd movements have declined (see, for example, Niamir-Fuller 2000), and various forms and degrees of settlement have occurred. Spontaneous settlement is usually caused by long droughts; encroachment of other land uses (Cullis and Watson 2004; Leloup 1994; Mkutu 2004); comparative lack of infrastructure and social services; disease control policies (Morton 2001); shifting of ownership (Niamir-Fuller 2000); and breakdown of customary pastoral social hierarchies, in addition to social insecurity (Morton 2001). Governments sometimes promote settlement to intensify and commercialize animal production and to facilitate social control and delivery of social and livestock specific services (Pratt, Le Gall, and de Haan 1997). Involuntary settlement of pastoralists by governments because of dam construction, famine, and civil war has also been reported (Larsen and Hassan 2003).

Since about the 1920s, vast areas of natural rangelands in arid and semiarid regions have been taken over by cropping systems, semiprivate and private livestock and game ranches, nature reserves, and infrastructure. The encroached rangelands included the better areas for grazing during the dry season, which provided easier access to water. Such areas are the key resources ensuring the overall sustainability of the pastoral system.

KEY DRIVERS

The demands of growing human populations everywhere else have been driving the increasing competitive and conflicting use of arid and semiarid regions.

For a long time, the multiple values and needs of traditional mobile pastoralism have been neglected or misunderstood. Until the 1970s, pastoralism was considered inefficient and backward, and livestock research and development focused on providing veterinary care and increasing beef productivity per animal. Only from the mid-1970s have field studies on pastoral systems emerged to help explain seasonal livestock movements, herd-sex structures and productivity, rangeland ecology, and the multiple functions of pastoralism (Blench and Marriage 1999; Breman and de Wit 1983; de Ridder and Wagenaar 1984). The advantages of opportune and flexible use of natural resources, rather than control of stocking rates, have only recently been accepted as the recommended scientific basis of livestock development (Behnke, Scoones, and Kerven 1993).

Various policies, such as the following examples, have undermined basic foundations of pastoralism:

- State boundaries were established that neglected the interests of local land-use patterns and societies.
- Pastoralists have been weakly represented at the national level. Ministries in charge of livestock generally do not address issues of accessibility of natural resources or availability of social services (that is, education, health care, and infrastructure).
- Inadequate land-use policies and legislation have neglected existing customary tenure systems and undermined relevant local authorities, in particular with regard to the use of natural rangelands (Kirk 2000).
- Unfavorable incentive policies have been practiced. Dumping of beef, in particular by the European Union, was favored by African governments. This practice reduced the income of West African pastoralists and caused them to take up arable farming. National government policies of subsidizing inputs have favored cropping systems over pastoral systems and fuel (Pratt, Le Gall, and de Haan 1997). Moreover, subsidizing livestock ranching at the expense of rangelands for pastoralists and wildlife is still ongoing (Cullis and Watson 2004).

LESSONS LEARNED

- Mobility of pastoral systems enhances ability to cope with droughts and prevents natural resources degradation.
- Rather than changing environmental conditions and the inherent malfunctioning of pastoral systems, the increas-

ing degradation and downward poverty cycle associated with these systems can be explained by misunderstanding, lack of knowledge, and neglect of the effectiveness and needs of mobile pastoral systems in arid and semi-arid areas.

- The multifunctionality of pastoral systems—such as the supply of live animals, milk, meat, manure, hides, transport, and animal traction—makes Sub-Saharan Africa's mobile pastoralist more productive than U.S. and Australian livestock systems under similar ecological environments (Breman and de Wit 1983; de Ridder and Wagenaar 1984). Fodder supply is achieved with minimal labor and low economic cost, chance of disease transmission between animals is low, and access to various markets and social communities and gatherings is easy (Niamir-Fuller 2000).
- The ecological, social, and economic interests of mobile pastoralists have been too often overlooked.

OPPORTUNITIES FOR SUSTAINABLE LAND MANAGEMENT

Rather than a backward, antiquated system, mobile pastoralism can be an efficient and sustainable system. Improving natural rangelands in arid and semiarid regions would improve the world's carbon storage capacity, biodiversity, and water quality.

Arid and semiarid lands represent about two-thirds of Africa's total land area of nearly 30 million square kilometers (UNEP 2000) and host about 189 million people. The semiarid and arid areas in the Horn make up 70 percent of the total land area of this type and provide an average of 20 to 30 percent of gross domestic product (GDP), with substantial subregional trade (Little 1996). In West Africa, the pastoral sector contributes between 10 percent and 20 percent of total GDP in Mali, Mauritania, and Niger, and there is active trade between those countries. Pastoral development could, therefore, be an important force in regional development.

Support to mobile pastoralists would be of immediate benefit to the approximately 30 million pastoral peoples living in arid areas (Thornton and others 2002). These people are some of the most deprived populations in the region, and they often remain far removed geographically, linguistically, culturally, academically, and economically from those who run the country (Pratt, Le Gall, and de Haan 1997).

More than most other groups, mobile pastoralists are involved in and affected by enduring social tensions that often result from competition over natural resource uses.

Such cases are of concern in national situations, such as those in Benin, Burkina Faso, Côte d'Ivoire, Sudan, and Tanzania, as well as in transnational situations, such as those between Kenya and Somalia or Mauritania and Senegal (see, for example, Shazali and Ahmed 1999; van Driel 2001). Pastoral development could, therefore, prevent some of the conflict or postconflict social upheaval and deprivation.

Enhancing the condition and availability of natural rangelands and water resources[1] for pastoral production would simultaneously improve the availability of wild foods, provide critical micronutrients, and diversify regional rural economies. Moreover, increasing the area and condition of rangelands adjacent to cropping areas would favor the sustainability and productivity of cropping systems through (a) reduced soil erosion resulting from the increased water retention capacity of the rangelands and (b) increased availability of animal manure per cropping area unit. Finally, mixed crop-rangeland systems would reduce the impact of food-crop failure induced by drought and crop-specific pests or diseases, thus contributing to the livelihood of the 180 million people in Sub-Saharan Africa who are food insecure (Ehui and others 2002).

RATIONALE FOR INVESTMENTS

Declining mobility is leading Sub-Saharan African pastoralists in a downward cycle of environmental degradation, poverty, and increased food-aid dependency. Standards of living are falling among the approximate 20 million mobile pastoralists in Africa, often resulting in settlement and the need to rely on alternative income sources, such as cropping and hired labor; on out-migration to urban centers; or, ultimately, food aid (Niamir-Fuller 2000). Absentee investors and owners are increasingly contracting pastoralists to herd their livestock while often putting restrictions on livestock movements to facilitate control (Fafchamps, Udry, and Czukas 1998).

Per capita ownership of livestock is declining significantly, and many pastoralist families are now below the minimum subsistence level. In addition, production per livestock unit is declining. For example, from 1975 to 1995, beef production per animal declined slightly from 135 kilogram per head to 129 kilogram per head (Ehui and others 2002). Frequent and almost permanent relief interventions in human food aid and feed supplements for livestock are the result (Morton 2001; Pratt, Le Gall, and de Haan 1997). For example, in the Horn of Africa, pastoralists usually represent the part of the national population that most depends on food aid. The insights described earlier suggest that investing in mobile pastoral development would address the following issues of general interest to economic development of the arid and semiarid areas of Sub-Saharan Africa:

- Maintain efficient natural resource use in arid and semi-arid areas.
- Support important subregional and national economies.
- Reduce poverty.
- Reduce social conflicts.
- Enhance food security.

RECOMMENDATIONS FOR PRACTITIONERS

Broad-Based Consultations and Partnerships

Raising awareness of all policy makers on national, subregional, and regional levels is required to define the long-term vision on the role of mobile pastoral systems as a tool of sustainable natural resources management. Timing (that is, dovetailing campaigns to raise awareness with the preparation of major policy papers, such as World Bank Poverty Reduction Strategy Papers, and donor assistance strategies) and broad-based ownership (that is, involvement of infrastructure and social service departments) are essential because of the cross-cutting nature of the issues. Adequate representation of pastoralists in defining a long-term vision and the subsequent follow-up is critical. The ALive program, with its Web site, facilitates communication among various stakeholders.

Research

Monitoring activities need to be supported to fill the gaps in knowledge on a country-by-country basis (for example, total number of pastoralists and their livestock, importance of absentee owners, benefits and costs to national economy, physical constraints to mobility, policies constraining mobility, pastoral organizations). Meanwhile, adequate indicators to monitor the situation of mobile pastoralism and its role in larger economies need to be defined; then, long-term measurement needs to be arranged. Research should also assess the lessons learned that are available in the literature regarding various attempts to improve the situation of pastoralists (for example, water-use fees, grazing fees, livestock corridors, integrated livestock-wildlife management, integrated livestock-forest management, and grazing reserves) while attempting to produce new, out-of-the-box incentives to be tested.

Incentive Policies

Public funds and mechanisms need to be used to support the viability and mobility of pastoral systems (for example,

by introducing countervailing import tariffs on meats and limiting distribution of subsidized livestock feed). Providing livestock feed causes declining mobility, thereby inducing long-term dependency and abuse of systems, which often reach only the more sedentary and wealthy livestock owners (Hazell 2000). Water-use fees would improve sustainability of water infrastructure and cause better spatial distribution of livestock. Permitting livestock in nature reserves may also be a viable option to enhance mobility.

Resource Access Policies

A critical priority is the development of appropriate legislation that ensures access and user rights (not necessarily property rights) to critical grazing and water resources; limits encroachment of other uses and users (for example, cropping and ranching); integrates various natural resources uses and users; and, in some areas, reclaims some of the important lost grazing and water resources for pastoral use. Although highly sensitive, such legislation is absolutely essential for environmentally and socially sustainable development of these areas. Where increased cropping and declining stock numbers have made long migration impossible, shorter treks, with a closer integration of crops and livestock, are probably the best strategy. Community institutions can facilitate and enforce contracts between the different land uses and users.

Infrastructure

Infrastructure needs concern mostly water, networks of pathways through crop areas, markets, and mobile communication and weather forecasting equipment to manage drought. Sustainability of those investments is a major issue that needs to be addressed through clear agreements with pastoral users on cost-sharing and maintenance responsibilities.

Services

Service needs concern the technical services, such as veterinary care and livestock marketing information, and cover adapted social services, such as health care and education. Needed investments include equipment and training to replace the current static service models for human and animal health and education with mobile service models. Major strategic decisions are required in education on the curriculum (with a focus on pastoral indigenous knowledge rather than more formal teaching and language) and "training-the-trainer" programs (Kratli 2001). In health care, the major strategic decision concerns the combination of human and animal basic health care systems, an issue that is often debated and has many synergies, but is rarely implemented.

NOTE

1. Natural rangelands and water resources contribute to many aspects of interest to economic and social development, such as biomass fuels, human and veterinary health care products, shelter materials, water transport, cultural values, and sometimes ecotourism.

REFERENCES

Behnke, R. H., I. Scoones, and C. Kerven, eds. 1993. *Range Ecology at Dis-equilibrium.* London: Overseas Development Institute.

Blench, R., and Z. Marriage. 1999. "Drought and Livestock in Semi-arid Africa and Southwest Asia." Working Paper 117, Overseas Development Institute, London.

Breman, H., and C. T. de Wit. 1983. "Rangeland Productivity in the Sahel." *Science* 221 (4618): 1341–47.

Cullis, A., and C. Watson. 2004. "Winners and Losers: Privatising the Commons in Botswana." Securing the Commons 9, International Institute for Environment and Development, London.

de Ridder, N., and K. T. Wagenaar. 1984. "A Comparison between the Productivity of Traditional Livestock Systems and Ranching in Eastern Botswana." *International Livestock Center for Africa Newsletter* 3 (3): 5–7.

Ehui, S. K., S. E. Benin, T. William, and S. Meijer. 2002. "Food Security in Sub-Saharan Africa to 2020. Socioeconomics and Policy Research." Working Paper 49, International Livestock Research Institute, Nairobi.

Fafchamps, M., U. Udry, and K. Czukas. 1998. "Drought and Saving in West Africa: Are Livestock a Buffer Stock?" *Journal of Development Economics* 55 (2): 273–305.

Hazell, P. 2000. "Public Policy and Drought Management in Agropastoral Systems." In *Property Rights, Risk, and Livestock Development,* ed. N. McCarthy, B. Swallow, M. Kirk, and P. Hazell, 86–101. Washington, DC: International Food Policy Research Institute.

Kirk, M. 2000. "The Context for Livestock and Crop-Livestock Development in Africa: The Evolving Role of the State in Influencing Property Rights over Grazing Resources in Sub-Saharan Africa." In *Property Rights, Risk, and Livestock Development,* ed. N. McCarthy, B. Swallow, M. Kirk, and P. Hazell, 23–54. Washington, DC: International Food Policy Research Institute.

Kratli, S. 2001. "Education Provision to Pastoralists." IDS Working Paper 126, Institute of Development Studies, University of Sussex, U.K.

Larsen, K., and M. Hassan. 2003. *Sedentarisation of Nomadic People: The Case of the Hawawir in Um Jawasir, Northern Sudan.* DCG Report 24, Drylands Coordination Group, Ås, Norway.

Leloup, S. 1994. "Multiple Use of Rangelands within Agropastoral Systems in Southern Mali." Ph.D. thesis, Wageningen University, Netherlands.

Little, P. D. 1996. "Cross-Border Cattle Trade and Food Security in the Kenya/Somalia Borderlands." Binghamton, NY: Institute for Development Anthropology.

Mkutu, K. 2004. *Pastoralism and Conflict in the Horn of Africa.* London: Africa Peace Forum, Saferworld, and University of Bradford.

Morton, J., ed. 2001. *Pastoralism, Drought, and Planning: Lessons from Northern Kenya and Elsewhere.* Chatham, U.K.: Natural Resources Institute, University of Greenwich.

Niamir-Fuller, M. 2000. "Managing Mobility in African Rangelands." In *Property Rights, Risk, and Livestock Development,* ed. N. McCarthy, B. Swallow, M. Kirk, and P. Hazell, 102–31. Washington, DC: International Food Policy Research Institute.

Pratt, D. J., F. Le Gall, and C. de Haan. 1997. "Investing in Pastoralism: Sustainable Natural Resource Use in Arid Africa and the Middle East." World Bank Technical Paper 365, World Bank, Washington, DC.

Shazali, S., and A. G. M. Ahmed. 1999. "Pastoral Land Tenure and Agricultural Expansion: Sudan and the Horn of Africa." Paper 185, International Institute for Environment and Development, London, U.K.

Thornton, P. K., R. L. Kruska, N. Henninger, P. M. Kristjanson, R. S. Reid, F. Atieno, A. N. Odero, and T. Ndegwa. 2002. *Mapping Poverty and Livestock in the Developing World.* Nairobi: International Livestock Research Institute.

UNEP (United Nations Environment Programme). 2000. *Global Environment Outlook 2000.* Nairobi: UNEP.

van Driel, A. 2001. *Sharing a Valley: The Changing Relations between Agriculturalists and Pastoralists in the Niger Valley of Benin.* Leiden, Netherlands: African Studies Centre.

SELECTED READINGS

ALive. 2006. "Investing in Maintaining Mobility in Pastoral Systems of the Arid and Semi-arid Regions of Sub-Saharan Africa." ALive Policy Note, World Bank, Washington, DC.

de Haan, C. 1994. "An Overview of the World Bank's Involvement in Pastoral Development. Pastoral Development." Network Paper 36b, Overseas Development Institute, London.

de Haan, C., T. Schillhorn van Veen, B. Brandenburg, J. Gauthier, F. Le Gall, R. Mearns, and M. Siméon. 2001. *Livestock Development: Implications for Rural Poverty, the Environment, and Global Food Security.* Washington, DC: World Bank.

Delgado, C., M. Rosegrant, H. Steinfeld, S. Ehui, and C. Courbois. 1999. "Livestock to 2020: The Next Food Revolution." Food, Agriculture, and the Environment Discussion Paper 28, International Food Policy Research Institute, Washington, DC.

McCarthy, N., B. Swallow, M. Kirk, and P. Hazell, eds. 2000. *Property Rights, Risks, and Livestock Development in Africa.* Washington, DC: International Food Policy Research Institute.

Savory, A. 1988. *Holistic Resources Management.* Washington, DC: Island Press.

WEB RESOURCES

LEAD electronic conference policy papers. Livestock, Environment And Development (LEAD) is a multi-institutional initiative of FAO formed to promote ecologically sustainable livestock production systems. It focuses on protecting the natural resources that are affected by livestock production and processing and on poverty reduction and public health enhancement through appropriate forms of livestock development. LEAD hosts an electronic conference on Maintaining Mobility and Managing Drought. This e-conference discusses and reviews two policy options papers to inform policy makers and decision makers in international aid and financial institutions on the latest developments in key areas important for pro-poor livestock development, and provide them with options on how to address them: http://www.virtualcentre.org/en/ele/econf_03_alive/policy.htm.

Sustainable Land Management in Marginal Dry Areas of the Middle East and North Africa: An Integrated Natural Resource Management Approach

The International Center for Agricultural Research in the Dry Areas (ICARDA), based in Aleppo, Syrian Arab Republic, has been working with farmers in the Middle East and North Africa to develop innovative crop diversification alternatives for smallholder farmers. In marginal drylands of the Khanasser valley, the rural poor live between the traditional agricultural areas and the arid rangelands with less than 200 millimeters of yearly rainfall. Pressures on these lands are considerable, landholdings are shrinking in size, and land productivity is decreasing—with resulting increased poverty and out-migration.

In the past, promising technologies were not adopted because they were developed in isolation from the requirements of the local communities and were based on an inadequate understanding of the asset base and flows as well as local informal institutions. This study shows that sharing knowledge and increasing public awareness of land degradation facilitate closer cooperation among the stakeholders involved in sustainable land management (SLM) and result in options targeted at the various sectors of the population, each with different access to natural, physical, human, and financial capital. Although income generation is the first priority of the land users, most of the technological options also contribute to more sustainable management of the land. The lessons learned in this pilot program are applicable more widely in the Middle East and North Africa.

KEY SUSTAINABLE LAND MANAGEMENT ISSUES

In marginal drylands of the Khanasser valley, the rural poor live between the traditional agricultural areas and the arid rangelands with less than 200 millimeters of yearly rainfall.

Extending more than 450 square kilometers, the valley's main habitats are agricultural lands and rangelands that are home to 58 villages of 5 to 270 households per village and a total population of approximately 37,000. Pressures on these lands include high population growth rates, erratic rainfall patterns and droughts, soil erosion from both wind and water, declining soil fertility, saline groundwater, lack of drought-tolerant germplasm and alternative crop-livestock options, lack of credit and financial capital, lack of information about new technologies and farming practices, unclear land property rights, policy disincentives to invest in dry areas, and lack of markets and market information. As a result of high population growth rates, landholdings are shrinking in size, and land productivity is decreasing—with resulting increased poverty and out-migration.

The farming systems are dryland rainfed mixed crop-livestock and pastoral, as defined by Dixon and Gulliver with Gibbon (2001). Agriculture, based on extensive sheep rearing and cultivation of barley mainly for forage, is still the main activity; however, livelihoods depend on both on- and off-farm income. Households in the Khanasser valley can be categorized into three main groups (La Rovere and others 2006):

- Agriculturalists who grow crops, fatten lambs, and undertake wage labor (about 40 percent of the households)
- Laborers who are semilandless and rely mostly on-farm earnings and migrations (50 percent of the households)
- Pastoralists who are extensive herders, migrating for wage labor or occasionally engaging in intensive lamb fattening (about 10 percent of the households).

This note was prepared by R. Thomas, F. Turkelboom, R. La Rovere, A. Aw-Hassan, and A. Bruggeman, International Center for Agricultural Research in the Dry Areas, Aleppo, Syrian Arab Republic.

The main coping strategies of households living in these marginal areas, therefore, include diversifying livelihood strategies, intensifying agriculture, finding off-farm employment, and exiting agriculture. This grouping immediately raises questions on who to target and with what. If the goal is primarily poverty alleviation, then interventions should focus on the poorest (laborers and pastoralists). If the goal is to expand food production, then the focus should be on agriculturalists. If the goal is to protect the land, the emphasis should be on the mainly government-controlled communal rangelands and the privately owned cultivated land (land used mainly by pastoralists and agriculturalists).

The tool used to help orient the project team was a simple analysis of the strengths, weaknesses, opportunities, and threats of the marginal dry areas. The input to the analysis came from contributions from land users, researchers,

extension agents, and decision makers. Table 5.5 summarizes the results of this exercise.

The study attempted comprehensively to address the complexity of this marginal dryland by identifying environmentally benign options that improve livelihoods, reduce poverty, and sustain the natural resource base. An interdisciplinary approach was taken to introduce new land-use options and to broaden interactions among local communities, researchers, and local and national governments by creating multistakeholder platforms (Campbell and others 2006). ·

LESSONS LEARNED

First, the study team analyzed previous experiences. In the past, promising technologies were not adopted because they were developed in isolation from the requirements of the

Table 5.5 Major Strengths, Weaknesses, Opportunities, and Threats for the Khanasser Valley as an Example of Marginal Drylands

Strengths	Weaknesses	Opportunities	Threats
• Indigenous knowledge and local innovations • Strong social networks and rich local culture • Comparative advantage for small ruminant production • Salt lake with rich bird biodiversity • Relatively unpolluted environment • Reasonable mobility and accessible markets • Improved basic services (electricity, roads, mobile-phone network)	• Cash-flow problems (resulting in lack of long-term investments) • Poor nutritional status of children • Limited experience with nontraditional farming enterprises • Lack of adapted crop germplasm • Decreasing productivity • Degraded natural resource base (soil, groundwater, vegetation) and degrading management practices • Land degradation masked by variations in rainfall • Poor extension services	• Investments of off-farm income into productive resources • Better education levels and expertise • Increased awareness of the risks of resource degradation • Cooperatives • Improved market knowledge through mobile phones and other media • Out-migration and off-farm opportunities • Sheep fattening • Potential to improve the traditional barley system • Improved germplasm • Diversification for cash and subsistence purposes • Agrotourism, ecotourism, and cultural tourism • Runoff water harvesting and efficient small-scale irrigation systems • Soil fertility improvement • Rangeland rehabilitation and medicinal plants collection • Better government services and increased attention to poverty alleviation and environmental services in marginal areas	• Aging and feminization of active Khanasser population • Declining social networks • Destruction of traditional "beehive houses" • Increased population pressure and too small landholdings • Depletion of groundwater resources • Recurrent droughts • Further decline of soil fertility and groundwater levels • Declining groundwater quality and salinization of irrigated fields • Population by intensive sheep fattening and untreated village sewage • Degradation of the fragile Jabul salt lake ecosystem • Unreliable export markets for sheep

Source: Authors' elaboration.

local communities and were based on an inadequate understanding of the asset base and flows and of local informal institutions. Clearly, a need existed to study livelihood strategies in greater detail for better targeting of agricultural and nonagricultural interventions. Multistakeholder processes are required that bring together local populations and decision makers to develop common understandings of the different perceptions of these marginal zones and to facilitate better organizational ability of community-based groups. In addition, the time lag between the announcement of a change in restrictions to cropping on marginal lands and the implementation of the new regulations pointed to the need to improve communication between policy makers and land users.

OPPORTUNITIES FOR SUSTAINABLE LAND MANAGEMENT: PRODUCTS AND SERVICES

Following this analysis, the team then developed and refined a set of options that had been researched previously in the area. After on-farm trials, the options were tried and tested jointly by researchers and interested land users who were organized into farmer interest groups on a voluntary basis. From this collaboration, the following feasible options were identified:

- Options that strengthen the traditional farming system:
  - New barley varieties selected by using a participatory breeding approach
  - Barley production with application of phosphogypsum to improve soil fertility and to increase and stabilize production in dry years
  - Dairy products from sheep for consumption or sale
  - Seed priming of barley seeds with nutrient solutions to improve crop establishment
- Diversification options:
  - Barley intercropped with *Atriplex* shrubs to stabilize forage production, increase biomass during dry years, and enhance protein content in sheep diets
  - Improved vetch production by selection of drought-tolerant varieties to reduce production risks
  - Improved management of rainfed cumin (a new cash crop) to stabilize and increase production and improve its marketing value
  - Olive orchards, using water harvesting and cultivating on foothill slopes, to increase production and reduce summer irrigation by groundwater
- Intensification options:
  - Improved lamb fattening by using lower-cost feeds

- Institutional options:
  - Traditional dairy institutions (Jabban) for sharing knowledge and providing informal credit
  - Village saving and credit associations (Sanadiq, established and operated by a parallel development project led by the United Nations Development Programme).

RATIONALE FOR INVESTMENT

The marginal zone of Syria represented by this case study covers about 11 percent of the country's land area and 14 percent of the population (about 2 million people). Poverty is greatest in areas located within this zone. The fact that many men migrate to urban areas results in labor shortages and in sociocultural decline from the loss of social structure and cultural heritage. Investments are needed both to restore the social and physical infrastructures and to reverse land degradation. The latter is a slowly changing variable not perceived as urgent by local populations but is a process that threatens long-term sustainability of the region. Importantly, this approach can be applied (with local adaptations) across large areas of North Africa, Iraq, the Islamic Republic of Iran, Jordan, and Central Asia that are characterized by similar agro-ecological and socioeconomic factors.

RECOMMENDATIONS FOR PRACTITIONERS

The study showed that knowledge sharing and increased public awareness of land degradation are required to facilitate closer cooperation among the stakeholders involved in SLM. As a result of closer integration among all stakeholders, the study team developed a set of options. The options are targeted at the various sectors of the population—each with different access to natural, physical, human, and financial capital. Although the team recognizes that income generation is the first priority of the land users, most of the technological options also contribute to more sustainable management of the land. The study demonstrated to government researchers, extension agents, and land users the value of collaboration. Consequently, plans are under way to replicate the Khanasser valley example in similar areas of Syria.

For each crop enterprise, specific technological objectives have been identified along with a corresponding agronomic approach. A summary of the objectives and the approaches taken to introduce technological interventions is shown in table 5.6.

For all these technologies and options, the study team prepared feasibility reports, including ex ante economic

Table 5.6 Technological Interventions Introduced in the Khanasser Valley

Enterprise	Objective of technology	Approach
Barley (rainfed)	Stabilize and enhance barley productivity.	Selection and improvement of barley varieties using a farmer-breeding participatory approach
Barley (rainfed)	Stabilize feed production, increase dry-year biomass, and enhance protein content.	Intercrop with the Atriplex (saltbush) shrub for sheep grazing.
Barley (rainfed)	Improve soil fertility, and increase and stabilize production in dry years.	Apply a phosphogypsum amendment residue of the fertilizer industry.
Wheat (irrigated)	Improve rainfall water productivity and yields.	Implement supplemental irrigation using sprinkler and surface methods.
Vetch	Reduce production risks, and increase feed availability.	Include improved drought-tolerant vetch varieties in traditional rotations.
Cumin (rainfed)	Stabilize and increase production, and improve its marketing outcome.	Improve management.
Olive orchards	Increase olive production, and reduce groundwater use for irrigation.	Cultivate olive trees on foothills by using water-harvesting practices
Sheep (lambs)	Intensify production.	Fatten lambs by using lower-cost feeds.
Sheep (extensive)	Enhance home consumption and sale of dairy surplus.	Improve small-scale dairy sheep institutions and strategies (for example, for marketing).
Sheep (dairy)	Improve sheep productivity.	Apply various small-ruminant technologies (for example, health, productivity)
Water harvesting	Improve water-use efficiency, and protect natural resources.	Combine with olive orchard management.
Phosphogypsum applications	Restore soil fertility.	Combine with barley crop improvements.

Source: Adapted from La Rovere and others 2007.

analyses (La Rovere and Aw-Hassan 2005; La Rovere and others 2007). The study team took this effort further, however, with analysis based on the characteristics of the different livelihood categories and assets of the defined population groups. Thus, the options were categorized as follows:

- Profitable in the short term and requiring more awareness and information
- Profitable but requiring investment and are prone to climatic risks
- Highly profitable but needing high investments
- Profitable only in the long run and needing initial investment.

MULTILEVEL ANALYTICAL FRAMEWORK

To help determine the main driving variables, the study used a toolbox approach that comprises diagnostic, problem-solving, and process tools (Turkelboom and others 2004). An example of a multilevel analytical framework used to identify the main constraints on the hill slopes of the valley is presented in figure 5.2. Biophysical and socioeconomic factors are examined in a framework consisting of a "spatial pillar" and a "stakeholder pillar" that are linked both vertically and horizontally. The tool lists the main pri-

oritized issues that constrain the adoption of technologies and resources and identifies potential solutions. This simple framework requires a multidisciplinary approach and helps foster greater understanding and communication among all parties.

REFERENCES

Campbell, B., J. Hagmann, A. Stroud, R. Thomas, and E. Wollenberg. 2006. *Navigating amidst Complexity: Guide to Implementing Effective Research and Development to Improve Livelihoods and the Environment.* Bogor, Indonesia: Center for International Forestry Research. http://www.icarda.cgiar.org/publications/navigatingamidstcomplexity.pdf.

Dixon, J., and A. Gulliver, with D. Gibbon. 2001. *Farming Systems and Poverty: Improving Farmers' Livelihoods in a Changing World.* Rome: Food and Agriculture Organization and World Bank. http://www.fao.org/farmingsystems/.

La Rovere, R., and A. Aw-Hassan. 2005. *Ex ante Assessment of Agricultural Technologies for Use in Dry Marginal Areas: The Case of the Khanasser Valley, Syria.* Integrated Natural Resource Management Technical Report 6. Aleppo, Syrian Arab Republic: International Center for Agricultural Research in the Dry Areas.

Figure 5.2   Application of the Multilevel Analytical Framework to the Management of Olive Orchards on Hill Slopes at Khanasser Valley

Spatial levels

> **Marginal drylands**
> - Climate suitability:
>   - Can olives grow properly in this type of climate?
>   - Selection of adapted varieties.

> **Khanasser valley:**
> - Land suitability: Can olives grow on stony hillsides?

> **(Sub)catchments:**
> - Runoff water use: Is there competition between upslope and downslope?

> **Field:**
> - What are the local management practices, technical knowledge, and knowledge gaps? Awareness, participatory research, and training about improved husbandry.
> - Soil and water management: Soil and water harvesting, irrigation, tillage, soil erosion, and use of ancient terraces.
> - Tree husbandry: Pruning, diseases, soil fertility management, and diagnosis of unproductive trees.

Stakeholder levels

> **Policy and institutions**
> - Policy regarding state land?
> - Olive policy in Syria?
> - Credit availability?
> - Institutional analysis plus services.

> **Trading links:**
> - Do marketing channels exist for olives?

> **Communities:**
> - Expansion of olive orchards?
> - Will olives affect equity?
> - Competition between grazing and olive orchards and potential for communal agreed arrangements.

> **Household livelihood strategies:**
> - Who is interested in growing olives and what are their motives?
> - Are there gender divisions related to olive orchards?
> - What are the technical knowledge sources?
> - For subsistence or cash? Enterprise budgets for olives.
> - Alternative tree crops: Are there adapted and viable alternatives?

Source: ICARDA.

La Rovere, R., A. Aw-Hassan, F. Turkelboom, and R. Thomas. 2006. "Targeting Research for Poverty Reduction in Marginal Areas of Rural Syria." *Development and Change* 37 (3): 627–48.

La Rovere, R., F. Turkelboom, A. Aw-Hassan, A. Bruggeman, and R. Thomas (Forthcoming). "A Comprehensive Assessment of Technological Options for Improving Rural Livelihoods in the Dry Marginal Areas of Syria." *International Journal of Agricultural Sustainability.*

Turkelboom, F., R. Thomas, R. La Rovere, and A. Aw-Hassan. 2004. "An Integrated Natural Resources Management (INRM) Framework for Coping with Land Degradation in Dry Areas." In *Ecosystem-Based Assessment of Soil Degradation to Facilitate Land Users' and Land Owners' Prompt Actions,* ed. P. Zdruli, P. Steduto, S. Kapur, and E. Akca, 91–109. Bari, Italy: Istituto Agronomico Mediterraneo.

SELECTED READING

Gonsalves, J., T. Becker, A. Braun, D. Campilan, H. de Chavez, E. Fajber, M. Kapiriri, J. Rivaca-Caminade, and R. Vernooy, eds. 2005. *Participatory Research and Development for Sustainable Agriculture and Natural Resource Management: A Sourcebook.* Ottawa: International Development Research Centre. http://www.idrc.ca/en/ev-84706-201-1-DO_TOPIC.html.

Pound, B., S. Snapp, C. McDougall, and A. Braun, eds. 2003. *Managing Natural Resources for Sustainable Livelihoods: Uniting Science and Participation.* Ottawa: International Development Research Centre. http://www.idrc.ca/en/ev-34000-201-1-DO_TOPIC.html.

Thomas, R., F. Turkelboom, R. La Rovere, T. Oweis, A. Bruggeman, and A. Aw-Hassan. 2004. "Towards Integrated Natural Resources Management (INRM) in Dry Areas Subject to Land Degradation: The Example of the Khanasser Valley in Syria." In *Combating Desertification: Sustainable Management of Marginal Drylands (SUMAMAD),* 85–93. UNESCO-MAB Dryland Series 3. Paris: United Nations Educational, Scientific, and Cultural Organization. http://www.icarda.cgiar.org/INRMsite/Towards_INRM.pdf.

Tyler, S. R. 2006a. *Comanagement of Natural Resources: Local Learning for Poverty Reduction.* Ottawa: International Development Research Centre. http://www.idrc.ca/en/ev-103297-201-1-DO_TOPIC.html#begining.

———. 2006b. *Communities, Livelihoods, and Natural Resources: Action Research and Policy Change in Asia.*

Ottawa: International Development Research Centre. http://www.idrc.ca/en/ev-97782-201-1-DO_TOPIC.html.

WEB RESOURCES

Integrated Natural Resource Management Web site. Integrated Natural Resource Management (INRM) is a research approach that aims at improving livelihoods, agroecosystem resilience, agricultural productivity, and environmental services. The Web site facilitates the sharing of experiences, approaches, and results among scientists working on INRM issues in the Consultative Group on International Agricultural Research and partner institutions. http://www.icarda.cgiar.org/INRMsite/.

Adaptation and Mitigation Strategies in Sustainable Land Management Approaches to Combat the Impacts of Climate Change

Climate change has the potential to undermine significantly efforts in the sustainable management of agricultural land, particularly in subtropical and tropical regions. The impacts of climate change of concern to agricultural land management include amplification of drought-flood cycles, increase in wind and rain intensity, shift in the spatial and temporal distribution of rainfall, and range expansion of agricultural pests and diseases. The degree of this maladaptation to climate variability could increase over the next several decades, with climate change potentially derailing future development efforts in climate-vulnerable regions such as Africa.

Developing more coherent links between land management and institutional change could create a more conducive environment for land improvement. For example, the recent revegetation phenomenon in the Sahel is rooted both in technical support for land improvement and in legal code reforms that provided local communities with control over resource management decisions.

In Africa, with its dependence on rainfed agriculture, the combined factors of variable rainfall, high temperatures, and poor soil fertility heighten the sensitivity of smallholder producers to shocks from extreme climate events. In the near to medium term, there is reasonably good potential to enhance rainfed production sustainability through improvements in water capture and storage, combined with better soil and fertility management. Fairly modest changes have the potential to triple cereal yields in high-risk farming environments.

There are also opportunities to link greenhouse gas (GHG) mitigation simultaneously with sustainable land use and adaptation to climate change. Other options include advances in probabilistic forecasting, embedding of crop models within climate models, enhanced use of remote sensing, and research into "weather within climate." These advances, however, will need to be matched with better means for disseminating forecasts to farming communities through multiple forums, such as those where information on water, health, housing, and disaster management is shared.

INTRODUCTION

Climate change has the potential to significantly undermine efforts to sustain and manage agricultural land, particularly in subtropical and tropical regions. The impacts of climate change—including (a) amplification of drought-flood cycles, (b) increase in wind and rain intensity, (c) shift in the spatial and temporal distribution of rainfall, and (d) range expansion of agricultural pests and diseases (IPCC 2007)— are of concern to agricultural land management. The disruptive impacts of climate change on agriculture are more likely to be experienced in terms of increased seasonal and interannual climate variability and higher frequency of extreme events than as mean changes in the climate.

These effects will not be uniformly distributed, nor will they be exclusively negative. High-latitude zones that do not limit moisture are expected to experience increased productivity from warmer temperatures and longer growing seasons, assuming relatively modest temperature increases (less than 3°C). In contrast, low-latitude zones that will undergo the smallest increase in warming will likely be subjected to the greatest negative influence from climate change and variability because of the multiple pressures of land degradation, poverty, and weak institutional capacity. This combination of stress factors increases the vulnerability of smallholder producers to shocks from extreme climatic events, such as El Niño episodes, thus leading to

This note was prepared by J. Padgham, U.S. Agency for International Development.

heightened risk of a poverty trap at the local level and diminished economic growth at the national level (Brown and Lall 2006). The degree of this maladaptation to climate variability could increase over the next several decades, with climate change potentially derailing future development efforts in climate-vulnerable regions such as Africa.

Climate change has the potential to intersect with sustainable land management (SLM) efforts directly (by affecting soil function, watershed hydrology, and vegetation patterns) and indirectly (by stimulating changes in land-use practices and altering the dynamics of invasive species). This note examines critical issues related to how climate change will affect soil and water management, and it explores the potential to improve land management through efforts to mitigate agricultural GHG emissions, to use seasonal climate forecasts to support agriculture management decisions, and to adapt to climate variability and change.

KEY SUSTAINABLE LAND MANAGEMENT ISSUES: SOIL AND WATER MANAGEMENT

Intensification of the hydrologic cycle, in which climate change is manifested by increased frequency and intensity of flooding and drought, as well as by more extreme storms with high-intensity rainfall, could significantly affect land management. Substantial increases in future soil erosion are projected because of the important role of extreme events that contribute to total soil erosion (Nearing, Pruski, and O'Neal 2004). Agricultural soils of the tropics are particularly vulnerable to erosion from extreme events because low soil organic matter levels and weak structures reduce their resilience to erosive forces; crop productivity in these areas is quite sensitive to cumulative soil loss. Socioeconomic factors that mediate land-use practices will also influence future changes in soil erosion risk. These factors include shifts in cropping patterns and land use in response to market signals that would occur, for instance, with increased demand for biofuels and rural out-migration.

Addressing the threat of increased soil erosion posed by climate change will require better quantification of the problem, greater attention to prioritizing which production systems and regions are vulnerable, and a redoubling of soil erosion management efforts:

- *Quantification.* Future approaches to soil erosion modeling and assessment will need to better capture the role of extreme events in soil erosion (Boardman 2006). Efforts to integrate meteorological time series from global climate models into soil erosion models are beginning to address this research gap. However, the complexity of these models will likely limit their use to wealthy regions. In developing regions, two-dimensional hillslope models and geographic information systems can be used more widely to quantify erosion and develop landslide hazard maps.

- *Prioritization.* Because limited resources will be available for addressing the multitudinous impacts of climate change, identification will be necessary of priority areas where serious soil erosion is occurring that could accelerate with climate change. Boardman (2006) suggested identifying soil erosion hotspots where anthropologically induced soil erosion is high because of topography, climate, and population growth. These areas include (a) the Andes and Central American highlands; (b) the Loess Plateau and Yangtze basin in China; and (c) the countries of Ethiopia, Lesotho, and Swaziland, as well as the Sahel in Africa.

- *Management.* Widening the adoption of practices and technologies that enhance soil coverage will become increasingly critical to future agricultural land management under climate change. The broad category of conservation agriculture contains many such interventions—cover crops, agroforestry, and improved fallows to reduce the period during which soil surfaces are exposed—which, along with conservation tillage and use of green manuring, can maintain or increase soil organic matter levels and conserve soil moisture (Lal 2005; Sanchez 2000).

The resilience of conservation farming systems in the Central American highlands to El Niño drought and the catastrophic soil losses from Hurricane Mitch provides strong evidence of conservation agriculture's soil stabilization potential. However, achieving broad-scale adoption of this set of practices is a significant challenge, given that factors such as land tenure instability, rural labor shortages, and nonfarm income sources tend to have a dissuasive influence on soil improvement measures (Knowler 2004).

Developing more coherent links between land management and institutional change could create a more conducive environment for land improvement. For example, the recent revegetation phenomenon in the Sahel is rooted both in technical support for land improvement and in legal code reforms that provided local communities with control over resource management decisions, such as in Niger, where ownership of trees was transferred from central to local control. This policy change appears to have been an important catalyst for investments in agroforestry and land rehabilitation. The area that has undergone revegetation is extensive, with estimates of between 2 million and 3 million hectares in Niger (U.S. Geologic Survey, unpublished data) and 0.5 million hectares in Burkina Faso (Reij, Tappan, and Belemvire 2005).

Regions that are highly dependent on climate-sensitive sectors are vulnerable to changes in water availability with climate change. Africa's dependence on rainfed agriculture exemplifies this situation because the combined factors of variable rainfall, high temperatures, and poor soil fertility heighten the sensitivity of smallholder producers to shocks from extreme climate events. A recent assessment by the Intergovernmental Panel on Climate Change (IPCC 2007) estimated that between 75 million and 250 million people in Africa will experience increased water stress by the end of this century as a result of elevated surface temperatures, increased rainfall variability, and aridity. Semiarid regions are the most vulnerable to rainfall reductions. For example, a 10 percent decrease in precipitation in regions receiving 500 millimeters per year is estimated to reduce surface drainage by 50 percent (de Wit and Stankiewicz 2006).

Long-term changes in precipitation patterns may simply reduce the total amount of land available for agriculture. In the near to medium term, however, there is reasonably good potential to sustain and enhance rainfed production through improvements in water capture and storage combined with better soil management. One of the key challenges will be to diminish the feedback between water management risk and declining soil fertility, wherein the prospect of crop failure from insufficient soil moisture hinders investments in soil fertility, which, in turn, diminishes the potential of soils to capture and retain water, thus increasing the vulnerability to drought. One way to address this issue is to focus on the manageable part of climatic variability by linking better in situ rainfall retention with incremental amounts of fertilizer to bridge ephemeral dry spells that occur during sensitive plant growth stages. Rockström (2004) reported that these types of fairly small-scale changes can double and triple cereal yields in high-risk farming environments.

LESSONS LEARNED

GHG emissions from agriculture represent a significant source of climate forcing. Globally, agriculture contributes between 70 and 90 percent of anthropogenic nitrous oxide, between 40 and 50 percent of anthropogenic methane, and 15 percent of anthropogenic carbon dioxide emissions

(DeAngelo and others 2005). Land clearance for agriculture, nitrogenous fertilizer, flooded rice production, and livestock constitute the main sources of agricultural GHGs.

Reducing the global warming potential of agriculture provides a number of opportunities to simultaneously link GHG mitigation with SLM and adaptation to climate change. From a GHG mitigative standpoint, avoiding agriculturally based emissions of nitrous oxide and methane through enhanced factor productivity and energy efficiency is more economical than modifying land-use practices to enhance carbon sequestration in soil (Smith and others 2007). Soil carbon sequestration, as a mitigative strategy, is less robust because carbon storage in soils is impermanent (that is, lasting decades); is sensitive to management changes; and can result in elevated nitrous oxide emissions.

OPPORTUNITIES FOR SUSTAINABLE LAND MANAGEMENT

Specific options for linking GHG mitigation with SLM include the following:

- *Change water management practices in paddy rice production.* Significant future reductions in methane emissions from rice can be achieved through improved water management. For instance, over the past two decades, 80 percent of paddy rice production in China has shifted from continuously flooding to ephemeral drainage at midseason. This change resulted in an average 40 percent reduction in methane emissions and an overall improvement of yield because of better root growth and fewer unproductive panicles (Li and others 2006). An additional 20 to 60 percent reduction in methane production is possible without sacrificing yield through adopting shallow flooding and through slowing methane production by substituting urea for ammonium sulfate fertilizer (DeAngelo and others 2005; Li and others 2006).
- *Improve nitrogen-use efficiency.* Reductions in methane emissions from rice do not necessarily lead to an overall reduction in net GHG emissions, because shifts between anoxic and oxic soil environments accelerate nitrification and denitrification processes, resulting in greater nitrous oxide production (DeAngelo and others 2005; Li and others 2006). Leakage of nitrogen from rice and other cropping systems can be reduced by better matching fertilizer application with plant demand (for example, by applying slow-release fertilizer nitrogen, split fertilizer application, and nitrification inhibitors). Enhanced nitrogen-use efficiency can also be achieved through the

practice of site-specific nutrient management in which fertilizer nitrogen is used only for supplying that increment not provided by indigenous nutrient sources. This method can both reduce nitrous oxide emissions and improve the economics of production through enhanced factor productivity.

- *Retain more biomass on agricultural lands.* Carbon sequestration on agricultural lands can be enhanced through the deployment of SLM practices such as agroforestry, conservation tillage, use of rotations and cover crops, and rehabilitation of degraded lands. Increasing carbon sequestration in soils, although less effective at reducing global warming potential than avoiding emissions, is essential for bolstering the long-term sustainable management of soil and water. Other carbon sequestration practices, such as agroforestry and improved fallows, also produce a number of ancillary benefits (for example, improved income, nutrition, and protection of biodiversity).

SEASONAL CLIMATE FORECASTS AND SUSTAINABLE LAND MANAGEMENT

Agricultural productivity and economic growth strongly track seasonal and interannual rainfall variability in countries that rely heavily on rainfed agriculture (Brown and Lall 2006). This relationship has important implications for SLM in highly variable climate regimes because investments in land improvement and yield-enhancing technologies are often stymied by uncertainty and risk around the timing, distribution, and quantity of rainfall. To the extent that climate change is manifested as increasing intra- and interannual climate variability, the influence of rainfall uncertainty in dampening SLM investments could become even greater.

Advances in improving the ability to provide useful seasonal climate forecasts and in developing pathways for disseminating and applying that information will be required to address this critical information gap. Forecasts that are timely and locally relevant can aid decision making. In good rainfall years, farmers and supporting institutions can invest in greater inputs to recover from or prepare for production downturns in poor rainfall years, when risk-avoidance strategies are prudent (Hansen and others 2006). Progress in climate-based crop forecasting will depend on (a) continued advances in probabilistic forecasting and downscaling, (b) embedding of crop models within climate models, and (c) enhanced use of remote sensing and research into "weather within climate." For seasonal climate forecasts to be effective, however, advances in forecasting skills will need

to be matched with better means of disseminating forecasts to farming communities through multiple forums, such as those where information on water, health, housing, and disaster management is shared (Vogel and O'Brien 2006).

RECOMMENDATIONS FOR PRACTITIONERS

Climate change is occurring within a background of larger global change with respect to population growth, urbanization, land and water use, and biodiversity. Thus, efforts to adapt to the impacts of climate change should do so in a manner that is consistent with these broader development issues. In this context, there are several opportunities to apply the products and services developed for SLM that will enhance adaptation to climate change in agriculture:

- *Address maladaptation to current climate variability.* There is significant scope for enhancing climate risk management in vulnerable regions, such as in El Niño–affected areas of southern and eastern Africa. It can be accomplished through (a) broader use of water conservation in agriculture; (b) better understanding of and support for local coping strategies; (c) resolving production bottlenecks, such as access to seed; (d) promoting changes in policies to give local communities greater stake in resource management decisions; and (e) providing access to seasonal climate information by local decision makers.

- *Invest in soil protection.* Conservation agriculture practices and measures that increase soil organic matter and reduce the time that soils are bare will become more important for enhancing the resilience of soils to greater erosive forces with climate change. Stabilizing the resource base and replenishing soil fertility through low-cost and locally relevant means is an important precursor to more technologically intensive adaptation measures, such as expansion of irrigation and use of drought-tolerant varieties (Sanchez 2005). SLM has significant knowledge and operational presence in this area.

- *Couple soil fertility improvements with soil water management.* In smallholder production systems, farmers tend to invest in soil fertility only after other production risks, especially those associated with access to water, are lessened. Reducing water risk is more cost-effective than attempting to address absolute water scarcity. SLM could assist in this process through several entry points, such as (a) targeting small investments in rainwater capture and storage for supplemental irrigation, (b) promoting practices that reduce runoff to bridge the gap between rains, and (c) linking fertility inputs to seasonal rainfall projections.

REFERENCES

Boardman, J. 2006. "Soil Erosion Science: Reflections on the Limitations of Current Approaches." *Catena* 68 (2–3): 73–86.

Brown, C., and U. Lall. 2006. "Water and Economic Development: The Role of Variability and a Framework for Resilience." *Natural Resources Forum* 30: 306–17.

DeAngelo, B., S. Rose, C. Li, W. Salas., R. Beach., T. Sulser, and S. Del Grosso. 2005. "Estimates of Joint Soil Carbon, Methane, and N_2O Marginal Mitigation Costs from World Agriculture." In *Non-CO_2 Greenhouse Gases: Science, Control, Policy, and Implementation: Proceedings of the Fourth International Symposium on Non-CO_2 Greenhouse Gases, NCGG4, Utrecht, the Netherlands, July 4–6, 2005*, ed. A. van Amstel, 609–17. Rotterdam, Netherlands: Millpress.

de Wit, M., and J. Stankiewicz. 2006. "Changes in Surface Water Supply across Africa with Predicted Climate Change." *Science Express* 10 (1126): 1–9.

Hansen, J. W., A. Challinor, A. Ines, T. Wheeler, and V. Moron. 2006. "Translating Climate Forecasts into Agricultural Terms: Advances and Challenges." *Climate Research* 33 (1): 27–41.

IPCC (Intergovernmental Panel on Climate Change). 2007. "Summary for Policymakers." In *Climate Change 2007: Impacts, Adaptation, and Vulnerability: Contribution of Working Group II to the Fourth Assessment Report of the Intergovernmental Panel on Climate Change*, ed. M. L. Parry, O. F. Canziani, J. P. Palutikof, P. J. van der Linden, and C. E. Hanson, 7–22. Cambridge, U.K.: Cambridge University Press. http://www.ipcc.ch.

Knowler, D. J. 2004. "The Economics of Soil Productivity: Local, National, and Global Perspectives." *Land Degradation and Development* 15 (6): 543–61.

Lal, R. 2005. "Climate Change, Soil Carbon Dynamics, and Global Food Security." In *Climate Change and Global Food Security*, ed. R. Lal, B. A. Stewart, N. Uphoff, and D. O. Hansen, 113–43. New York: Taylor and Francis.

Li, C., W. Salas, B. DeAngelo, and S. Rose. 2006. "Assessing Alternatives for Mitigating Net Greenhouse Gas Emissions and Increasing Yields from Rice Production in China over the Next Twenty Years." *Journal of Environmental Quality* 35: 1554–65.

Nearing, M. A., F. F. Pruski, and M. R. O'Neal. 2004. "Expected Climate Change Impacts on Soil Erosion Rates: A Review." *Journal of Soil Water Conservation* 59 (1): 43–50.

Reij, C., G. Tappan, and A. Belemvire. 2005. "Changing Land Management Practices and Vegetation on the Central Plateau of Burkina Faso (1968–2002)." *Journal of Arid Environment* 63 (3): 642–59.

Rockström, J. 2004. "Making the Best of Climatic Variability: Options for Upgrading Rainfed Farming in Water Scarce Regions." *Water Science and Technology* 49 (7): 151–56.

Sanchez, P. A. 2000. "Linking Climate Change Research with Food Security and Poverty Reduction in the Tropics." *Agriculture Ecosystems and the Environment* 82 (1–3): 371–83.

———. 2005. "Reducing Hunger in Tropical Africa While Coping with Climate Change." In *Climate Change and Global Food Security*, ed. R. Lal, B. A. Stewart, N. Uphoff, and D. O. Hansen, 3–19. New York: Taylor and Francis.

Smith, P., D. Martino, Z. Cai, and D. Gwary, H. Janzen, P. Kumar, B. McCarl, S. Ogle, F. O'Mara, C. Rice, B. Scholes, O. Sirotenko, M. Howden, T. McAllister, G. Pan, V. Romanenkov, U. Schneider, and S. Towprayoon. 2007. "Policy and Technological Constraints to Implementation of Greenhouse Gas Mitigation Options in Agriculture." *Agriculture Ecosystems and the Environment* 118 (1–4): 6–28.

Vogel, C., and K. O'Brien. 2006. "Who Can Eat Information? Examining the Effectiveness of Seasonal Climate Forecasts and Regional Climate-Risk Management Strategies." *Climate Research* 33 (1): 111–22.

SELECTED READINGS

Klein, R. S., L. Eriksen, L. Naess, A. Hammill, T. Tanner, C. Robledo, and K. O'Brien. 2007. "Portfolio Screening to Support the Mainstreaming of Adaptation to Climate Change into Development Assistance." Working Paper 102. Tyndall Centre for Climate Change Research, Norwich, U.K.

Lai, R., B. A. Stewart, N. Uphoff, and D. O. Hansen, eds. 2005. *Climate Change and Global Food Security.* New York: Taylor and Francis.

Low, P. S., ed. 2005. *Climate Change and Africa.* Cambridge, U.K.: Cambridge University Press.

Sivakumar, M., H. Das, and O. Brunini. 2005. "Impacts of Present and Future Climate Variability and Change on Agriculture and Forestry in the Arid and Semiarid Tropics." *Climatic Change* 70 (1–2): 31–72.

Tirpak, D., and M. Ward. 2005. "The Adaptation Landscape." COM/ENV/EPOC/IEA/SLT 12, Organisation for Economic Co-operation and Development, Paris, France.

High-Value Cash Crops for Semiarid Regions: Cumin Production in Khanasser, Syrian Arab Republic

Cumin is an innovative cash crop in the Middle East and North Africa. It requires relatively little land, little water, and few soil nutrients because of its low biomass. Farmers are attracted to it because of these low input requirements and its relatively short cycle of about 100 days. The International Center for Agricultural Research in the Dry Areas, based in Aleppo, Syrian Arab Republic, has been working with farmers to develop innovative crop diversification alternatives for smallholder farmers. This note shows the potential for introducing a reliably profitable cash crop to a conventional monocropping system in an area of low rainfall. Cumin provides a profitable rotation crop for poor farmers reliant on barley cash crops. The requirements of the new crop were carefully investigated to ensure that it was a consistent and reliable alternative.

PRESENTATION OF INNOVATION

Currently, cumin is the only rainfed cash crop available for Khanasser farmers as an alternative to barley monocropping. Preliminary results indicate that yields of barley after cumin are more sustainable than barley monocropping and that residual water is available for the following barley crop. When grown under supplemental irrigation, cumin requires less water than wheat. The inclusion of cumin contributes to diversification of the cropping system and farm income, and manual weeding and harvesting of the crop generate local employment opportunities.

PROJECT OBJECTIVE AND DESCRIPTION

Cumin is a cash crop with a short growing cycle and demands few moisture and nutrient inputs. Cumin is suit-able for households with even small amounts of agricultural land; however, they will need to have adequate family labor.

Proper agronomic management reduces the risk for farmers. Some suggested management practices include the following:

- Planting in mid-January
- Mixing seeds and fertilizer, and planting them together (using cereal drill)
- Using a seed rate of 30 kilograms per hectare
- Fertilizing:
  - At planting, 50 kilograms per hectare of triple super phosphate and 50 kilograms per hectare of urea
  - If spring rains are adequate, 50 kilograms of ammonium nitrate (33 percent) can be top-dressed
- Weed control:
  - Hand weeding at early stages of cumin growth
  - Herbicide application of Treflan 15 days before planting and Afalon or Gesagard soon after emergence.

BENEFITS AND RESULTS OF THE ACTIVITY

Cumin provides an alternative rainfed cash crop with acceptable yields ranging from 50 to 1,000 kilograms per hectare with averages around 250 kilograms per hectare. Gross income per season is about LS 28,990 per hectare (US$576 per hectare) with a net annual profit of about LS 16,245 per hectare (US$323 per hectare). Yields and profits are higher if the crop is irrigated. Only small land areas of 0.08 to 1.60 hectares are required for profitable activities; however, this figure varies with fluctuating market prices.

This profile was prepared by F. Turkelboom and R. Thomas, International Center for Agricultural Research in Dry Areas, Aleppo, Syrian Arab Republic.

LESSONS LEARNED AND ISSUES FOR SCALING UP

- Inputs have a high cost.
- Good management knowledge is needed to obtain good returns and reduce risks of failure.
- Cumin planted in succession is susceptible to the buildup of cumin wilt disease (but this disease does not affect the following barley crop).
- Fluctuations in cumin prices make the profits from growing cumin uncertain, but during the period studied, prices always remained above the minimum profitability thresholds (and they have recently improved).
- Cumin prices remain competitive even in marginal areas, although they depend on international trade and need close monitoring.
- Farmers need better access to market and price information before they make planting or marketing decisions.
- Management recommendations that reduce production risks should be transferred to farmers through local extension services and farmer interest groups.

ECONOMIC ASSESSMENT

For rainfed production systems, the investment cost is currently US$248 per hectare with a net return on capital of 106 percent. Net return on land is estimated at US$263 per hectare, on hired labor at 5 percent and on family labor at 17 percent. Cumin is attractive to farmers because of its low water requirements, short duration, and ability to contribute directly to household cash flow. Market price fluctuations represent a high risk.

SELECTED READINGS

La Rovere, R., and A. Aw-Hassan. 2005. *Ex ante Assessment of Agricultural Technologies for Use in Dry Marginal Areas: The Case of the Khanasser Valley, Syria.* Integrated Natural Resource Management Technical Report 6. Aleppo, Syrian Arab Republic: International Center for Agricultural Research in the Dry Areas.

La Rovere, R., A. Aw-Hassan, F. Turkelboom, and R. Thomas. 2006. "Targeting Research for Poverty Reduction in Marginal Areas of Rural Syria." *Development and Change* 37 (3): 627–48.

La Rovere, R., F. Turkelboom, A. Aw-Hassan, A. Bruggeman, and R. Thomas (Forthcoming). "A Comprehensive Assessment of Technological Options for Improving Rural Livelihoods in the Dry Marginal Areas of Syria." *International Journal of Agricultural Sustainability.*

Economic and Sustainable Land Management Benefits of the Forage Legume: Vetch

The International Center for Agricultural Research in the Dry Areas (ICARDA), based in Aleppo, Syrian Arab Republic, has been working with farmers to develop innovative crop, forage, and livestock diversification alternatives for smallholder farmers. The objectives of ICARDA's work on forage systems are to introduce leguminous forage species (for example, vetch) to the farming systems of poor livestock farmers in rural and urban communities. This effort is intended to improve production and make use of the nitrogen-fixing ability of this legume on soils that have been depleted of nutrients and soil organic matter.

Vetch is an annual forage legume that is planted in rotation with barley in winter. It is either grazed or cut for haymaking in early spring. Vetch seed can be harvested in late spring. Similarly, vetch straw is produced in late spring and used as a protein supplement to cereal straw for sheep meat and milk production. Vetch can be grown in dry areas with annual rainfall ranging from 200 to 400 millimeters although it is riskier than the more drought-tolerant barley.

PRESENTATION OF INNOVATION

Field experimentation with farmers has shown that yields of barley straw and grain increase by 25 to 40 percent when grown in rotation with vetch, as compared to continuous barley cropping. In addition, feeding vetch hay or grain as a supplement to low-quality cereal straw improves lamb growth by 20 to 30 percent. Lambs grazing on vetch in early spring gain as much as 100 to 150 grams per day.

When vetch is planted in rotation with barley, soil fertility is increased by 10 to 15 percent—mainly through increases in soil nitrogen and phosphorus. Additional income can be earned by selling vetch seed and straw. In comparisons with other tested options, the production and marketing risks of vetch are lower than those for cumin and wheat. Investment cost is US$126 per hectare with a net return on capital of 160 percent, and net return on land is US$202 per hectare.

LESSONS LEARNED

More information is required on the beneficial effects of vetch on soil fertility over the long term to increase the attractiveness of this option. Agronomic management can be improved considerably by paying more attention to seeding rates and planting methods. Farmers need access to better storage and use practices of vetch hay and would benefit from reduced costs of weeding. Vetch appears to fit well within the diversification strategies used by farmers under mixed or intensive systems.

ISSUES FOR SCALING UP: INVESTMENTS

Future research on vetch should include efforts to empower farmers to use the technology and improve the establishment and harvest of the crop. Greater support is required to establish and maintain viable forage seed systems. This effort can be accomplished by paying more attention to the creation of market opportunities for fodder and forage seed. Efforts are required to improve seed quality of high-yielding varieties and to make these varieties more readily available to farmers.

SELECTED READING

La Rovere, R., and A. Aw-Hassan. 2005. *Ex ante Assessment of Agricultural Technologies for Use in Dry Marginal Areas: The Case of the Khanasser Valley, Syria.* Integrated Natural Resource Management Technical Report 6. Aleppo, Syrian Arab Republic: International Center for Agricultural Research in the Dry Areas.

This profile was prepared by R. Thomas, F. Turkelboom, and R. LaRovere, International Center for Agricultural Research in Dry Areas, Aleppo, Syrian Arab Republic.

Participatory Barley-Breeding Program for Semiarid Regions

In a conventional crop-breeding program, the most promising lines are released as varieties, and their seed is produced under controlled conditions; only then do farmers decide on adoption. The process often results in many varieties being released, and only a few are adopted. The International Center for Agricultural Research in the Dry Areas (ICARDA) based in Aleppo, Syrian Arab Republic, has been working with farmers to develop innovative crop, forage, and livestock diversification alternatives for smallholder farmers.

The Decentralized-Participatory Plant Breeding (D-PPB) approach pioneered by ICARDA focuses on an alternative way of conducting plant breeding that is more efficient in bringing new varieties to farmers regardless of their farm size, location, wealth, or education. These varieties are adapted to the physical and socioeconomic environment. The component activities include (a) training of farmers, researchers, and extension personnel; (b) field trials; (c) seed production; and (d) dissemination workshops and publications.

PRESENTATION OF INNOVATION

The D-PPB process turns the delivery phase of a plant breeding program upside down. The program is based on the following concepts:

- The traditional linear sequence of scientists to extensionists to farmers is replaced by a team approach with scientists, extension personnel, and farmers participating in variety development.
- Selection is conducted in farmers' fields using agronomic practices they decide on.
- Farmers are the key decision makers.

The general scheme starts with planning meetings where farmers assist in designing a research agenda in which they will participate. Under the D-PPB approach, the initial farmers' adoption drives the decision of which variety to release. Hence, adoption rates are higher and risks are minimized, because farmers gain intimate knowledge of varietal performance as part of the process. The investment in seed production is nearly always paid off by farmers' adoption.

BENEFITS AND RESULTS OF THE ACTIVITY

Agriculturalists and land-poor laborers are benefiting from quicker access to improved barley varieties as a result of the D-PPB approach. Indirectly, pastoralists and their sheep herds benefit from better barley. The cyclical nature of D-PPB programs has enriched farmers' knowledge and has improved their negotiation capability, thereby empowering farming communities. Key project benefits include the following:

- Improved varieties are released quicker, and adoption rates are higher.
- Different varieties are being selected in different areas of Syria in direct response to different ecological constraints.
- Farmers spontaneously tested new varieties as early as three years after starting the program. Thousands of hectares have been planted with two newly released varieties, and about 30 varieties are under large-scale testing.
- In advanced yield trials, several lines outyielded the local varieties; yield gains were modest in Mugherat (10 to 11 percent) and higher in Khanasser (22 to 28 percent).

Farmers in Mugherat and Khanasser selected tall varieties and varieties that grow faster in winter. The visual selection of farmers in Mugherat was more closely corre-

---

This profile was prepared by S. Ceccarelli and S. Grando, International Center for Agricultural Research in the Dry Areas, Aleppo, Syrian Arab Republic.

lated with grain yield (r = 0.503) than that of farmers in Khanasser (r = 0.059).

LESSONS LEARNED AND ISSUES FOR WIDER APPLICATION

- Farmers are excellent partners: their contribution to the program increases with their understanding of the process, which becomes more and more demand driven.
- The quality of participation is unrelated to culture, religion, education, age, wealth, or gender.
- As the program develops, the breeder becomes more and more a facilitator and a provider of genetic variability.
- Participatory plant breeding increases crop biodiversity, promotes the use of land races and wild relatives, and is ideal for organic conditions.
- In the case of Syria (the only country where a detailed study was conducted), the cost-benefit ratio of participatory plant breeding is less than half (0.38) that of conventional plant breeding.
- Participatory plant breeding offers the possibility of improving more than one crop within the same program (one of the first requests of farmers across many countries).
- Participatory plant breeding allows quick response to both agronomic and climatic changes.
- Participatory plant breeding is a good entry point (easy to organize) for integrated participatory research.
- Participatory plant breeding is a good training ground for future plant breeders and can be used in university curricula.

ISSUES FOR SCALING UP: INVESTMENTS

In several countries, the D-PPB approach generated changes in the attitude of policy makers and scientists toward the benefits of participatory research. At the same time, variety release systems are considered too rigid.

Extension services need to take on new tasks. The role of extension in the D-PPB approach is in participating with farmers and researchers, in developing technology, and in involving additional farmers in the process, rather than in transferring research results from researchers to farmers.

The difficulty of national program scientists in dealing with farmers as partners is an ongoing concern. Changes within the national agricultural research and extension systems are slow.

SELECTED READINGS

Ceccarelli, S., and S. Grando. 2005. "Decentralized-Participatory Plant Breeding: A Case from Syria." In *Participatory Research and Development for Sustainable Agriculture and Natural Resource Management,* vol. 1, ed. J. Gonsalves, T. Becker, A. Braun, D. Campilan, H. De Chavez, E. Fajber, M. Kapiriri, J. Rivaca-Caminade, and R. Vernooy, 193–99. Ottawa: International Development Research Centre.

———. 2007. "Decentralized-Participatory Plant Breeding: An Example of Demand-Driven Research." *Euphytica* 155 (3): 349–60.

Ceccarelli, S., S. Grando, E. Bailey, A. Amri, M. El Felah, F. Nassif, S. Rezgui, and A. Yahyaoui. 2001. "Farmer Participation in Barley Breeding in Syria, Morocco, and Tunisia." *Euphytica* 122 (3): 521–36.

Ceccarelli, S., S. Grando, M. Baum, and S. M. Udupa. 2004. "Breeding for Drought Resistance in a Changing Climate." In *Challenges and Strategies of Dryland Agriculture,* ed. S. C. Rao and J. Ryan, 167–90. Crop Science Society of America Special Publication 32. Madison, WI: American Society of Agronomy.

Ceccarelli, S., S. Grando, and R. H. Booth. 1996. "International Breeding Programmes and Resource-Poor Farmers: Crop Improvement in Difficult Environments." In *Participatory Plant Breeding: Proceedings of a Workshop on Participatory Plant Breeding, 26–29 July 1995, Wageningen, Netherlands,* ed. P. Eyzaguirre and M. Iwanaga, 99–116. Rome: International Plant Genetic Resources Institute.

Ceccarelli, S., S. Grando, M. Singh, M. Michael, A. Shikho, M. Al Issa, A. Al Saleh, G. Kaleonjy, S. M. Al Ghanem, A. L. Al Hasan, H. Dalla, S. Basha, and T. Basha. 2003. "A Methodological Study on Participatory Barley Breeding: II. Response to Selection." *Euphytica* 133 (2): 185–200.

Mangione, D., S. Senni, M. Puccioni, S. Grando, and S. Ceccarelli. 2006. "The Cost of Participatory Barley Breeding." *Euphytica* 150 (3): 289–306.

Climate Risk Management in Support of Sustainable Land Management

Changes in climate patterns, such as the ones projected by climate change scenarios for many parts of the developing world, have the potential to change current land management practices fundamentally and to alter the risk profile of agriculturally based economies. Thus, with additional increasing commercialization and expansion of agriculture and its integration into international markets and supply chains, new risk management approaches are required that are adapted to the agricultural and rural sectors in developing countries and to the pervasive risks affecting those sectors. This profile outlines the fundamental elements of a climate risk management approach for agricultural systems.

INTRODUCTION

Farming and land management activities are exposed to seasonal climate risks arising from interannual climate variability and anthropogenic perturbations of the climate system, which are likely to result in more frequent extreme weather events. A key element of agricultural and rural risk management includes the efficient use of inherently variable natural resources (for example, runoff) and measures to increase the resilience of land and crop management systems against seasonal climate threats (for example, droughts and floods). Unmitigated risks are likely to result in increased crop and yield losses and, in extreme cases, in loss of the natural resource base (for example, soil erosion).

Land management practices and agricultural expansion can alter (increase or decrease) the exposure to natural perils and the potential impacts associated with them. Extreme climatic events can result in irreversible damage to land management and farming systems and, by extension, to

human livelihoods. Coping strategies of rural and agriculturally based communities in response to such events often lead to unsustainable land management practices. For instance, after cyclones destroyed vanilla plantations in Madagascar in 2004, many rural communities turned to shifting cultivation that infringes on protected areas and causes soil erosion. Thus, sustainable farming, of which risk management is an important component, is essential to sustainable land management and the preservation of the natural resource base.

Longer-term changes in climate patterns, such as the ones projected by climate change scenarios for many parts of the developing world, have the potential to change current land management practices fundamentally and to alter the risk profile of agriculturally based economies. These changes represent an additional layer of risk and uncertainty, and increasingly they need to be considered as part of a sound climate risk management framework.

PROJECT OBJECTIVE AND DESCRIPTION

Agricultural actors in developing countries—including commercial producers and smallholder farmers, rural communities, suppliers, traders, and planners—have long dealt with the risks in agricultural production and have adopted traditional and ad hoc means to cope with them. At the same time, with increasing commercialization and expansion of agriculture and its integration in international markets and supply chains, risk patterns and exposure can change dramatically and require risk management approaches that are adapted to the agricultural and rural sector in developing countries and to the pervasive risks affecting it.

This profile was prepared by A. Lotsch, World Bank, Agriculture and Rural Development Commodity Risk Management Group, Washington, D.C.

The Commodity Risk Management Group has worked with partners in several countries in Africa, Asia, and Latin America with the objective of assisting agricultural producers and farmers, rural lending institutions, and governments in developing means to identify, quantify, and manage risks arising from both market forces (such as commodity price volatility) and climatic events (such as seasonal droughts, floods, and storms). With respect to land management systems, the overarching objectives of risk management include protection of agriculturally based livelihoods; sustainable use of natural assets (for example, soil, water, and plant genetic material); and management of undesirable outcomes from climate-related stress (for example, plant diseases).

Although markets can have a long-term effect on the development of land management systems through trade and commodity prices (thereby altering risk profiles), seasonal variations in climate—particularly extreme events—tend to have more direct effects on the natural resource base and agricultural assets. This profile focuses mostly on risks arising from seasonal weather variability and extreme events. The fundamental elements of a climate risk management approach for agricultural systems are outlined here and include several novel technologies and approaches to managing long-term and seasonal climate risks.

PRESENTATION OF INNOVATION

The development of risk management solutions requires a systematic and stepwise approach. The principal framework for risk assessments in the productive sector includes risk identification, risk quantification, and design of risk management instruments.

Risk Identification

Several perspectives may be chosen to identify risks affecting agricultural production:

- *Spatio-temporal.* Identify the regions or locations that are affected by climatic stress and the season during which such stress has the most significant impacts.
- *Supply chain.* Identify the elements in an agricultural supply chain in which value added is at risk because of variability in climate. Additional risks in a supply chain may arise directly or indirectly from weather perturbations, such as diseases and product quality, and from logistical and operational disruptions.
- *Institutional.* Identify the operations or assets of institutions that are at risk, such as the lending portfolio of a microfinance institution or the delivery of goods and services (for example, business interruption for input suppliers).

Risk Quantification

After risks and their systemic links have been identified, the potential losses arising from such risks need to be quantified. For quantitative risk, modeling framework risk is commonly defined as a function of (a) the climate or weather hazard, (b) the exposure of agricultural assets to natural hazards, and (c) the vulnerability of these assets to such hazards. Specifically,

- *Hazards* are described by their spatial and temporal statistical properties (for example, likelihood of cyclones of a certain strength making landfall in a particular location).
- *Exposure* describes the absolute amount of assets (for example, plantations) and economic activity that may experience harm because of the effects of natural events.
- *Vulnerability* (or sensitivity) captures the degree to which assets and productive activities are susceptible to negative impacts of natural hazards.

This breakdown of risk is important because it illustrates that risk can arise from (a) temporary or permanent changes in hazard patterns (for example, climate cycles); (b) changes in the exposure (for example, agricultural expansion and intensification); and (c) changes in the vulnerability profiles (for example, crop choices). That is, risk can be reduced most effectively by managing the exposure and reducing the vulnerability (increasing the resilience) of land management systems, whereas changing hazard patterns that are largely controlled by climatic processes is more difficult.

Risk Management

Last, an appropriate risk management mechanism needs to be developed to reduce (mitigate), transfer, or share the residual risk. The appropriate management solution is a function of (a) the magnitude of the risk; (b) the likelihood that a negative outcome may be realized; (c) the institutional (informal or formal) capacity to cope with the risk; and (d) the nature of the underlying hazard (for example, droughts represent a covariate risk that tends to affect large areas simultaneously and generally results in long-term and indirect losses, whereas floods tend to be more localized and cause direct damage to crops and infrastructure such as irrigation systems).

Several existing and new technologies have been used and piloted in recent years to support risk modeling and management in developing countries. These include (a) geo-information technologies, such as space- or air-borne remote sensing and cyclone and flood modeling; (b) probabilistic and quantitative risk modeling; and (c) innovative approaches to transfer (insure) risk through market-based approaches. These innovations can enhance and complement more conventional approaches to risk management in the productive sectors, such as water storage, crop diversification, or flood mitigation schemes. Some of these innovations are featured here in relation to the risk framework described:

■ *Remote-sensing technologies.* Remote-sensing technologies can provide cost-effective and rapid means to collect hazard information. Satellite-based sensors provide repeated observations of atmospheric and terrestrial conditions and can cover large geographic areas with moderate resolution sensors or small areas with very high spatial resolution. Examples for applications of remote-sensing technology include (a) flood mapping and detection, (b) measurement of tropical rainfall, (c) monitoring of vegetation and crop conditions, and (d) cyclone tracking. Although remote-sensing technology provides a very powerful tool in many risk applications, a key limitation is that it is a relatively new technology that provides limited historical observations, which are critical in modeling the long-term patterns of climatic hazards. (For some sensors, reliable time series are available from the mid-1980s; however, the more advanced technologies generally provide fewer than 10 years of temporal observations.)

■ *Bio-geophysical and atmospheric models.* Bio-geophysical and atmospheric models are frequently used when direct observations of hazards are not available. Careful calibration of models allows the simulation of hazard patterns over a longer time period, which is critical to quantify trends and return periods of extreme climate events, such severe droughts or floods. Examples of state-of-the-art modeling in support of hazard analysis include (a) floodplain and inundation models using numerical water balance and drainage, (b) cyclone models that dynamically simulate the trajectories and wind speed of cyclones, and (c) regional circulation models that can be used to simulate seasonal climate patterns and provide seasonal forecasts.

■ *Risk models.* Risk models combine the information about hazards in a probabilistic framework with information about the vulnerability and exposure of assets to estimate the likely damages and financial losses arising from extreme climatic events. Advances in geo-information technology, such as geographic information systems, facilitate the assimilation and analysis of hazard, vulnerability, and financial models in an integrated framework. Many of these systems have become user friendly and can be deployed on desktop computer systems to be used in an interactive and dynamic fashion by decision makers in support of risk assessment and management.

■ *Innovative approaches for risk transfer.* Most developing countries lack agricultural insurance. Traditional multi-peril crop insurance (MPCI) programs, which compensate farmers on the basis of yield loss measured in the field, have major drawbacks: (a) adverse selection (that is, farmers know more about their risks than the insurer, leading the low-risk farmers to opt out and leaving the insurer with only bad risks); (b) moral hazard (that is, farmers' behaviors can influence the extent of damage that qualifies for insurance payouts); and (c) high administrative costs, especially in small farmer communities, and difficulties of objective loss adjustment. As a result, a strong movement exists to develop index-based insurance solutions, which have several advantages over MPCI. Index-based insurance products are contingent claims contracts for which payouts are determined by an objective parameter, such as rainfall, temperature, and regional yield level, that is highly correlated with farm-level yields or revenue outcomes. Farmers with index contracts receive timely payouts because the compensation is automatically triggered when the chosen index parameter reaches a prespecified level. The automatic trigger reduces administrative costs for the insurer by eliminating the need for tedious field-level damage assessment, while the objective and exogenous nature of the index prevents adverse selection and moral hazard. Index products are most suitable for covariate risks (risks affecting larger areas or groups of people simultaneously), and most index product development to date has concentrated on rainfall deficit (that is, drought), which is particularly difficult to insure by traditional methods.

BENEFITS AND RESULTS OF THE ACTIVITY

Several benefits accrue from following a systematic approach to assessing risks in the productive sector in relation to sustainable land management and from applying the specific technologies described in this profile:

- The disaggregation of risk into hazard, vulnerability, and exposure provides a clear framework under which experts from different disciplines, including climate experts and meteorologists, social scientists, engineers, and agronomists, can collaborate on risk assessments. In addition, it defines a clear functional relationship between natural hazards and negative outcomes of risk.

- A clear risk management framework identifies the areas where investments would have the highest marginal effect to reduce risk. For instance, systematic risk modeling reveals how increasing exposure (for example, agricultural expansion in floodplains) contributes to the overall risk compared to the vulnerability arising from poor farming practices.

- A risk management framework is scalable, and the same general framework can be used with varying geographic and sectoral detail. That is, simple risk models can be developed when data availability and quality are an issue, and more detailed and sector-specific models can easily be incorporated if appropriate data are available.

- Quantifying and mapping risks has an important awareness-raising effect because risks are frequently not explicitly addressed. Risk assessments can provide a powerful tool to introduce measures to manage risks before damages and losses occur, rather than after a disaster and severe event.

- Climate risk management provides a framework to promote new technology, such as better computer-based land-monitoring systems, and to build capacity for public and private sector entities, such as planning departments or the domestic insurance market.

LESSONS LEARNED AND ISSUES FOR WIDER APPLICATION

- Good data are the most critical inputs for any risk modeling. Unfortunately, adequate data are rarely found in most client countries, or poor data management systems prevent the data from being readily used. Despite sophisticated satellite technology and models, no substitute exists for high-quality data collection on the ground by agencies such as hydrometeorological services and statistical bureaus. In many countries, particularly in Africa, the capacity to collect data on natural hazards, including weather data, is deteriorating rapidly. Investments in hydrometeorological infrastructure and data management systems are fundamental to supporting climate risk management, which is virtually impossible without solid data and statistical capacity at all administrative levels.

- National and local agencies could use readily available public data sources, such as the ones derived from satellite data, more effectively. Capacity building in technical agencies, such as agrometeorological services, has the potential to unlock the wealth of underused data sources that can generate a variety of public goods.

- Simple hazard and risk assessments can be performed in most countries by compiling data from existing sources (for example, land-use inventories or climatological time series) and integrating them systematically in a common framework (through spatial-reference data layers in a geographic information system). This approach can provide a powerful starting point for engaging local agencies and stakeholders and can stimulate more focused sector- or asset-specific risk analyses.

- Insurance markets in the productive sectors, in particular agriculture, are largely underdeveloped in most client countries. Index-based insurance products using quantitative risk modeling can potentially provide more adapted risk management solutions for the agricultural sector in developing countries. Deploying them effectively, however, requires capacity building in the domestic insurance sector, leveraging of local capacity to model risk, investments in sustainable data collection and management systems, and risk education and sensitization among stakeholders (such as producers, suppliers, and lending institutions in an agricultural supply chain).

INVESTMENT NEEDS AND PRIORITIES

Key investments for better climate risk management include the following:

- Upgrading of hydrometeorological infrastructure, including synoptic weather stations, gauging stations for river runoff and surface water, and agrometeorological sites. This fundamental investment requires a long-term perspective, including the development of institutions and agencies that have the mandate and resources to manage such systems and create added value through dissemination of climate information.

- Capacity building at the national and below-national levels to collect, manage, disseminate, and use data for climate and disaster risk management. Such capacity building includes basic training of technical personnel, development of risk assessment protocols (before and after seasonal events), and statistical capacity building.

- Development of multisector risk management frameworks that clearly delineate and facilitate public and private sector responsibilities in risk management, including insurance through market-based instruments and disaster response by public entities. A key element of such a framework is effective multilevel and multisector stakeholder coordination.

- Systematic development and updating of baseline data and natural hazards and risks arising from them. This effort would include development of land management information systems, with routine inventories of the natural resource base, inventories of the key assets in the productive sectors, and updating of vulnerability profiles using some of the technologies described in this profile.

- Improvement of rural infrastructure and capacity. Hard solutions for improving transportation, water storage facilities, information and communication infrastructure, drainage and irrigation systems are needed, as well as soft solutions for improving market development and diversification, community-driven risk management plans, or capacity extension services.

SELECTED READINGS

Hartell, J., H. Ibarra, J. Skees, and J. Syroka. 2006. *Risk Management in Agriculture for Natural Hazards.* Rome: Istituto di Servizi per il Mercato Agricolo Alimentare. http://www.sicuragro.it/pages/..%5CItalia%5CDownloads%5CDerivati%20meteo%20Ismea%20-%20Ver%20Inglese.pdf.

Hellmuth, M. E., A. Moorhead, M. C. Thomson, and J. Williams, eds. 2007. *Climate Risk Management in Africa: Learning from Practice.* New York: Columbia University.

King, M. D., C. L. Parkinson, C. Partington, and R. G. Williams. 2007. *Our Changing Planet: A View from Space.* New York: Cambridge University Press.

UNDESA (United Nations Department of Economic and Social Affairs). 2007. "Developing Index-Based Insurance for Agriculture in Developing Countries." Sustainable Development Innovation Brief 2, UNDESA, New York. http://www.un.org/esa/sustdev/publications/innovationbriefs/no2.pdf.

WEB RESOURCES

Dartmouth Flood Observatory Web site. This Web site contains an active archive of large floods, from 1985 to the present. http://www.dartmouth.edu/~floods.

International Task Force on Commodity Risk Management in Developing Countries. Lighting Africa is a World Bank Group initiative. Its aim is to provide up to 250 million people in Sub-Saharan Africa with access to non-fossil fuel based, low cost, safe, and reliable lighting products with associated basic energy services by the year 2030. Web site: http://www.itf-commodityrisk.org.

Land Degradation Surveillance:
Quantifying and Monitoring Land Degradation

Diagnostic surveillance approaches used in the public health sector can now be adapted and deployed to provide a reliable mechanism for evidence-based learning and the sound targeting of investments in sustainable land management (SLM) programs. Initially, a series of case definitions are developed through which the problem can be quantified. Then, sample units are screened to determine whether they meet the case criteria. This process involves conducting prevalence surveys requiring measurement of a large number of sample units. The land management surveillance approach uses a combination of cutting-edge tools, such as satellite remote sensing at multiple scales; georeferenced ground-sampling schemes based on sentinel sites; infrared spectroscopy for rapid, reliable soil and plant tissue analysis; and mixed-effects statistical models to provide population-based estimates from hierarchical data.

The approach provides a scientifically rigorous framework for evidenced-based management of land resources that is modeled on well-tested scientific approaches used in epidemiology. It provides a spatial framework for testing interventions in landscapes in a way that samples the variability in conditions, thereby increasing the ability to generalize from outcomes. The baseline that the protocol generates provides a scientifically rigorous platform for monitoring outcomes of intervention projects at a landscape level. The approach is particularly well suited to providing high-quality information at low cost in areas such as Sub-Saharan Africa, where existing data on land resources are sparse. It is being used in a United Nations Environment Programme (UNEP) capacity-building project to guide strategies for land restoration in five West African dryland countries and in a World Bank Global Environment Facility

(GEF) project in Kenya, led by the Kenya Agricultural Research Institute, which is designed to tackle land degradation problems in the Lake Victoria basin. Soil health surveillance has been recommended as part of a strategy endorsed by the New Partnership for Africa's Development (NEPAD) for saving Africa's soils and is proposed for Sub-Saharan Africa as a component of the Global Digital Soil Map of the World project.

INTRODUCTION

Many of the problems associated with managing land stem from a lack of systematic and operational approaches for assessing and monitoring land degradation at different scales (village to global). As a result, there is no mechanism for sound targeting of interventions and no basis for reliable evidence-based learning from the billions of dollars that have been invested in SLM programs. Recent scientific and technical advances are enabling diagnostic surveillance approaches used in the public health sector to be deployed in SLM. Land degradation surveillance provides a spatial framework for diagnosis of land management problems, systematic targeting and testing of interventions, and assessment of outcomes.

A broad range of stakeholders, such as regional and national policy makers, donors, environmental convention secretariats, and civil society, are asking these key questions:

- What is the state of the nation's land at a particular point in time?
- How much agricultural land in Sub-Saharan Africa is currently suffering from productivity declines and off-site impacts attributable to soil degradation?

This profile was prepared by K. D. Shepherd, T.-G. Vågen, and T. Gumbricht, World Agroforesty Centre (ICRAF), Nairobi, Kenya, and M. G. Walsh, Earth Institute, Columbia University, New York.

- What caused the degradation in places where it exists, and how can further degradation be prevented?
- Can land degradation be reversed, and if so, what are the costs to individuals and to society?
- Are there cost-effective and socially acceptable means for treating degraded lands to increase their productivity, while avoiding harmful side effects to the environment, such as the pollution of surface waters and accelerated greenhouse gas emissions?

PROJECT OBJECTIVES AND DESCRIPTION

Surprisingly, the world does not have clear answers to these questions at present. The basic premise of this project is that a problem cannot be managed unless progress can be measured from a baseline toward a well-defined target. Thus, a land health surveillance system must accomplish the following:

- Provide high spatial resolution and practical, timely, and cost-effective information about where specific land degradation processes occur in a given region or country and how those processes are changing over time.
- Identify areas at risk of degradation and the commensurate preventive measures in a spatially explicit way.
- Provide a framework for rigorous scientific testing and implementation of locally relevant rehabilitative soil management interventions, addressing what works, what does not, where, how, and at what cost to individuals and society.
- Anticipate and respond to external requests from a wide audience (that is, farmers, conservationists, scientists, and policy makers).

PRESENTATION OF DIAGNOSTIC SURVEILLANCE AND OPERATIONAL FRAMEWORK

Human health surveillance techniques are a normal part of public health. Health surveillance is based on case definitions that define prevalence (percentage of people affected) and incidence (new cases). This project proposes an analogous land health surveillance system that provides the scientific and factual database essential to informed decision making and appropriate policy action (Shepherd and Walsh 2007).

Soil health diagnostic surveillance aims are as follows:

- Provide diagnostic information on land degradation problems to guide resource allocation and management decisions.

- Identify cause-and-effect relationships needed for primary prevention, early detection, and rehabilitation of degraded land at different spatial scales.
- Provide a scientifically rigorous platform for testing and monitoring land management interventions.
- Provide a conceptual and logical framework for understanding coupled social-ecological systems.

A diagnostic surveillance framework (box 5.1) can provide a basis for a quantitative, evidence-based approach to land management. After a problem has been identified, a critical step is to describe a case definition through which the problem can be quantified. Problems such as disease in populations generally exist as a continuum of severity; however, for practical reasons, dichotomizing the diagnostic continuum into "cases" and "noncases" or "affected" and "nonaffected" is often helpful. The lack of rigorous stipulation of diagnostic criteria for key land degradation problems is a major impediment in formulating a sound development policy. Adequate definitions of *degraded land* and *nondegraded land* are a prerequisite to assessing the extent of land degradation.

After case definitions are stipulated, a screening test is required to measure the problem in individuals or sample units and classify them as "case" or "noncase." The availability of rapid, reliable (that is, highly repeatable and reproducible), and cost-effective screening tests (for example, equivalent to blood tests used in medicine) is key to using the surveillance framework to conduct prevalence surveys involving measurement of a large number of sample units. In clinical medicine, large investments are made in development of screening tests, and even the case definition may be defined in relation to the screening test. For example, for some disorders, an operational case definition is used that assigns an arbitrary cut-off value of the screening test as a decision threshold for treatment.

The surveillance approach is put into effect using a combination of cutting-edge tools (figure 5.3), including satellite remote sensing at multiple scales; georeferenced ground-sampling schemes based on sentinel sites; infrared spectroscopy for rapid, reliable soil and plant tissue analysis; and mixed-effects statistical models to provide population-based estimates from hierarchical data. The methods provide accurate information on the areas where land degradation is taking place, on the different manifestations of land degradation and soil constraints, on the extent of the problems, and on the sort of intervention strategies that are required to prevent or reverse degradation. The methods have been designed to be simple and cost-effective so that

The diagnostic surveillance framework involves the following steps:

1. Identify the specific land degradation problem or groups of problems.
2. Develop a rigorous case definition of *affected* and *nonaffected* states.
3. Develop a screening test (or set of tests) so that subjects can be assigned rapidly to affected or nonaffected states. Infrared spectroscopy can play a key role as a screening tool for identification of cases.
4. Apply the screening test to subjects in randomized sampling schemes designed to provide unbiased prevalence data on the specified problem.

5. Conduct measurements. Simultaneous measurement of environmental and socioeconomic correlates permits problem risk factors to be identified. Controllable risk factors point to the main management levers for controlling the problem.
6. Confirm risk factors through follow-up surveys that measure changes in the problem over time (incidence) and assess intervention outcomes. Assessment of outcomes may lead to a new or refined problem definition.

The accompanying figure shows the relationship of these steps.

Source: International Centre for Research in Agroforestry.

Diagnostic Surveillance Framework

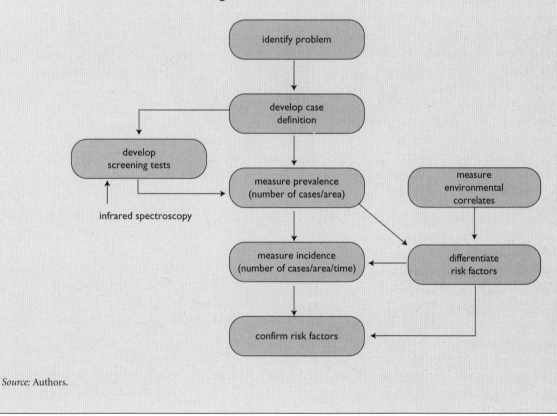

Source: Authors.

they can be implemented in isolated areas and in countries with limited resources.

At a regional or national scale, land degradation risk domains are first established using low-resolution time-series satellite information on vegetation cover. These domains are further sampled using sentinel sites, consisting of 10-by-10-kilometer blocks. Within sentinel sites, high-resolution imagery and ground sampling are used to gather data on vegetation and soil condition at randomized points. Infrared spectroscopy is used for rapid, reliable, and low-cost

Figure 5.3 Successive Samples of Land Degradation Problem Domains at a Hierarchy of Scales Using Satellite Imagery, Ground Sampling, and Laboratory Analysis of Soils by Infrared Spectroscopy

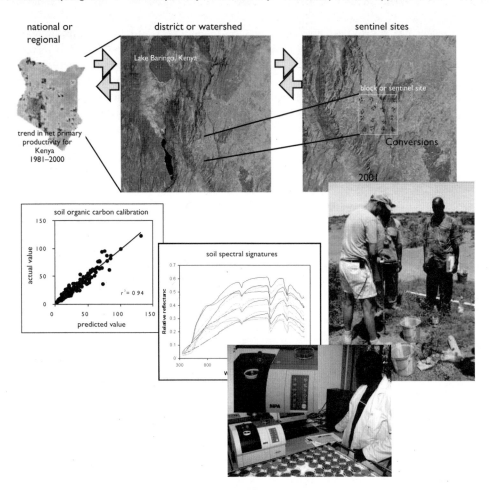

Source: ICRAF.

soil analysis and development of soil condition indexes. Degradation indexes are related to risk factors such as vegetation type and cover and are then mapped out through calibration to the satellite imagery using statistical inference. This information is used to spatially target land management strategies for systematic testing. The sentinel sites provide not only a framework for change detection through follow-up surveys (for example, after five years) but also a spatial platform for testing recommended land management options. For example, spatially distributing tree planting trials in each sub-block ensures that species are tested over a wide range of land conditions; consequently, growth performance can be correlated with site indexes, which can be used to predict tree performance at new sites. The steps used in the framework are described in more detail in box 5.2

The land degradation surveillance framework is being used in a UNEP capacity-building project to guide strategies for land restoration in five West African dryland countries

(see http://www.worldagroforestry.org/wadrylands/index .html) and in a World Bank GEF project in Kenya, led by the Kenya Agricultural Research Institute, which is designed to tackle land degradation problems in the Lake Victoria basin. Soil health surveillance has been recommended as part of a NEPAD-endorsed strategy for saving Africa's soils (Swift and Shepherd 2007) and is proposed for Sub-Saharan Africa as a component of the Global Digital Soil Map of the World project (see http://www.globalsoilmap.net/). Further information on infrared spectroscopy for sensing soil quality is available at http://www.worldagroforestrycentre.org/sens ingsoil/.

BENEFITS AND RESULTS OF THE ACTIVITY

The activity provides a scientifically rigorous framework for evidenced-based management of land resources, modeled on well-tested scientific approaches used in epidemiology.

Box 5.2   Steps in the Land Degradation Surveillance Framework

The land degradation surveillance framework involves the following steps:

1. At a regional or national scale, establish land degradation risk domains using low-resolution time-series satellite information on vegetation cover in combination with long-term rainfall records. The risk domains indicate areas where land may have been degraded or recovered over the past 25 years and are used as a sampling frame for more detailed studies. Alternatively, stratification and sampling of the Landsat World Reference System grid can be used as a sampling frame. Ancillary data on population, infrastructure, climatic zones, and the like are integrated to build quantitative scenario analyses.

2. Sample contrasting areas using moderate-resolution (for example, Landsat, ASTER, SPOT) satellite imagery, which provides data on major land-cover conversions. Processing of full-coverage imagery at this scale provides data on prevalence of woody cover and bare soil areas. Variation within these areas is further sampled through sentinel sites to provide more detailed information on land condition. Sentinel sites consist of 10-by-10-kilometer blocks, which are logistically convenient for field sampling while being large enough to encompass major landscape variability.

3. For the sentinel sites, obtain high-resolution (0.6 to 2.4 meter) satellite imagery, which allows individual fields, trees, and erosion features to be observed. Within the sites, a standardized, georeferenced ground survey is used to provide direct measurement of land condition. The 10-by-10-km blocks are spatially stratified into 2.5-kilometer sub-blocks. Within each sub-block, an area of 1 square kilometer is sampled using a cluster of 10 randomized 1,000-square-meter observation plots. Direct observations are made in four 100-square-meter subplots. Socioeconomic surveys also use the cluster design (for example, sampling of households or villages nearest to cluster centroids).

4. Within plots, observe landform, topography, visible signs of soil erosion, land use, vegetation type and cover, and vegetation density and distribution, and take soil samples. Vegetation type is classified using the Food and Agriculture Organization Land Cover Classification System, supplemented with woody biomass estimates. Single-ring infiltration measurements are made on a selection of plots (three in each cluster). A field crew of four people can complete a block in

about 14 to 16 field days. The number of plots can be adjusted, if desired, to meet different objectives.

5. Characterize soil samples using infrared spectroscopy. This technique is widely used in industry for rapid and routine characterization of materials and has been adapted for rapid, reliable, and low-cost soil analysis. This no-chemical method is attractive for laboratories in developing countries because it minimizes sample preparation and requires only a source of electricity. Furthermore, many agricultural inputs and products can be analyzed using the same instrument. Subsets of samples are sent to specialized laboratories for conventional soil analysis and isotope analysis. These expensive analyses, conducted on relatively few samples, are calibrated to the infrared spectral data and predicted for all samples. Also, spectral indicators of soil condition are derived that successfully screen soils into intact or degraded categories.

6. Compile standard data-entry sheets that can be enabled for Web-based data entry. The data are compiled in a central database. Individual users are provided with password access to their own data.

7. Use specialized statistical analyses for handling hierarchical data to derive population-based estimates for indicators of land condition and to analyze the effect of environmental covariates (for example, vegetation cover and soil spectral indicators) at different spatial scales. Robust statistical inference mechanisms with spatial models, pedotransfer functions, and expert systems are under development.

8. Use the georeferenced sampling scheme to allow ground observations (for example, soil condition index) to be calibrated directly to satellite imagery and to be spatially interpolated and mapped.

9. Produce electronic atlases showing areas that are already degraded, areas at risk, and intact areas, with matched recommendations on intervention strategies.

10. Propose spatially explicit land management strategies for systematic testing (for example, enrichment planting of trees to meet specific tree-density targets).

11. Through the sentinel sites, provide not only a framework for change detection through follow-up surveys (for example, after five years) but also a spatial platform for testing land management interventions. For example, spatially distributing tree planting trials in the blocks ensures that species are tested over a wide range of land conditions, so that growth performance can be related back to site indexes, which can be used to predict tree performance at new sites.

Source: International Centre for Research in Agroforestry.

Currently, no comparable system is in operation. The systematic application of the approach will provide unbiased prevalence data on land degradation problems and permit quantification of land degradation risk factors, thereby enabling preventive and rehabilitative measures for SLM to be appropriately targeted. The approach provides a spatial framework for testing interventions in landscapes in a way that samples the variability in conditions, thereby increasing the ability to generalize from outcomes. The baseline that the protocol generates provides a scientifically rigorous platform for monitoring effects of intervention projects at a landscape level. The hierarchical sampling frame and statistical methods used allow systematic aggregation of results and population-level inferences to be made about land properties at different scales. The approach is particularly well suited to providing high-quality information at low cost in areas such as Sub-Saharan Africa, where existing data on land resources are sparse.

LESSONS LEARNED AND ISSUES FOR WIDER APPLICATION

The most difficult area for adoption is the advanced data analysis techniques used. An efficient solution to this barrier could be establishment of regional analytical centers, which would provide sampling schemes (global position system points, standardized forms, and protocols), as well as remote-sensing information and processing of field data posted by field teams on the Internet. In addition, the centers would fulfill a technical and scientific capacity-building and support role.

INVESTMENT NEEDS AND PRIORITIES

Widespread application of this approach principally requires investment in capacity building of national teams in the approaches and methods. Operating costs for implementing a national surveillance system in the field are modest, and existing soil or natural resource survey departments could easily take up this role. The advanced data analysis techniques used are the most difficult area for adoption. An efficient solution to this barrier could be establishment of regional analytical centers that would provide sampling schemes (global position system points, standardized forms, and protocols); remote-sensing information; and processing of field data posted by field teams on the Internet. The centers would also fulfill a technical and scientific capacity-

building and support role. A government would need to take the following steps to implement a national-level surveillance program:

- Provide exposure training in the approaches and methods to a national team of scientists.
- Equip a national soil laboratory with a near-infrared spectrometer (about US$75,000), provide basic training, ensure basic facilities for soil processing and storage, and provide limited conventional soil analysis.
- Provide resources for two survey teams for about 12 months of fieldwork every five years (each team will need one surveyor and two field assistants, as well as a vehicle, a global positioning system, an auger set, and field operating funds) to establish sentinel sites (for example, 50 sites) throughout the country.
- Train a national remote-sensing and geographic information system lab in data analytical techniques with support from the regional surveillance center.
- Orient national agronomic testing and socioeconomic research programs to work through the sentinel sites.
- Establish additional sentinel sites for setting up baselines and monitoring outcomes for individual development projects aimed at land improvement.

REFERENCES

Shepherd, K. D., and M. G. Walsh. 2007. "Infrared Spectroscopy—Enabling an Evidence-Based Diagnostic Surveillance Approach to Agricultural and Environmental Management in Developing Countries." *Journal of Near Infrared Spectroscopy* 15: 1–19.

Swift, M. J., and K. D. Shepherd, eds. 2007. *Saving Africa's Soils: Science and Technology for Improved Soil Management in Africa.* Kenya, Nairobi: World Agroforestry Centre.

SELECTED READING

Infrared Diagnostics for Agriculture and the Environment. 2008. "Sensing Soil Condition: Infrared Diagnostics for Agriculture and the Environment." World Agroforestry Centre, Nairobi. http://www.worldagroforestrycentre .org/sensingsoil/.

Vågen, T-G., K. D. Shepherd, and M. G. Walsh. 2006. "Sensing Landscape Level Change in Soil Quality Following Deforestation and Conversion in the Highlands of Madagascar Using Vis-NIR Spectroscopy." *Geoderma* 133: 281–94.

WEB RESOURCES

Global Digital Soil Map of the World. Global Digital Soil Map of the World project seeks to make a new digital soil map of the world using state-of-the-art and emerging technologies for soil mapping and predicting soil properties at fine resolution. The map will be supplemented by interpretation and functionality options that aim to assist better decision-making in various global issues, such as food production and hunger eradication, climate change, and environmental degradation: http://www.globalsoilmap.net/.

West Africa Drylands Project. The West Africa Drylands project emphasizes the application of science-based tools to help accelerate learning on sustainable dryland management and increase adaptive capacity at all scales, from local communities to regional and international policy bodies. Learn more about the project on its web site: http://www.worldagroforestry.org/wadrylands/index.html.

PART III

Web-Based Resources

CHAPTER 6

Web-Based Tools and Methods for Sustainable Land Management

his section provides information to help locate key resources on tools and methods being developed by international, national, and civil society agencies that work on different aspects of land and natural resource management.

GLOBAL FIELD AND MARKET INTELLIGENCE ON CEREAL AND OILSEEDS

The U.S. Department of Agriculture (USDA) and Foreign Agricultural Service (FAS) have a site where users can access near real-time data and growing conditions for major cereal, fiber (such as cotton), and oilseed crops in most countries (figure 6.1).

To use the USDA-FAS Crop Explorer, go to http://www .pecad.fas.usda.gov/cropexplorer/.

REMOTE-SENSING TOOL FOR WATER RESOURCES MANAGEMENT

The USDA and FAS, in cooperation with the National Aeronautics and Space Administration (NASA) and the University of Maryland, are routinely monitoring lake and reservoir height variations for approximately 100 lakes located around the world. The Global Reservoir and Lake Monitor project (figure 6.2) is the first of its kind to use near real-time radar altimeter data over inland water bodies in an operational manner.

Surface elevation products are produced by a semiautomated process and placed at this Web site for USDA and public viewing. Monitoring heights for approximately 100 reservoirs and lakes around the world will greatly assist the Production Estimates and Crop Assessment Division of the FAS in locating regional droughts quickly, as well as improve crop production estimates for irrigated regions located downstream from lakes and reservoirs. All targeted lakes and reservoirs are located within major agricultural regions around the world. Reservoir and lake height variations may be viewed by placing the cursor on and clicking the continent of interest.

The link to Global Reservoir and Lake Monitor project is http://www.pecad.fas.usda.gov/cropexplorer/global_reser voir/.

HYDROLOGICAL DATA AND DIGITAL WATERSHED MAPS

The Conservation Science Program of the World Wildlife Fund (WWF) is currently developing a new and innovative global hydrological database, called HydroSHEDS. HydroSHEDS stands for **Hydro**logical data and maps based on **SH**uttle **E**levation **D**erivatives at Multiple **S**cales (figure 6.3). For many parts of the world, these data and the tools built to use them open a range of previously inaccessible analyses and applications related to freshwater conservation and environmental planning. HydroSHEDS is based on

151

Figure 6.1   USDA-FAS Crop Explorer

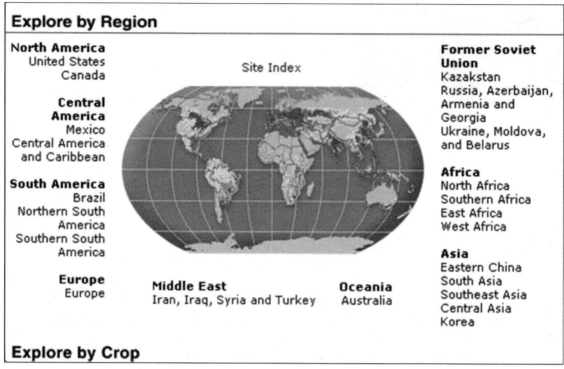

Source: http://www.pecad.fas.usda.gov/cropexplorer/.

Figure 6.2   USDA-FAS Global Reservoir and Lake Monitor

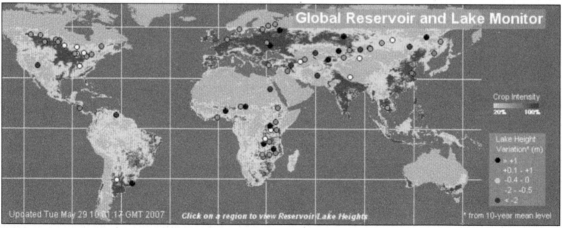

Source: http://www.pecad.fas.usda.gov/cropexplorer/global_reservoir/.

high-resolution elevation data obtained during a Space Shuttle flight for NASA's Shuttle Radar Topography Mission.

At the most basic level, HydroSHEDS allows scientists to create digital river and watershed maps. These maps can then be coupled with a variety of other geospatial data sets or applied in computer simulations, such as hydrologic models, to estimate flow regimes. HydroSHEDS allows scientists and managers to perform analyses that range from basic watershed delineation to sophisticated flow modeling.

HydroSHEDS can be used for a wide range of applications. WWF has already applied the data to create aquatic habitat classification maps for remote and poorly mapped

Figure 6.3 HydroSHEDS Database

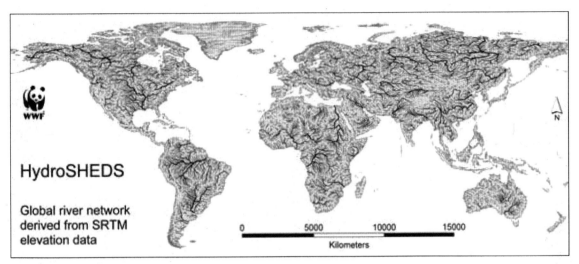

HydroSHEDS

Global river network
derived from SRTM
elevation data

Source: http://hydrosheds.cr.usgs.gov.

regions, such as the Amazon headwaters and the Guiana Shield. Ultimately, taxonomists will be able to link their field-site locations directly to digital river maps. WWF researchers hope to use HydroSHEDS in the future to assess the possible impacts of climate change on freshwater ecosystems.

HydroSHEDS has been developed by the Conservation Science Program of WWF, in partnership with the U.S. Geological Survey, the International Centre for Tropical Agriculture, the Nature Conservancy, and the Center for Environmental Systems Research at the University of Kassel in Germany. Major funding for this project was provided to WWF by JohnsonDiversey Inc.

Data for Asia, Central America, and South America are now available. Other continents are scheduled for completion by 2009. HydroSHEDS data are freely available for noncommercial use.

For more information and data, visit http://hydrosheds .cr.usgs.gov.

BASIN AND WATERSHED SCALE HYDROLOGICAL MODELING

The hydrology of a regional-scale river system can be modeled as a geospatially explicit water mass balance for each grid cell within the basin contributing to stream flow and downstream routing. As such, a model can be divided into two major components: (a) a vertical component that calculates the water balance at each individual grid cell and (b) a horizontal component that routes the runoff generated by each grid cell to the ocean. This split into two separate com-

ponents has a number of advantages. It separates indirect water routing from direct water diversions. The former includes impacts of land-use change and climate change and is expressed mainly through the vertical model—that is, the water balance at the grid cell level. The latter includes increased withdrawals and diversions for agricultural, industrial, and domestic use and affects mainly the horizontal model, which represents the flow routing. The separation into the grid cell and channel components creates an easy interface to treat non-point-source and in-channel chemical processes separately.

To learn more about the variable infiltration capacity (VIC) macroscale hydrologic model, visit http://www.hydro .washington.edu/Lettenmaier/Models/VIC/VIChome.html.

The Distributed Hydrology Soil Vegetation Model (DHSVM) is a distributed hydrologic model that explicitly represents the effects of topography and vegetation on water fluxes through the landscape. It is typically applied at high spatial resolutions on the order of 100 meters for watersheds of up to 104 square kilometers and at subdaily time scales for multiyear simulations (figure 6.4).

To learn more about DHSVM, visit http://www .hydro.washington.edu/Lettenmaier/Models/DHSVM/index .shtml.

RIVER BASIN DEVELOPMENT AND MANAGEMENT

The International Water Management Institute is documenting the historical development of nine river basins from different parts of the world to derive generic understanding

Figure 6.4 The Distributed Hydrology Soil Vegetation Model

Source: Lettenmaier, University of Washington, Seattle.

about how societies manage water resources under growing population and basin closure, which problems are faced, and which range of solutions (technical and institutional) are available for a given physical and societal context (see figure 6.5). The studies first address the past transformations of each basin, periodize changes, and draw lessons on how population growth and water resource development relate to food production and environmental degradation and preservation. Second, they investigate in more detail the present situation and define the scope for improvement in management, allocation, environmental services, and income generation. A third part deals with projections and scenarios, with the aim of informing current or future stakeholders' dialogues and providing decision makers with a state-of-the-art analysis and understanding of the basin challenges and opportunities.

To learn more about the conceptual framework, basin studies, and tools, visit http://www.iwmi.cgiar.org/assessment/Research_Projects/River_Basin_Development_and_Management/.

TRACKING FLOODS GLOBALLY: THE DARTMOUTH FLOOD OBSERVATORY

The Dartmouth Flood Observatory detects, maps, and measures major flood events worldwide using satellite remote sensing. The record of such events is preserved as a "World Atlas of Flooded Lands."

An "Active Archive of Large Floods, 1985 to present," describes these events individually. Maps and images accompany many of the floods described and can be accessed by links in the yearly catalogs (see, for example, figure 6.6). As the archive of reliable data grows, the possibility increases of predicting where and when major flooding will occur and of analyzing trends over time.

Surface Water Watch is a satellite-based surface-water monitoring system. Orbital AMSR-E (Advanced Microwave Scanning Radiometer for the Earth Observing System) microwave measurements over selected river reaches and wetlands are used to measure discharge and watershed runoff. The system can be used to determine where flooding is under way today, to predict inundation extents, and to assess the current runoff status of watersheds. For rivers in cold regions, river ice status is also being monitored.

To access the Dartmouth Flood Observatory and its products, visit http://www.dartmouth.edu/~floods/.

THE CARNEGIE LANDSAT ANALYSIS SYSTEM

Problems in detecting selective logging with remote sensing are complicated by the fact that tree species diversity in

Figure 6.5   River Basin Development and Management Comparative Study

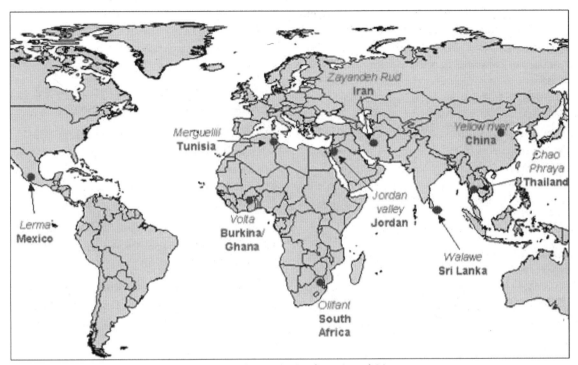

Source: http://www.iwmi.cgiar.org/assessment/Research_Projects/River_Basin_Development_and_Management.

Figure 6.6   Dartmouth Flood Observatory Map

Source: http://www.dartmouth.edu/~floods/.

some tropical rainforests (for example, the Brazilian Amazon or the Congo) is very high, and most species are locally rare. Logging is highly selective because markets accept only a few species for timber use. This situation contrasts with logging practices in other parts of the world where clearcutting or nearly complete harvests predominate. These large differences in logging intensity result in variation of forest disturbance and collateral damages caused by harvesting activities.

The Carnegie Landsat Analysis System (CLAS) uses high spatial resolution satellite data for regional and global studies of forest disturbance. CLAS is an automated processing system that includes (a) atmospheric correction of satellite data; (b) deconvolution of spectral signatures into subpixel fractional cover of live forest canopy, forest debris, and bare substrates; (c) cloud, water, and deforestation masking; and (d) pattern recognition algorithms for forest disturbance mapping.

Figure 6.7 compares an example of the CLAS high-resolution detection of selective logging in the eastern Amazon during 2001 to 2002 from the CLAS processing (right),

with deforestation mapping provided by standard Landsat processing (Program for the Estimation of Deforestation in the Brazilian Amazon, or PRODES).

For more information on CLAS and associated publications, visit http://asnerlab.stanford.edu/.

PLANT BIODIVERSITY: RAPID SURVEY, CLASSIFICATION, AND MAPPING

The Center for Biodiversity Management (CBM) provides users worldwide with free access to state-of-the-art biodiversity assessment methodology and related software. The software highlighted here, VegClass 2.0 and DOMAIN, are available free at http://www.cbmglobe.org/softwaredev.htm.

VegClass 2.0: Field Tool for Vegetation Data Entry and Classification

VegClass 2.0 is a computer-assisted data-entry and analytical package for general vegetation classification and analysis. It is built around a novel system of classifying vegetation accord-

Figure 6.7 Comparison of CLAS High-Resolution Processing with Standard Landsat Processing

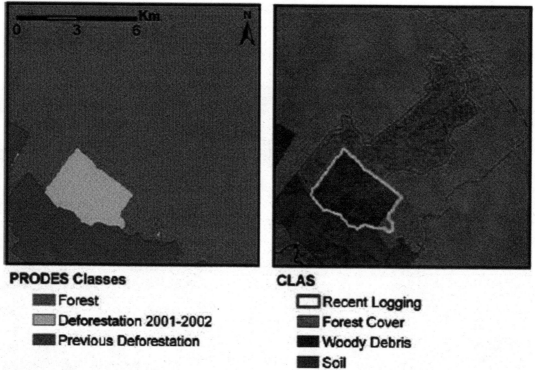

Source: Asner and others 2005.
Note: The image on the left shows deforestation mapping under standard Landsat processing for PRODES. The image on the right shows deforestation mapping using CLAS high-resolution processing.

ing to morphological adaptations to environment as well as species, vegetation structure, and additional recording-site physical features. The software allows the user to choose from a range of variables to suit a particular purpose and scale. References to the theory and practice underlying this software are available in scientific literature, as well as on the Internet. The software runs on personal computers with Microsoft Windows® software. The instructions are in simple English. With minimal training, users of VegClass will find it a powerful tool for both entering and compiling field data. VegClass uses a formal protocol that allows transfer of data summaries into a wide range of industrial computerized spreadsheet and relational database formats, such as Microsoft Excel® and Access®.

Apart from being useful in the field, VegClass is an excellent tool for training purposes and has been successfully used in a number of developing countries in tropical West Africa (Cameroon) and the sub-Sahel (Mali); southern Africa (Mozambique); Indomalesia (India, Indonesia, the Philippines, Thailand, and Vietnam); and Latin America (Brazil, Costa Rica, and Peru). Because it provides a ready means of producing standardized data sets, VegClass is rapidly becoming popular in vegetation surveys in different countries. It provides a unique, generic means of recording and comparing data within and between regions, and it is a unique tool for global and local comparative purposes. VegClass has been supported by the Center for International Forestry Research as well as by CBM.

DOMAIN: Habitat Mapping Package

DOMAIN is a user-friendly software program that makes possible the exploration of potential habitats for plant and animal species. Unlike many other potential mapping programs, DOMAIN allows the use of relatively few spatially referenced data points, such as known species locations. When these data points are overlaid on known environmental variables, such as soil type, elevation, and certain climate variables, the program constructs an environmental DOMAIN map showing different levels of similarity. The program is now widely used in more than 80 countries.

AGRICULTURAL PRODUCTION REGIONS AND MODIS: NASA'S MODERATE RESOLUTION IMAGING SPECTRORADIOMETER

Mosaic images were created by the NASA MODIS (Moderate-Resolution Imaging Spectroradiometer) Rapid Response Sys-

tem team to overlap the agricultural regions shown by the rectangles in panel a of figure 6.8. New MODIS mosaics are produced daily for each agricultural region in false color and true color from the Terra and Aqua satellites at 1-kilometer, 500-meter, and 250-meter resolution. These near real-time images can be viewed and downloaded after clicking on a region (panel b of figure 6.8).

To access daily images, go to http://www.pecad.fas.usda.gov/cropexplorer/modis_summary.

INTEGRATED GLOBAL OBSERVATIONS FOR LAND

Since its creation in 1998, the Integrated Global Observing Strategy (IGOS) has sought to provide a comprehensive framework to harmonize the common interests of the major space-based and in situ systems for global observation of the Earth.

Integrated Global Observations for Land (IGOL) is the land theme of IGOS and has the responsibility of designing a cohesive program of activities that will provide a comprehensive picture of the present state of terrestrial ecosystems and build capacity for long-term monitoring of those ecosystems. Global Observation of Forest and Land Cover Dynamics is strongly involved in developing the IGOL theme. The current IGOL aims at an integrated and operational land observation system that focuses on the following areas (figure 6.9):

- Land cover, land-cover change, and fire
- Land use and land-use change
- Agricultural production, food security, sustainable agriculture, and forestry
- Land degradation and soils
- Ecosystems and ecosystem goods and services
- Biodiversity and conservation
- Human health and effects of land properties on vectors
- Water resource management, water use for agriculture, and human use of water
- Disaster early warning systems (for fires, floods, and droughts)
- Climate change impacts on land properties
- Energy (biomass and fuelwood)
- Urbanization and infrastructure

To visit IGOS, go to http://www.eohandbook.com/igosp/. The IGOL Web site is at http://www.fao.org/gtos/igol.

Figure 6.8   MODIS Image Gallery

a. MODIS world map

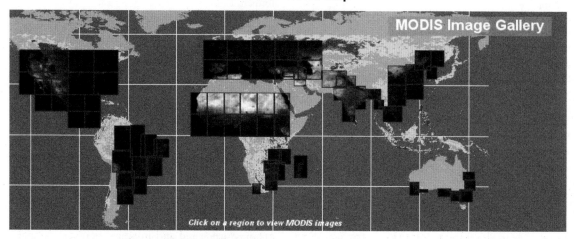

b. MODIS mosaic image

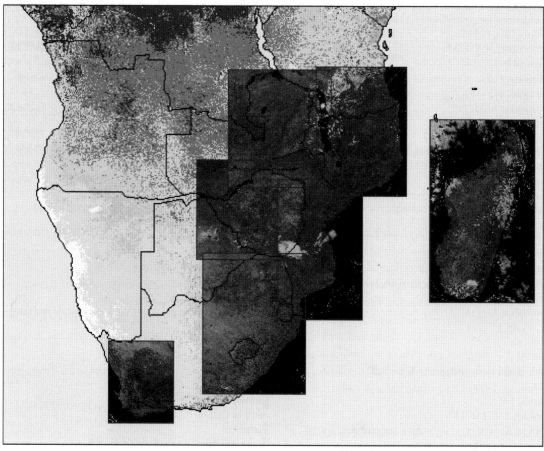

Source: http://www.pecad.fas.usda.gov/cropexplorer/modis_summary/.

Figure 6.9   Integrated and Operational Land Observation System

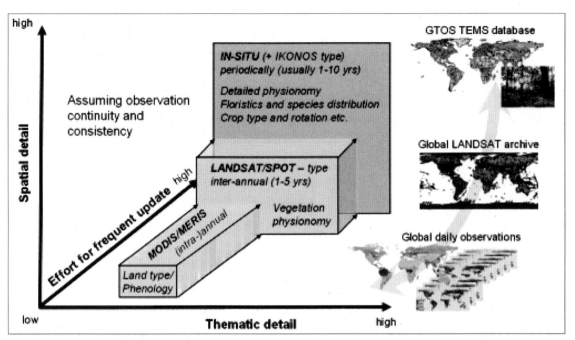

Source: Food and Agriculture Organization.

REFERENCE

Asner, G. P., D. E. Knapp, E. N. Broadbent, P. J. C. Oliveira, M. Keller, and J. N. Silva. "Selective Logging in the Brazilian Amazon." *Science* 310 (5747): 480–82.

GLOSSARY

Many of the definitions in this glossary have been sourced from the Intergovernmental Panel on Climate Change, http://www.ipcc.ch/pdf/glossary/ipcc-glossary.pdf.

Abatement: Processes and technologies leading to the reduction of greenhouse gas emissions.

Adaptation: Adjustment in natural or human systems, in response to actual or expected climatic stimuli or their effects, that moderates, harms, or exploits beneficial opportunities.

Afforestation: Act or process of establishing a forest where one has not existed in recent history.

Afforestation Grant Scheme: Scheme proposed by the government whereby landowners would be invited to tender for grants for establishing new post-2007 Kyoto-compliant forests.

Agricultural plains, lowland plains, or plains: Lower part of river basins between the headwaters and the coastal areas (except in urban areas). They are mainly flat or rolling lands with large streams or rivers. In Asia and parts of Latin America, they typically contain large contiguous areas with rainfed agriculture and irrigation systems. Huge areas are under low-intensity grazing or ranching in Latin America and Africa.

Agriculture: All human activities where natural resources are used to produce the raw materials for food, feed, and fiber. Use of equipment, fertilizer, and fossil energy in the process is common and so is the use of irrigation water. Agriculture includes crop production, livestock production, fisheries, and timber. In most cases, the products are sold to markets.

Agro-ecological system: Total of natural resources, people, and their interactions in an area, where the processes within the system are relatively independent of those in other agro-ecological systems.

Annex I countries: Group of countries included in annex I to the United Nations Framework Convention on Climate Change. Annex I includes all developed countries in the Organisation for Economic Co-operation and Development and economies in transition (including the Russian Federation and Ukraine).

Annex B countries or parties: Group of countries included in annex B of the Kyoto Protocol that agreed to a target for their greenhouse gas emissions. Annex B includes all the annex I countries except Belarus and Turkey.

Biofuel: Fuel produced from plants, animal products, and waste. Biofuels include alcohols, biodiesel, "black liquor" from the paper manufacturing process, wood, and soybean oil.

Carbon credits: Tradable unit that represents the right to emit 1 ton of carbon dioxide equivalent emissions.

Carbon dioxide (CO_2): Naturally occurring gas that is a byproduct of burning and a breakdown of fossil fuels and biomass, land-use changes, and other industrial processes. It is the principal human-induced greenhouse gas that affects the Earth's temperature.

Carbon dioxide equivalent (CO₂e): Quantity of a given greenhouse gas multiplied by its global warming potential, which equates its global warming impact relative to carbon dioxide. It is the standard unit for comparing the degree of warming that emissions of different greenhouse gases can cause.

Carbon (C) sequestration: Process by which carbon from the air (in CO_2) is absorbed by growing plants and trees and is left in dead plants (dead roots, exudates, mulch) in the soil. C sequestration increases soil organic matter. It counteracts buildup of CO_2 in the air and hence climatic change and is also an aspect of land rehabilitation: the more carbon is retained in the soil, the better its fertility, water-holding capacity, and resilience.

Climate change: Change in climate, attributed directly or indirectly to human activity, that alters the composition of the global atmosphere and that is additional to natural climate variability observed over a comparable time period.

Coastal areas: Land area between the coast of the sea or the ocean and a line approximately 100 kilometers inland with all water bodies in it, plus the marine zone, where most fisheries, aquaculture, and tourism take place.

Co-benefits: Benefits of policies that are beyond the scope of the original policy.

Commitment period: Range of years within which parties to the Kyoto Protocol are required to meet their greenhouse gas emissions target, which is averaged over the years of the commitment period. The first commitment period is 2008 to 2012. The targets are set relative to greenhouse gas emissions in the base year (in New Zealand's case, 1990), multiplied by five.

Deforestation: Direct human-induced conversion of forested land to nonforested land (that is, as agriculture).

Degradation: For the purposes of this sourcebook, sum of the processes that render land or water economically less valuable for agricultural production or for other ecosystem services. Continued degradation leads to zero or negative economic agricultural productivity. Degraded land and water can have a significant nonagricultural value, such as

in nature reservations, in recreational areas, and for houses and roads, even though for these purposes nondegraded lands are far superior. *Soil degradation* refers to the processes that reduce the capacity of the soil to support agriculture.

Desertification: Form of land degradation in which vegetation cannot reestablish itself after removal by harvesting, burning, or grazing. It occurs because of overexploitation and may occur in nearly every climate, but particularly in semiarid environments. Strong winds increase the vulnerability to desertification.

Devegetation: Removal of natural vegetation and crops that leave the land surface bare and exposed to degradation by water, wind erosion, and leaching. Deforestation is the form of devegetation where tress and shrubs are removed. Reestablishment of plant and tree species in devegetated areas is often difficult because of harsh environmental conditions for germination and establishment. Grazing of emerging plants can modify the vegetation composition significantly so that mainly unpalatable, weedy species are present in low density, rendering land unfit for agriculture. Devegetation can lead to desertification.

Ecological footprint: Virtual area cultivated or exploited to grow the crops and livestock that supply the food an average person consumes annually. Typically, this area is not contiguous, and part of this area may be far away—even in other countries. Its size ranges from 100 square meters to 1 hectare, or even beyond these values, depending on the type of food consumed (vegetarian or rich in animal protein) and the productivity of the farming system (dependent on the intensity of management practices and the quality of the natural resources). The size of the ecological footprint can be used to compare consequences of different lifestyles in different zones.

Ecosystem services: Various benefits that ecosystems provide to people, including food, clean water, nature, and wildlife as well as protection against natural disasters such as flooding. Agriculture is always part of an ecosystem, and agriculture can be seen as an ecosystem service.

Emission unit or allowance: Tradable unit representing the right to emit 1 ton of carbon dioxide equivalent emissions.

Encroachment: Use of land for agriculture in protected natural areas. Although predominant in headwaters and coastal areas, it is also common in plains. The term refers to people moving onto new land, which happens when they have few alternatives for food production in unprotected areas. In other situations, people have been living in and cultivating the encroached area for a long time, albeit in smaller numbers, and the notion of protected area was recently imposed on them.

Emissions: Intentional and unintentional release of greenhouse gases into the atmosphere.

Environmental flow: Flow of water required to maintain healthy wetlands and other ecosystems.

Environmental security: Condition of natural resources in a particular area. Full environmental security is achieved when the resources provide full environmental services to the human beings who depend on this area and when this condition is sustainable. Rehabilitation of degraded areas to achieve this situation is feasible only if the damage threshold has not been exceeded.

Erosion: Process of movement of soil particles, with organic matter and nutrients contained in them, because of rain, water movement, or wind. Erosion is accompanied by deposition nearby or at a distance. Erosion is a natural process that can be accelerated by soil cultivation or deforestation. Construction of infrastructure (that is, roads and paths) can contribute much toward accelerating erosion.

Evapotranspiration: Process by which water passes from the liquid state in soil and plants into a gaseous state in the air. Only the fraction that passes through plants can contribute to crop production.

Food security: For the purposes of this sourcebook, production of food, access to food, and use of food. For global food security, the emphasis is that sufficient food should be produced in the world to meet the full requirements of all people: total global food supply equals the total global demand. For household food security, the focus is on the ability of households, both urban and rural, to purchase or produce the food they need for a healthy and active life. Disposable income is a crucial issue. Women are typically gatekeepers of household food security. For national food security, the focus is on sufficient food for all people in a nation. National food security can be ensured through any combination of national production and food imports and exports. Food security always has components of production, access, and use.

Forest: Minimum area of 1 hectare of land with tree-crown cover (or equivalent stocking level) of more than 30 percent, with trees able to reach the potential of a minimum height of 5 meters at maturity in situ. A forest may consist either of closed forest formations, where trees of various stories and undergrowth cover a high proportion of the ground, or open forest formations. Young natural stands and all plantations that have yet to reach a crown density of 30 percent or tree height of 5 meters are included under this definition. So, too, are areas normally forming part of forest that are temporarily unstocked as a result of human interventions, such as harvesting or natural causes, but are expected to revert to forest.

Fossil fuel: Fuel that is sourced from fossilized biomass such as oil and gas.

Globalization: Process by which more and more goods and services are traded internationally. It encompasses greater commercialization of farming and more dependence on trade for achieving food security.

Grain equivalent: Weight of grain (typically wheat) that would be required to replace a certain amount of food. Daily food has an endless variety of composition, water content, and edible parts and is produced from many crops. The term *grain equivalent* is used to express all these parts in a single dimension.

Greenhouse gas (GHG): Greenhouse gases are constituents of the atmosphere, both natural and human induced, that absorb and reemit infrared radiation. Greenhouse gas emissions covered by the emissions limitation commitment for the first commitment period of the Kyoto Protocol are carbon dioxide (CO_2), methane (CH_4), nitrous oxide (NO_2), hydrofluorocarbons (HFCs), perfluorocarbons (PFCs), and sulfur hexafluoride (SF_6).

Greenhouse gas intensity/global warming potential: Index that approximates the time-integrated warming effect of a unit mass of a given greenhouse gas in today's atmosphere, relative to that of carbon dioxide.

Gross domestic product (GDP): National income earned by production in a country.

Groundwater: Water extracted from the soil depth beyond the rooting zone, generally with manual or motorized pumps.

Groundwater depletion: Process of extraction of groundwater from below the rooting zone, sometimes from depths below 50 meters, at a rate faster than groundwater recharge takes place.

Headwaters (or upland watersheds): Upper parts of river basins, where water is collected in small streams that merge into larger ones. They often flow into a reservoir or major river. Headwaters are typically hilly and mountainous areas originally forested or covered with perennial vegetation; in many cases, they are the home of nature reservations. People in headwaters, sometimes living in tribes or other groupings of minorities, include the poorest people with often less formal rights than those downstream.

Heterogeneity and diversity: Gradual changes in the nature and intensity of natural resources in space or in time and to sociological and cultural diversity among the people living there. This natural phenomenon is the cause of problems and opportunities, but it makes effective management always highly site and situation specific. People at "peaks" can do very well. Poor people are generally found at the "troughs."

Holistic and participatory approaches: Successful approaches in reducing degradation and improving food security. These approaches consider how to make the best use of, or to increase, all resources that people should have at their disposal: natural, human, physical, social, and financial resources.

Hotspots: Areas where the particular degradation problem is relatively intensive and significant.

Intergovernmental Panel on Climate Change (IPCC): Organization established by the World Meteorological Organization and the United Nations Environment Programme to assess scientific, technical, and socioeconomic information relevant for the understanding of climate change, its potential effects, and options for its adaptation and mitigation.

Kyoto-compliant land: Land that was not forestland as of December 31, 1989.

Kyoto forest: Forest that has been established by direct human activity on land that was not forestland as of December 31, 1989.

Kyoto Protocol: Protocol to the United Nations Framework Convention on Climate Change that requires ratifying countries listed in its annex B (industrial nations) to meet greenhouse gas reduction targets during the period from 2008 to 2012 (see http://unfccc.int/kyoto_protocol/items/2830.php for further information).

Land managers: Farmers (includes arable, horticultural, and pastoral farmers) and foresters.

Land use: Refers to the type of management; major categories of land use are annual crops, perennial crops, fallows, pastures, and herding on rangelands.

Low-emissions technologies: Technologies that lead to reduced emissions of greenhouse gases (as opposed to conventional technologies).

Methane (CH_4): Hydrocarbon that is a greenhouse gas produced through anaerobic (without oxygen) decomposition of waste in landfills, animal digestion, decomposition of animal wastes, production and distribution of natural gas and oil, coal production, and incomplete fossil fuel combustion.

Mitigation: Any action that results, by design, in the reduction of greenhouse gas emissions by sources or removals by sinks.

Nitrification inhibitor: Product that reduces the conversion of various forms of nitrogen into nitrate and nitrous oxide.

Nitrous oxide (NO_2): Powerful greenhouse gas emitted through soil management practices, animal wastes, fertilizers, fossil fuel combustion, and biomass burning.

Nutrient depletion or mining: Process that slowly depletes the soil of its mineral constituents (that is, mainly phosphorus, potassium, and nitrogen). These plant nutrients are essential to crops. Depletion may take 5 to 50 years before the soil can no longer support economically sustainable cropping. The process is common on marginal soils where crop residues are not recycled. The nutrient balance, which assumes a negative value under depletion, refers to the difference of the inputs of nutrients into a farm (or catchment, region, or country) from fertilizers, manure, biological nitrogen fixation, and rainfall and the outputs (in crop harvests, leaching, and erosion). Plants also absorb micronutrients (including calcium, magnesium, iron, zinc, and copper) in small quantities. Correction of the negative balance was long considered unnecessary, but micronutrient deficiencies are increasingly showing up in food crops and in human nutrition. Appropriate fertilizers can remediate this problem.

Offset: To compensate for the effects of activities through other means. Offsetting greenhouse gas emissions could include planting trees, using nitrification inhibitors, or improving the energy efficiency of farm operations.

On-site and off-site effects: Effects observed at the same location or area (on-site effects) or beyond (off-site effects). Off-site effects are often not included in economic evaluations of practices.

Participatory: "With the people": designing and implementing intervention strategies should be done with all stakeholders.

Permanent forest sink initiative: Initiative that allows landowners to get the economic value of removing carbon dioxide from the atmosphere and sequestering (storing) it in the form of new forests.

Plains and lowland plains: Area downstream of headwaters and upstream of coastal zones, excluding urban and peri-urban areas. Plains are usually flat and contain most agricultural activities.

Post-2012 negotiations: Negotiations already commenced that aim to result in an international framework for addressing climate change following the first commitment period of the Kyoto Protocol.

Potential productivity: Biological production in conditions where inputs are not limiting and management is optimal. Potential productivity is used as a reference value for the current level of productivity and yield gap.

Price-based instruments (measures): Intervention that encourages or discourages practices by changing the price of or creating a price for activities that emit or absorb greenhouse gases.

Resilience: Property of complex ecosystems and society to withstand external pressure without significant internal change. Pressure beyond a threshold causes the system to collapse.

Revenue recycling: Return to the economy of revenue derived from a policy measure.

Rumen: Stomach of a ruminant animal.

Ruminant animal: Cloven-hoofed mammal that digests its food in two steps. Ruminant animals include cows, sheep, deer, and goats.

Salinization: Process of building up concentrations of salt in water or soil to levels that reduce or prevent crop growth.

Seawater intrusion: Process of seawater moving through the subsoil into the land. If seawater reaches the surface, salinization of soil and surface water occurs. The process occurs when fresh water near the coast is extracted from the soil.

Sequestration: Uptake and storage of carbon. Carbon can be sequestered (stored) by plants as organic material or by industrial processes, such as pumping deep underground.

Sink: Any process, activity, or mechanism that removes a greenhouse gas or a precursor of a greenhouse gas from the atmosphere.

Sink credit: Unit derived from a forest sink activity that results in a net removal of greenhouse gases.

Soil organic matter (SOM): Remainder of plants, animals, and microbes in the upper layers of the soil. SOM contains carbon (40 percent), nitrogen (0.1 to 1.0 percent), phosphorus, potassium, and other plant micronutrients. SOM enhances the soil's water-holding capacity.

Technology transfer: Set of processes that covers the exchange of knowledge and goods among different stakeholders. Technology transfer leads to the dissemination of technology for adapting to or mitigating climate change.

Threshold: Criteria that define which firms, sites, or other business units are required to participate in a policy measure.

Tradable permit regime: Situation whereby a government allocates permits to industry members to cover all or some of their current greenhouse gas emissions. Members are liable for emissions above the level of emission permits they hold.

United Nations Framework Convention on Climate Change (UNFCCC): Convention negotiated in 1992 that aims to stabilize greenhouse gas concentrations at levels that avoid dangerous human interference with the climate system.

Urban and peri-urban areas: Parts of a river basin where people and management of land and water are strongly affected by large concentrations of people. The term refers to cities with more than a few hundred thousand inhabitants and particularly to mega-cities of several million people, plus the area with horticulture and animal husbandry that surround them. Most of these cities are in the lower parts of basins, often at or close to the coast. Important exceptions include the highland cities of Mexico, the Andes, and the Himalayas.

Peri-urban and urban agriculture (PUA) refers to very intensive, small- or large-scale agriculture (particularly horticulture, floriculture, and poultry and pig production) that occurs in or near cities. It is characterized by its strong ties to urban life and markets—more so than by geography. PUA is a major consumer of city wastes (liquid and solid) but contributes to groundwater pollution and health hazards.

Voluntary greenhouse gas reporting (VGGR): System whereby sector participants voluntarily report their emissions to a central registry in accordance with a prescribed and standard format.

Wastewater: Water from households and cities that has been used domestically and often contains urine and feces of humans and animals plus organic remainders of food preparations. Wastewater may contain valuable plant nutrients but is often a carrier of diseases and heavy metals.

Water: All surface water in rivers, lakes, reservoirs, wetlands, and aquifers.

Water productivity: Quantity of produce, measured in weight or monetary terms per unit of water. Water productivity can be determined at the plot, farm, catchment, and basin scale.

Water quality: Change in the availability of water (increases or reductions) in quantity, the contents of particles and dissolved materials, and contamination with diseases.

INDEX

Boxes, figures, notes, and tables are indicated by b, f, n, and t respectively. The term "sustainable land management" is abbreviated as SLM throughout the index.

abatement, definition of, 161
adaptation, definition of, 161
afforestation
    definition of, 161
    Kyoto Protocol, 65, 66
    large-scale programs in China, India, and Indonesia, 68
Afforestation Grant Scheme, 161
AfriAfya, 37
Africa
    See also specific countries and regions
    bean farming in, 83–87
    climate change and, 126, 128
    climate risk management in, 137
    fertilizer use in, 17
    fodder shrubs in, 88–94
    food production in, 96
    hillside agriculture in, 78, 81
    humid and subhumid areas in, 25
    indigenous fruit trees in. *See* indigenous fruit trees (IFTs)
    malaria in, 9
    mixed-maize farming systems in, 25
    no-till systems in, 17
    poverty traps in, 34
    production landscape in, 10f, 11
    soil degradation in, 34
    soybean farming in, 34–38
    water and feed challenges in, 27
        See also livestock
agricultural diversification. *See* diversification; *specific topics*
agricultural insurance products, 138, 139
Agricultural Investment Sourcebook (World Bank), 3
agricultural plains, definition of, 161
agricultural productivity, 3, 5

    See also specific topics
agriculture, definition of, 161
agriculture, forestry, and other land use (AFOLU), carbon effects of, 65, 66, 67
    See also carbon emissions reduction
agro-ecological systems, definition of, 161
air quality and global change, 8–9
    See also climate change
Ajayi, O.C., 60, 61
Akinnifesi, F.K., 60, 61
ALive program, 117
Alternatives to Slash-and-Burn (ASB) Programme, 39–44, 41t, 65–70, 68f, 68n1
Amede, T., 96
Amezquita, E., 78
Andhra Pradesh Rural Livelihoods Project, 112
animal health, mobile service models for, 117
Annex I countries. *See* United Nations Framework Convention on Climate Change (UNFCCC)
aquaculture. *See* integrated agriculture-aquaculture (IAA)
Arimi, H., 88
ASB. *See* Alternatives to Slash-and-Burn Programme
Asia
    See also specific countries
    carbon emissions reduction in, 68
    climate risk management in, 137
    hillside agriculture in, 78, 81
    humid and subhumid areas in, 25
    HydroSHEDS and, 153
    indigenous fruit trees (IFTs) in, 60
    malaria in, 9
    no-till systems in, 17
    production landscape in, 10f
    water and feed challenges in, 27
Asian Development Bank, 112
Attica, 6b
available natural resource base, 15

Aw-Hassan, A., 120
Ayarza, M., 78

barley
   breeding program. *See* participatory approaches
   production, 122, 123*t*
Barrious, E., 78
bean farming, 83–87
   key SLM issues, 83–84
   lessons learned, 84
   opportunities for SLM, 84–85
   rationale for investment, 85–86
   recommendations for practitioners, 86
   Web resources for, 87
beef, dumping of, 114
bees, natural habitat loss and, 8
Bekele, S., 96
Belize, PES in, 54
Benin, mobile pastoralists in, 116
biodiversity
   community watershed model, 111
   conservation of, 111
   decline in, 6
   in humid and subhumid areas, 25
   tree crops and, 18
   Web-based tools for surveying, classification, and mapping,
      156–57
biofuel, 3, 9, 109, 118*n*1, 161
bio-geophysical and atmospheric models, 138
biological nitrogen fixation (BNF), 104, 105*t*
biotechnology, 17, 18
Blackie, M.J., 12
Blümmel, M., 96
BNF (biological nitrogen fixation), 104, 105*t*
Bosma, R.H., 71
Brazil
   carbon emissions reduction in. *See* carbon emissions reduction
   CLAS and, 156
   indigenous fruit trees (IFTs) in, 61
   PES in, 53
   rainforest conservation and poverty reduction, balancing in,
      39–44
      ASB matrix, 40*t*, 40–41
      integrated natural resources management (INRM) approach,
         40
      key drivers for degradation dynamics, 40–41
      key SLM issues, 39–40
      lessons learned, 41
      opportunities for SLM, 42
      rationale for investment, 42
      recommendations for practitioners, 42
      Web resources for, 43–44
   VegClass 2.0 and, 157
Bruggeman, A, 120
Burkina Faso
   mobile pastoralists in, 116
   Zai systems as forage niches in, 100
bushmeat hunting, 9

California, wastewater aquifer recharging in, 49
Cameroon
   carbon emissions reduction in. *See* carbon emissions reduction
   fallow land management in, 56–59
      description of innovation, 57
      effects on vegetation community and biodiversity, 57–58, 58*t*
      lessons learned, 58–59
      overview, 56–57
      patterns of variation in species composition, 58
   rainforest conservation and poverty reduction, balancing in,
      39–44
   See also rainforest conservation
   VegClass 2.0 and, 157
Canada's International Development Research Center, 35
CaNaSTA (Crop Niche Selection for Tropical Agriculture), 2
   8–29
capacity building, 139
Capacity Observation of Forest and Land Cover Dynamics, 157
carbon credits, 161
carbon dioxide (CO$_2$), 6, 161–62
carbon dioxide equivalent (CO$_2$e), 162
carbon emissions reduction, 65–70
   ASB option, 66–67
   benefits and effect of activity, 67
   emissions, definition of, 163
   emission unit or allowance, 162
   lessons learned, 67–68, 68*f*
   project objective and description, 65–66
   Web resources for, 69–70
carbon sequestration, 162
Carnegie Landstat Analysis System (CLAS), 154, 156, 156*f*
Castro, A., 78
CDM (clean development mechanism), 65–70
Ceccarelli, S., 134
Center for Biodiversity Management (CBM), 156–57
Center for Environmental Systems Research, 153
Center for International Forestry Research, 157
Central America
   See also Latin America and Caribbean countries; *specific
      countries*
   conservation farming in, 127
   co-researching with farmers in, 29–30
   ecologically mediated disease in, 9
   HydroSHEDS and, 153
   livestock in, 27–33
      diagnosis of farm and market contexts, 29, 29*t*
      forage use and production criteria, 29, 29*t*
      fostering innovation and learning processes, 29–30
      key SLM issues, 27–28, 28*f*
      lessons learned, 28–30
      matching forage, 28–29
      opportunities for SLM in, 30–31, 31*b*
      pasture rehabilitation and intensification, 30, 31*b*
      rationale for investment in, 31
      recommendations for practitioners, 31–32
      sharing knowledge and scaling out activities, 30
      Web resources for, 33
   PES in, 54

slash-and-burn agricultural practices in, 78–80
    See also no-burn agricultural zones
Central Asia, marginal dry areas in, 122
Challenge Program for Water and Food, 81
Chianu, J.N., 34
China
    carbon emissions reduction in, 68
    community watershed model in, 108, 109, 112
    groundwater declines and land use in, 45–50
        See also groundwater declines
    regional climate change in, 8
CIAT. *See* International Center for Tropical Agriculture (Centro
        Internacional de Agricultura Tropical)
civil society organizations, 5, 92
clean development mechanism (CDM), 65–70
climate-based crop forecasting, 126, 129
climate change
    See also carbon emissions reduction; global change
    adaptation and mitigation strategies for, 126–30
        key SLM in soil and water management, 127–28
        opportunities for SLM, 128–29
        overview, 126–27
        recommendations for practitioners, 129–30
        seasonal climate forecast and SLM, 129
    definition of, 162
    lessons learned, 128
climate risk management, 136–40
    benefits and results of activity, 138–39
    investment needs and priorities, 139–40
    lessons learned, 139
    overview, 136
    presentation of innovation, 137–38
    project objective and description, 136–37
    risk identification, 137
    risk management, 137–38
    risk quantification, 137
    Web resources for, 140
coastal areas and waters
    artisinal fishing and farming systems, 15, 15t
    definition of, 162
    degradation of, 8
co-benefits, definition of, 162
Coca Cola Foundation, 112
Colombia
    forage use in, 29–30
    PES in, 54
commitment period, definition of, 162
commodity prices, effect of decrease of, 3–4, 11
Commodity Risk Management Group, 137
community watershed model, 108–13
    benefits and results of activity, 109–12
    biodiversity and, 111
    crop productivity and, 110
    investment needs, 112–13
    lessons learned, 112
    natural resource management at landscape level and, 111–12
    overview, 108–9, 110t
    partnerships and institutional innovations and, 112

policy and financial incentives, 113
    recommendations for practitioners, 112
    water availability and, 110–11, 111f
Confederation of Indian Industry, 112
Conference of the Parties to the United Nations Framework
        Convention on Climate Change (UNFCCC), 65
Congo, Republic of, PABRA in, 85
conservation farming practices, 17, 26, 30, 127
    See also specific topics
Conservation Science Program (WWF), 151–53, 153f
conservation tillage practices, 16, 17, 129
Consortium for Integrated Soil Management, 81
consultations and partnerships, 117
Consultative Group on International Agriculture Research
        centers, 4
co-researching with farmers, 29–30
Costa Rica
    carbon emissions reduction in, 68
    PES in, 53–54
    VegClass 2.0 and, 157
Côte d'Ivoire, mobile pastoralists in, 116
Crop Niche Selection for Tropical Agriculture (CaNaSTA),
        28–29
crops
    crop-livestock integration, 17, 26
    high-value cash crops, 131–32
    horticultural crops, 17
    intercropping system, 35
    tree crops. *See* tree crops
cryptosporidiosis, 9
cumin production, 131–32
cut-and-carry forage systems, 30–31
cyanobacteria, 8

dairy products, 122, 123t
Dartmouth Flood Observatory, 154, 155f
Decentralized-Participatory Plan Breeding (D-PPB), 134–35
deforestation
    carbon emissions reduction from, 65–70
    definition of, 162
    forage production and conservation and, 31
    in humid and subhumid areas, 25
    infectious diseases and, 9
    rainforest conservation and poverty reduction and, 39–40
degradation
    See also land and soil degradation; water conservation and use
    carbon emissions reduction from, 65–70
    definition of, 162
    land degradation surveillance, 141–44
desertification
    in Cameroon, 56
    definition of, 162
    pastoral systems and. *See* mobile pastoralism
devegetation, definition of, 162
disease and global change, 8, 9
Distributed Hydrology Soil Vegetation Model (DHSVM), 153
diversification
    See also specific topics

food shrubs and, 93
    in highland and sloping areas, 77
    in humid and subhumid areas, 26
    intensification and, 17–18
    livestock and, 17
    in marginal dry areas, 122
    production, 16b, 26
diversity of land management systems and poverty
    reduction, 13–16
Dixin, Y., 108
Dixon, J., 16, 23, 25, 120
DOMAIN, 156, 157
Donovan, C., 12
D-PPB (Decentralized-Participatory Plan Breeding),
    134–35
dry areas. See marginal dry areas
dry seasons, 27–28, 28f
dualistic farming systems, 15, 15t
Dumanski, J., 12
Dunstan, S.C.S., 98
Duong, L.T., 71

East Africa
    See also specific countries
    fodder shrubs in, 88–94
        benefits and effect of activity, 90, 91t
        issues for wider application, 92–93
        lessons learned, 90–92
        presentation of innovation, 89–90
        project objective, 88
        study area description, 88–89
ecological footprint, definition of, 162
ecologically mediated diseases, 9
ecosystem services, 3, 4b, 162
ecotourism, 118n1
education, mobile service models for, 117
El Niño, 78, 79, 126, 127, 129
El Salvador, PES in, 54
emigration, 77
emissions. See carbon emissions reduction
Empresa Brasileria de Pesquisa Agropecuária, 41
encroachment, definition of, 162–63
environmental assessment, 18b
environmental flow, 163
environmental security, 163
erosion
    definition of, 163
    food shrubs and, 93
    livestock and, 98
    quantification and management of, 127
    reduction of, 8, 17
Ethiopia, PABRA in, 85
Europe
    infectious diseases in, 9
    production landscape in, 9, 10f, 11
European Union (EU), 115
evapotranspiration, 7, 7f, 47, 47f, 49, 163
exit from agriculture, 16b, 26

fallow lands, management of. See forests
FAO. See Food and Agriculture Organization
farming systems
    See also specific types
    as baseline for targeting investments, 15–16
    comparison of, 15, 15f, 16b
    good practices for, 23
    overview, 23
    World Bank's rural development strategy and, 14
Farming Systems and Poverty: Improving Farmers' Livelihoods in a
    Changing World (FAO & World Bank), 13–14
FAS (Foreign Agriculture Service), 151, 152f
Fernandez-Rivera, S., 98
Ferreria, O., 78
fertilizer use, 7–8, 17
    See also manures; specific topics
fiber production systems, 5–6
flood tracking, 154, 155f
fodder, livestock. See forage production and conservation;
    livestock
Food and Agriculture Organization (FAO), 13–14, 78,
    79, 81
food and fiber production systems, requirements for, 5–6
food-borne illnesses, 9
food production, 4, 7–8, 9
    See also specific countries, regions, and topics
food security, definition of, 163
forage production and conservation
    ensiling alternatives, 30
    environmental effects, 31
    fodder shrubs in East Africa, 88–94
        benefits and effect of activity, 90
        issues for wider application, 92–93
        lessons learned, 90–92
        presentation of innovation, 89–90
        project objective, 88
        study area description, 88–89
    legume forage banks, 99
    legumes as, 30, 88, 99, 133
    little bag silage (LBS), 30
    livestock in Central America and, 27–33
        diagnosis of farm and market contexts, 29, 29t
        forage use and production criteria and, 29, 29f
        fostering innovation and learning processes, 29–30
        key SLM issues, 27–28, 28f
        lessons learned, 28–30
        matching forage, 28–29
        opportunities for SLM in, 30–31, 31b
        pasture rehabilitation and intensification, 30, 31b
        rationale for investment in, 31
        recommendations for practitioners, 31–32
        sharing knowledge and scaling out activities, 30
        Web resources for, 33
    pasture rehabilitation and intensification, 30, 31b
    smallholder livestock systems and. See livestock
    vetch as, 133
    Zai systems as forage niches, 100
Foreign Agriculture Service (FAS), 151, 152f

forests
  See also deforestation
  agroforests, 42
  fallow land management and species diversity in, 56–59
    description of forest fallow management innovation, 57
    effects on vegetation community and biodiversity, 57–58, 58*t*
    lessons learned, 58–59
    patterns of variation in species composition, 58
  global change and, 8
  permanent forest sink initiative, 165
  resources, 18*b*
  tree crops. *See* tree crops
fossil fuel, definition of, 163
Franzel, S., 61, 88, 91
freshwater agriculture and aquaculture. *See* integrated agriculture-aquaculture (IAA)
freshwater resources. *See* water conservation and use

GEF. *See* World Bank Global Environment Facility
GHG. *See* greenhouse gas
Gibbon, D., 16, 23, 120
Global Assessment of Human-Induced Soil Degradation (GLASOD), 28, 32*n*1
global change, 6–9, 7*f*
  See also climate change
  drivers and impact of, 6–9
  food production and, 7–8
  forest resources and, 8
  freshwater resources and, 8
  historical perspective on, 6*b*
  infectious diseases and, 9
  regional climate and air quality, 8–9
Global Digital Soil Map of the World, 141, 144, 147
global field and market intelligence on cereals and oilseeds, 151, 152*f*
globalization, 6, 163
Global Reservoir and Lake Monitor project, 151, 152*f*
glossary, 161–66
good land management, importance of, 3–4
governmental agencies, 5
grain equivalent, definition of, 163
Grando, S., 134
Green Evolution strategy, 11–12
greenhouse gas (GHG)
  definition, 163
  emissions
    definition of, 163
    forage production and conservation and, 31
    livestock and, 99
    mitigation, 126–30
  good practice guidelines for inventories, 65, 66
  intensity/global warming potential, 163
  voluntary greenhouse gas reporting (VGGR), 166
Green Revolution, 7
gross domestic product (GDP), definition of, 163
groundwater declines, 45–50
  definitions, 163, 164
  investment needs and priorities, 50

key drivers for degradation dynamics, 46–48
key SLM issues, 45, 46*b*
opportunities for both water and land management, 48–49
policy-water use nexus, 46–48, 47*f*, 48*f*
rationale for investment, 49
trends in resource use, 45–46, 46*f*
Web resources for, 50
Gulliver, A., 16, 23, 25, 120
Gumbricht, T., 141

habitat
  infectious diseases and wildlife habitat, 9
  loss of native, 8
    See also specific topics
  mapping package for, 157
  modification, 9
  natural habitats protection, 18*b*
  pollinators and, 8
Haileslasie, A., 96
headwaters, definition of, 164
health care, mobile service models for, 117–18
health surveillance, 142
heterogeneity and diversity, definition of, 164
Hiernaux, P., 98
high-value cash crops, 131–32
HIV, 9, 86
holistic approaches, 164
  See also participatory approaches
Holmann, F., 27
Honduras
  forage in, 30
  no-burn agricultural zones in, 78–82
    See also no-burn agricultural zones
  pasture rehabilitation and intensification in, 30, 31*b*
  PES in, 54
horticultural crops, 17
hotspots, definition of, 164
household income security associations, 11
household strategies to improve livelihoods, 15, 16*b*, 25–26
Hurricane Mitch, 9, 28, 78, 79, 127
hydometeorological infrastructure, upgrading of, 139
hydrologic cycle, changes in, 6, 7*f*, 127
hydronomic zoning, 47–48, 48*f*, 49
  See also groundwater declines
HydroSHEDS, 151–53, 153*f*

IAA. *See* integrated agriculture-aquaculture
ICAR (Indian Council for Agricultural Research), 112
ICARDA. *See* International Center for Agricultural Research in the Dry Areas
ICRAF (International Centre for Research in Agroforestry), 65
ICRISAT (International Crops Research Institute for the Semi-Arid Tropics), 103–7
IFTs. *See* indigenous fruit trees
IGNRM. *See* integrated genetic and natural resource management
IGOL (Integrated Global Observations for Land), 157
IGOS (Integrated Global Observing Strategy), 157
IITA. *See* International Institute of Tropical Agriculture

ILRI (International Institute for Land Reclamation and
        Improvement), 96
imaging spectroradiometer, 157
incentive policies, 115, 117
index-based insurance products, 138
India
    carbon emissions reduction in, 68
    community watershed model in, 108–13
        See also community watershed model
    VegClass 2.0 and, 157
Indian Council for Agricultural Research (ICAR), 112
indicators for SLM and landscape resilience, 13, 14b
indigenous fruit trees (IFTs), 60–64
    benefits for SLM, 61
    investment needs, priorities, and scaling up, 63
    lessons learned, 61–63
    overview, 60
    policy considerations, 63
    tree domestication innovation, 61, 61f
indigenous peoples action plan, 18b
Indonesia
    carbon emissions reduction in, 68
        See also carbon emissions reduction
    rainforest conservation and poverty reduction, balancing in,
        39–44
        See also rainforest conservation
        ASB matrix, 40t, 40–41
    VegClass 2.0 and, 157
infectious diseases, 8, 9, 86
infrastructure development, 117, 139
INM. See integrated nutrient management
Innovative Activity Profiles
    carbon emissions reduction, 65–70
    climate risk management, 136–40
    definition of, 4
    fallow lands in Cameroon, 56–59
    farming systems good practices and, 16, 23
    fodder shrubs in East Africa, 88–94
    forest tree crops, 60–64
    high-value cash crops, 131–32
    integrated agriculture-aquaculture (IAA) in Vietnam,
        71–75
    land degradation surveillance, 141–44
    legume forage, 133
    participatory barley-breeding program, 134–35
Institut des Sciences Agronomiques du Rwanda, 85
insurance products for agriculture, 138, 139
integrated agriculture-aquaculture (IAA), 71–75
    adoption of aquaculture practices, 72–73, 73t
    investment needs and priorities, 75
    on-farm resource flows and role of ponds, 73–74
    overview, 71–72, 72f
    project description, 72
integrated crop-livestock production, 17, 26
integrated genetic and natural resource management (IGNRM),
        108–9, 111
Integrated Global Observations for Land (IGOL), 157
Integrated Global Observing Strategy (IGOS), 157

integrated natural resources management (INRM) approach, 40,
        68n1, 108–13
integrated nutrient management (INM), 103–7
    biological nitrogen fixation (BNF), 104, 105t
    investment needs of local and national governments or other
        donors, 107
    key SLM issues, 103, 104t
    lessons learned, 103–4
    opportunities for SLM, 104–6, 106t
    policy recommendations, 107
    rationale for investment, 106
    recommendations for practitioners, 106–7
integrated pest and disease management (IPDM), 86
integrated pest management (IPM), 16, 17, 26
integrated plant nutrition, 16
Integrated Silvopastoral Approaches to Ecosystem Management,
        54
intensification, 17–18, 30, 31b, 122
Intergovernmental Panel on Climate Change (IPCC), 65, 66–67,
        128, 164
intermediate land uses, advantages of, 65–70
International Center for Tropical Agriculture (Centro
        Internacional de Agricultura Tropical, CIAT)
    bean farming and, 83, 85
    HydroSHEDS and, 153
    livestock in Central America and, 27–33
    non-burn agricultural zones in Honduras and, 78, 81
    soybean farming and, 34
International Centre for Research in Agroforestry (ICRAF), 65
International Crops Research Institute for the Semi-Arid Tropics
        (ICRISAT), 103–7
International Institute for Land Reclamation and Improvement
        (ILRI), 96
International Institute of Tropical Agriculture (IITA), 35, 36
International Maize and Wheat Improvement Center, 36
International Union for the Protection of New Plant Varieties, 63
International Water Management Institute (IWMI), 45–50,
        153–54, 155f
international waterways, projects in, 18b
Investment Notes
    bean farming in Africa, 83–87
    best practices and, 16
    climate change, adaptation and mitigation strategies for,
        126–30
    definition of, 4
    farming systems good practices in, 23
    groundwater declines, 45–50
    integrated natural resource management for watershed
        function in semiarid tropics, 108–13
    integrated nutrient management (INM), 103–7
    livestock in Central America, 27–33
    marginal dry lands, 120–25
    mobile pastoralism, 114–19
    no-burn agricultural zones in Honduras, 78–82
    payment for environmental services (PES), 51–55
    rainforest conservation and poverty reduction, 39–44
    smallholder livestock systems in Sub-Saharan Africa, 96–102
    soybean farming in Africa, 34–38

investments, future directions for, 16–18
  See also specific topics
involuntary resettlement, 18b
IPAD (impact assessment of policy reforms to agricultural
  development) project, 72
IPCC. *See* Intergovernmental Panel on Climate Change
IPDM (integrated pest and disease management), 86
IPM. *See* integrated pest management
Iran and Iraq, marginal dry areas in, 122
irrigated farming systems, 15, 15t
irrigation, 7–8, 9, 17
  See also ground water declines; *specific topics*

Jabban, 122
Jaenicke, H., 61
Janssen, W., 61
JohnsonDiversey Inc., 153
Jordan, marginal dry areas in, 122

Kasyoki, J., 39, 65
Kendy, E., 45
Kenya
  farmer groups in, 86
  fodder shrubs and livestock productivity in. *See* forage
    production and conservation
  land degradation surveillance in, 141
  mobile pastoralists in, 116
  PABRA in, 83, 85, 86
  soybean farming in, 34–38
Kenya Agricultural Research Institute, 36, 141, 144
Kenya Forestry Research Institute, 36
Kenyatta University, 36
knowledge and information services, 18
Kwesiga, F.R., 61
Kyoto-compliant land, definition of, 164
Kyoto forest, definition of, 164
Kyoto Protocol, 65–70, 164
  annex B countries or parties, 161
  annex X proposed, 67
  post-2012 negotiations, 165

Lake Basin Development Authority, 36
land and soil degradation
  See also specific countries and topics
  carbon emissions reduction from, 65–70
    See also carbon emissions reduction
  definition of, 162
  Global Assessment of Human-Induced Soil Degradation
    (GLASOD), 28, 32n1
  historical perspective on, 6b
  soil degradation, defined, 162
  soil protection, investment in, 129
  soil rooting depth and permeability, improvement in, 16
  surveillance, 141–44
    benefits and results of activity, 144, 146
    diagnostic surveillance and operational framework, 142–44,
      143b, 144f, 145b
    investment needs and priorities, 146

lessons learned, 146
    overview, 141–42
    project objectives and description, 142
    Web resources for, 147
land management
  land managers, definition of, 164
  systems and poverty alleviation, 13–16
  trade-offs, 12–13
landscape resilience. *See* resilience
land use
  See also sustainable land management (SLM); *specific types of
    uses (e.g., crops, livestock)*
  confronting effects of, 13
  definition of, 164
La Rovere, R., 120, 133
Latin America and Caribbean countries
  See also Central America
  climate risk management in, 137
  food production in, 96
  hillside agriculture in, 78, 81
  humid and subhumid areas in, 25
  HydroSHEDS and, 153
  indigenous fruit trees in. *See* indigenous fruit trees (IFTs)
  land degradation in, 27
  malaria in, 9
  no-till systems in, 17
  payment for environmental services in, 51–55
    See also payment for environmental services (PES)
  production landscape in, 9, 10f
  rainfed farming systems in, 77
  VegClass 2.0 and, 157
  water and feed challenges in, 27
LBS (little bag silage), 30
Leakey, R.B., 61
legume forage banks, 99
legumes as forage, 30, 88, 99, 133
Leloup, S., 114
Lewis, J., 39
lines of credit, 31
little bag silage (LBS), 30
livestock
  in Central America, 27–33
  diversification of, 17
  fodder shrubs and, 88–94
  integrated crop-livestock production and, 17, 26
  livestock-land and livestock-water systems, 96–102
  in mixed farming systems, 25, 77
  mobile pastoralism, 114–19
  pasture-livestock system in Brazil, 41
  ruminants, 77, 97, 165
  smallholder livestock systems in Sub-Saharan Africa,
    96–102
    implications for SLM, 97–99
    investment needs, 101
    key SLM issues, 96–97
    lessons learned, 99
    opportunities for scaling up, 99–101
    recommendations for practitioners and policy makers, 101

water and nutrient implications, 97–99
zero-grazing systems, 88
Löffler, H., 98
Lotsch, A., 136
lowland plains, definition of, 161, 165

malaria, deforestation and, 9
Malawi
  farmers groups in, 86
  PABRA in, 83
Malaysia, infectious diseases in, 9
Mali
  pastoral sector in, 116
  VegClass 2.0 and, 157
manures
  green, 85
  management of, 100–101
  organic, 105–6
marginal dry areas, 120–25
  key SLM issues, 120–21, 121t
  lessons learned, 121–22
  multilevel analytical framework, 123, 124f
  opportunities for SLM, 122
  rationale for investment, 122
  recommendations for practitioners, 122–23, 123t
  Web resources for, 125
marginal land farmers, commodity prices' effect on, 3–4, 11
market and private escort development, 18
market supply chains, 18
Matakala, P., 61
Matlon, P.J., 98
Mauritania, pastoral sector in, 116
May, P.H., 51
Mbili intercropping system, 35
MesoAmerican Biological Corridor, 54
methane (MH₄), 164
Mexico
  carbon emissions reduction in, 68
  PES in, 54
microorganisms in soil, 103–4
Middle East, 131
  See also specific countries
Millennium Development Goals, 3
Misra, A.K., 99
mitigation, definition of, 164
mixed-crop livestock systems. See crops
mixed farming systems, 25
mixed-maize farming systems, 25
mobile pastoralism, 114–19
  key drivers, 115
  key SLM issues, 115
  lessons learned, 115–16
  opportunities for SLM, 116
  overview, 114
  rationale for investments, 116–17
  recommendations for practitioners, 117–18
  trends of resource use, 115
  Web resources for, 119

MODIS (Moderate Resolution Imaging Spectroradiometer, NASA), 157, 158f
monsoons, 108
"mother and baby" trial design, 12
Mozambique, VegClass 2.0 and, 157
MPCI (multi-peril crop insurance), 138
multilateral and bilateral organizations, 5
multi-peril crop insurance (MPCI), 138

NARSs (national agricultural research systems), 112
National Aeronautics and Space Administration (NASA), 151, 152
  MODIS (Moderate Resolution Imaging Spectroradiometer), 157, 158f
National Agricultural Research Organization of Uganda, 91
national agricultural research systems (NARSs), 112
National Forestry Financing Fund (Fondo Nacional de Financiamiento, FONAFIFO, Costa Rico), 53–54
national organizations, 5
Nature Conservancy, 153
New Partnership for Africa's Development (NEPAD), 141
Ngobo, M., 56
Nhan, D.K., 71
Nicaragua
  forage in, 30
  PES in, 54
Niger, agroforestry in, 127–28
Nigeria
  pastoral sector in, 116
  soybean farming in, 35, 35f
Nipah virus, 9
nitrification inhibitor, definition of, 164
nitrogen-use efficiency, improvement in, 128–29
nitrous oxide (NO₂), 164
no-burn agricultural zones, 78–82
  key SLM issues in, 78–79
  lessons learned, 79–80
  opportunities for SLM, 80
  rationale for investment, 80–81
  recommendations for practitioners, 81
  Web resources for, 82
nongovernmental agencies, 5, 112
nongovernmental organizations (NGOs), 91
North Africa
  cumin production in, 131
  marginal dry areas in, 122
North America
  infectious diseases in, 9
  production landscape in, 9, 10f, 11
no-till systems, 17
  See also conservation tillage practices
NRM (participatory natural resource management), 111–12
nutrient depletion or mining, definition of, 164–65

off-farm income, 16b, 26, 73, 77, 120
offset, definition of, 165
Ohiokpehai, O., 34
on-site and off-site effects, definition of, 165

organic farming, 17
organic manures, 105–6
ozone (O₃), 9

PABRA (Pan-African Bean Research Alliance), 83–87
paddy rice production, changes in, 128
Padgham, J., 126
participatory approaches
    barley-breeding program, 122, 123*t*, 134–35
    definition of, 165
    domestication and, 60, 61
        See also indigenous fruit trees (IFTs)
    experimentation process and, 11–12, 86
    natural resource management as, 111–12
pastures. *See* forage production and conservation; livestock
Pathak, P., 108
Pavon, J., 78
payment for environmental services (PES), 51–55
    capacity-building opportunities for, 54*n*1
    costs and benefits for services, 52*t*, 53
    key SLM issues, 51, 52*b*
    lessons learned, 51–53, 52*t*
    opportunities for SLM, 52*t*, 53–54
    recommendations for practitioners, 54
    types of services generated by good land-use practices, 52*b*
    Web resources for, 55
Peden, D., 96, 99
peri-urban and urban agriculture (PUA), 166
permanent forest sink initiative, definition of, 165
Peru
    carbon emissions reduction in. *See* carbon emissions reduction
    indigenous fruit trees (IFTs) in, 61
    VegClass 2.0 and, 157
PES. *See* payment for environmental services
pest control. *See* integrated pest management (IPM)
Peters, M., 27
Philippines
    carbon emissions reduction in. *See* carbon emissions reduction
    VegClass 2.0 and, 157
plains, definition of, 161, 165
plants
    improvement of varieties of, 16–17, 63
    integrated plant nutrition, 16
    Web-based tools and methods, 156–57
Plato on land degradation, 6*b*
Pond-Live Project (Vietnam), 72
    See also Vietnam
ponds in integrated agriculture-aquaculture (IAA), 73–74
potential productivity, definition of, 165
poverty reduction, balancing with rainforest conservation, 39–44
    See also rainforest conservation
poverty traps, 34
Powell, J.M., 98
precision agriculture, 17
pressure-state-response framework, 13, 14*b*
price-based instruments (measures), definition of, 165
ProAmbiente (Brazil), 53

PRODES (Program for the Estimation of Deforestation in the Brazilian Amazon), 156
production landscapes, 4, 9–12, 10*f*
Program for Sustainable Hillside Agriculture in Central America, 54
public policy and regulatory systems, 18, 53

QSMAS (Quesungual Slash-and-Mulch Agroforestry System, Honduras), 78–82

rainfed farming systems
    dry and cold farming systems, 95–147
        climate change, adaptation and mitigation strategies for, 126–30
        climate risk management, 136–40
        high-value cash crops, 131–32
        integrated natural resource management for watershed function in semiarid tropics, 108–13
        integrated nutrient management (INM), 103–7
        land degradation surveillance, 141–44
        legume forage, 133
        marginal dry areas, 120–25
        mobile pastoralism, 114–19
        overview, 15, 15*t*, 23
        participatory barley-breeding program, 134–35
        smallholder livestock systems in Sub-Saharan Africa, 96–102
    in highlands and sloping areas, 77–94
        bean farming in Africa, 83–87
        fodder shrubs in East Africa, 88–94
        no-burn agricultural zones in Honduras, 78–82
        overview, 15, 15*t*, 23
    in humid and subhumid areas, 25–75
        carbon emissions reduction, 65–70
        fallow lands in Cameroon, 56–59
        forest tree crops, 60–64
        groundwater declines, 45–50
        integrated agriculture-aquaculture in Vietnam, 71–75
        livestock in Central America, 27–33
        overview, 15, 15*t*, 23, 25
        payment for environmental services, 51–55
        rainforest conservation and poverty reduction, 25, 39–44
        soybean farming in Africa, 34–38
    principles pertaining to, 16
rainforest conservation
    balancing with poverty reduction, 25, 39–44
        ASB matrix, 40*t*, 40–41
        integrated natural resources management (INRM) approach, 40
        key drivers for degradation dynamics, 40*t*, 40–41
        key SLM issues, 39–40
        lessons learned, 41
        opportunities for SLM, 42
        rationale for investment, 42
        recommendations for practitioners, 42
        Web resources for, 43–44
    humid area farming systems and, 25
Ramakrishna, Y.S., 108

Rao, C.S., 103
Rao, I., 78
Reaching the Rural Poor (World Bank), 3
reclamation of cultivated land, 16
reduction of emissions from deforestation and degradation
    (REDD), 65–70
regional climate and global change, 8–9
Rego, T.J., 108
regulatory frameworks, 18, 53
remote-sensing technologies, 138, 151, 152f
    See also Web-based tools and methods for SLM
research and development
    See also specific topics
    farmers groups, 86
        See also participatory approaches
    forage production and conservation and, 31–32
    mobile pastoralism and, 117
resettlement action plan, 18b
resilience
    definition of, 165
    landscape resilience, 13, 14b
resource access policies, 117
revenue recycling, definition of, 165
risk models, 138
    See also climate risk management
risk transfer approaches, 138
Rivera, M., 78
river basin development and management, 153–54, 155f
Rockefeller Foundation, 37
Rondon, M., 78
rumen, definition of, 165
ruminant animals, 77, 97, 165
    See also livestock
rural development strategy, 3
Rwanda
    community watershed model in, 112
    fodder shrubs and livestock productivity in. *See* forage
      production and conservation
    PABRA in, 85

Sahrawat, K.L., 103
salinization, definition of, 165
Sanadiq, 122
Sanchez, N., 78
Sanginga, N., 34
savings and credit cooperative societies, 11
SCALE (Systemwide Collaborative Action for Livelihoods), 92
seawater intrusion, definition of, 165
Selection of Forages for the Tropics (SoFT), 28
self-help groups (SHGs), 11, 109–10, 111, 112
Senegal, mobile pastoralists in, 116
sequestration, definition of, 165
Shallow, B., 65
*Shaping the Future of Water for Agriculture: A Sourcebook for
    Investment in Agricultural Water Management*
    (World Bank), 3
Shepherd. K.D., 141
SHGs. *See* self-help groups

Shuttle Radar Topography Mission (NASA), 152
Sileshi, G., 60, 61
simian foamy virus, 9
Singh, P., 108
sink, definition of, 165
sink credit, definition of, 165
Sir Dorabji Tata Trust, 112
slash-and-burn agricultural practices, 25, 78–80
    See also Alternatives to Slash-and-Burn (ASB) Programme; no-
      burn agricultural zones
SLM. *See* sustainable land management
smallholders
    livestock systems in Sub-Saharan Africa, 96–102
    needs of, 11
Smyth, A.J., 12
Snapp, S.S., 12
SoFT (Selection of Forages for the Tropics), 28
soil degradation. *See* land and soil degradation
soil health surveillance, 141, 142
soil microorganisms, 103–4
soil organic matter (SOM)
    See also specific countries and topics
    build up of, 16
    definition, 165
Somalia, mobile pastoralists in, 116
South America. *See* Latin America and Caribbean countries
South Asia
    food production in, 96
    production landscape in, 9, 10f
    rainfed farming systems in highland and sloping areas in, 77
Southeast Asia
    food production in, 96
    forest resources in, 8
    rainfed farming systems in highland and sloping areas in, 77
soybean farming in Africa, 34–38
    key SLM issues, 34
    lessons learned, 34–35, 35f
    opportunities for SLM, 35
    rationale for investment, 35–36
    recommendations for practitioners, 36–37
    Web resources for, 37–38
species diversity in forests. *See* forests
Sreedevi, T.K., 108
Stewart, J., 88
Sub-Saharan Africa
    See also specific countries
    community watershed model in, 108
    land degradation surveillance in, 141, 144
    livestock in, 88
    production landscape in, 10f
    smallholder livestock systems in, 96–102
        See also livestock
    soil nutrient losses in, 34
    soybean farming in, 36
Sudan, mobile pastoralists in, 116
Sujala Watershed Project, 112
Surface Water Watch, 154
surveillance of land and soil degradation, 141–44

sustainability, concept of, 12
sustainability index, 12
Sustainable Aquaculture for Poverty Alleviation program
    (Vietnam), 71
sustainable land management (SLM)
    See also specific regions, countries, and topics
    definition of, 5–6, 6*f*
    indicators of, 13, 14*b*
    investments, future direction for, 16–18, 18*b*
    need and scope of, 4, 5
    outcome measures, 4
    production landscape and, 11
    rainfed farming systems, principles for, 16
        See also rainfed farming systems
Syria
    high-value cash crops in, 131–32
    marginal dry areas in, 120–25
        key SLM issues, 120–21, 121*t*
        lessons learned, 121–22
        multilevel analytical framework, 123, 124*f*
        opportunities for sustainable management, 122
        rationale for investment, 122
        recommendations for practitioners, 122–23, 123*t*
        Web resources for, 125
    mobile pastoralism in, 114–19
        key drivers, 115
        key SLM issues, 115
        lessons learned, 115–16
        opportunities for SLM, 116
        overview, 114
        rationale for investments, 116–17
        recommendations for practitioners, 117–18
        trends of resource use, 115
        Web resources for, 119
    participatory barley-breeding program in, 122, 134–35
    vetch as forage in, 133

Tadesse, G., 99
Tanzania
    farmers groups in, 86
    fodder shrubs and livestock productivity in. *See* forage
        production and conservation
    mobile pastoralists in, 116
    PABRA in, 83, 86
Tchoundjeu, Z., 61
technology, 16–18
    See also Web-based tools and methods for SLM
    low cost, 11
    low-emissions, 164
    remote-sensing, 138, 151, 152*f*
    transfer, 165
Thailand
    carbon emissions reduction in. *See* carbon emissions
        reduction
    community watershed model in, 108–13
        See also community watershed model
    VegClass 2.0 and, 157
Thanh, D.N., 71

Thomas, R., 120, 131, 133
threshold, definition of, 165
tillage practices, 16, 17, 129
Tomich, T., 39
tradable permit regime, definition of, 165
trade-off analysis, 12–13
traditional farming system in marginal dry areas, 122
tree crops
    indigenous fruit trees (IFTs), 60–64
    investment in, 18
    in mixed farming systems, 25
    rainforest conservation and, 42
Tropical Soil Biology and Fertility Institute (TSBF), 34, 36
trust and respect, building of, 12
Turkelboom, F., 120, 131, 133

Uganda
    farmers groups in, 86
    fodder shrubs and livestock productivity in. *See* forage
        production and conservation
    PABRA in, 83, 85, 86
U.K. Department for International Development, 112
United Nations Development Programme, 122
United Nations Environment Programme (UNEP), 141, 144
United Nations Framework Convention on Climate Change
    (UNFCCC), 65, 165–66
    annex I countries, 66, 67, 161
    non-annex I countries, 67
United States, forest resources in, 8
upland watersheds, definition of, 164
urban and peri-urban areas, definition of, 166
urban-based farming systems, 15, 15*t*
urban "heat islands," 8
urbanization, effect of, 8, 14*b*, 49, 97, 129, 157
U.S. Geological Survey, 153
USDA (U.S. Department of Agriculture), 151, 152*f*

Vågen, T.-G., 141
Valentim, J., 39
Valladares, D., 78
Vanlauwe, B., 34
van Noordwijk, M., 65
variable infiltration capacity (VIC) macroscale hydrologic model,
    153
VegClass 2.0, 156–57
vehicle emissions, 9
Verchot, L., 65
Verdegem, M.J.C., 71
vermicompost, 105–6, 106*t*, 109
vetch as legume forage, 133
Vietnam
    community watershed model in, 108–13
        See also community watershed model
    integrated agriculture-aquaculture in, 71–75
        See also integrated agriculture-aquaculture (IAA)
    VegClass 2.0 and, 157
voluntary greenhouse gas reporting (VGGR), 166
Vosti, S., 39

Walsh, M.G., 141
Wambugu, C., 88, 91
Wangkahart, T, 108
Wani, S.P., 103, 108
wastewater
    aquifer recharging with, 49
    definition of, 166
water conservation and use
    See also coastal areas and waters; groundwater declines;
        watersheds; *specific countries and topics*
    definition of water, 166
    global change and, 8
    quality, 166
    rainwater management and, 16
    water-harvesting structures (WHSs), 110
watersheds
    basin and watershed scale hydrological modeling, 153
    community watershed model, 108–13
        See also community watershed model
    hydrological data and digital watershed maps, 151–53,
        153f
Web-based tools and methods for SLM, 4, 151–59
    See also specific topics
    basin and watershed scale hydrological modeling, 153
    Carnegie Landstat Analysis System (CLAS), 154, 156, 156f
    Dartmouth Flood Observatory, 154, 155f
    global field and market intelligence on cereals and oilseeds,
        151, 152f
    hydrological data and digital watershed maps, 151–53, 153f
    Integrated Global Observing Strategy (IGOS), 157
    NASA's MODIS (Moderate Resolution Imaging
        Spectroradiometer), 157, 158f
    plant biodiversity, 156–57
    remote-sensing tool for water resource management, 138, 151,
        152f
    river basin development and management, 153–54, 155f

Weise, M., 56
Welchez, L.A., 78
West Africa
    See also specific countries
    dry lands project in, 141, 144, 147
    pastoral sector in, 116
Western Europe, production landscape in, 9
wetland rice-based farming systems, 15, 15t
White, D., 27, 83
WHSs (water-harvesting structures), 110
Williams, T.O., 98
Witcover, J., 39
women
    bean farming and, 86
    self-help groups (SHGs), 11, 109–10, 111, 112
    soybean farming in Africa and, 34
World Agroforestry Centre, 61, 65, 91, 92
World Bank
    community watershed model and, 112
    Global Environment Facility (GEF), 53, 141, 144
    Innovative Activity Profiles and, 4
    Investment Notes and, 4
    Poverty Reduction Strategy papers, 117
    rural development strategy of, 3, 13–14
    SLM and natural resource management investments and, 18,
        18b
    SLM projects and, 4–5
World Wildlife Fund (WWF), 151–53, 153f

Zai systems as forage niches, 100
zero-grazing systems, 88
Zhong Li, 108
Zimbabwe, integrated nutrient management in, 106
zones and zoning
    hydronomic zoning, 47–48, 48f, 49
    no-burn agricultural zones, 78–82

ECO-AUDIT
Environmental Benefits Statement

The World Bank is committed to preserving endangered forests and natural resources. The Office of the Publisher has chosen to print **Sustainable Land Management Sourcebook** on recycled paper including 30% post-consumer recycled fiber in accordance with the recommended standards for paper usage set by the Green Press Initiative, a non-profit program supporting publishers in using fiber that is not sourced from endangered forests. For more information, visit www.greenpressinitiative.org.

Saved:
- 11 trees
- 7 million BTUs of total energy
- 942 pounds of total greenhouse gases
- 3,911 gallons of waste water
- 502 pounds of solid waste